# Called to Believe
*A Brief Introduction to Doctrinal Theology*

# Called to Believe

*A Brief Introduction to Doctrinal Theology*

Steven P. Mueller, editor

WIPF & STOCK · Eugene, Oregon

CALLED TO BELIEVE
A Brief Introduction to Doctrinal Theology

ISBN: 1-59752-995-8

# Contents

# Introduction

"I am the way, and the truth, and the life" (John 14:6)

Our gracious God has revealed himself to us through Jesus Christ and in his word. He reveals our need for salvation and he reveals our Savior. Since we cannot save ourselves or even come to him by ourselves, he sends his Holy Spirit who calls us to faith, gathers us in the body of Christ, and keeps us in the faith throughout our lives. Through word and sacrament he daily forgives us, strengthens our faith, and blesses us. He helps us in this life, and because of the death and resurrection of Jesus, has promised eternal life and salvation to all who receive him.

This is the truth revealed by God and believed by his children. We hold it in our hearts and minds, teach it to one another, and confess it before all the world. This book examines these truths, providing a detailed examination of the major doctrines of the Christian faith. It seeks to offer an orderly presentation of biblical teaching that is articulated and applied in our twenty-first century context.

The authors of this book are all Lutheran pastors and professors. Together, we believe that the Bible is the inspired, inerrant word of God, and that its chief purpose is to reveal Jesus Christ to us: the world's true and only redeemer. We believe that God's word is the only infallible guide for Christian life and teaching. This book reflects these convictions.

We have made several assumptions about our readers. First, this book is written for an adult Christian audience. It aims to assist college students and other Christian adults, providing an aid for understanding and growth in knowledge and faith. It presumes a basic understanding of the central teachings of Christianity, and an awareness of the biblical text. Readers who lack this background may benefit from a more foundational approach to Christianity before reading this book. Similarly, those of a more advanced level may benefit from this book, but will also note that there are many other resources available for their continued study, including the more detailed text from which this book is abridged, *Called to Believe, Teach, and Confess: An Introduction to Doctrinal Theology* (Wipf and Stock, 2005). This more thorough text includes more doctrinal topics and a more detailed discussion of most doctrines.

## Reading Order

With that understanding, we have followed an outline similar to that of the Ecumenical Creeds. After an initial discussion of theological method, we will address the doctrine of Scripture and its doctrines of Law and Gospel. Next we examine the doctrines of God, his creation, and humanity, and our sinfulness. With this contextual foundation laid, we consider the central doctrines of Christianity: the grace of God, the person and work of Christ, and his work of justification. After examining the work of the Holy Spirit as he brings us to faith and preserves us in that faith, we read about God's plan for our ongoing life in Christ in sanctification, the means of grace, baptism, and the Lord's Supper. We then examine God's institution of the church and the way that he has ordered our human relationships in society. Finally, we examine things which take place at the end of our own lives and at the end of this world. Any ordering of theology may have both advantages and disadvantages, since theology is not a grouping of isolated elements, but an organic whole. This is a serviceable order, but these topics may be placed in different orders as well.

You may, of course, choose to read these chapters in a different order. We recommend that you begin with chapter one, which addresses theological method and presuppositions. From that point, you may find it helpful to rearrange the chapters in your reading. It may be profitable, for example, to begin with the person and work of Jesus Christ and then move outward to other doctrines. You may jump immediately to topics that are of particular interest. Of course, it is helpful to remember that the chapters build on each other. You may need to read some other sections to provide a context for your topic.

## Some Suggestions for Reading

*Reading the Bible with this Book*

The authors of this text have included a variety of references to the scriptures. These references are not simply documentary citations, but an integral part of the text. At times, a passage is directly quoted, at other times it is only cited. But we strongly encourage you to look up these verses, read them, and see for yourself. When you read these verses and see the context in which they were written, you will often gain a deeper understanding of the word of God and of its application to the doctrine you are studying. You may find it helpful to mark some of these passages in your Bible or to commit key verses to memory. Ideally, you will continually consult your Bible as you read this book. Unless otherwise noted, we have used the English Standard Version of the Bible for all quotations. You may wish to use this helpful translation or choose another version (or, if you are able, the original Hebrew and Greek), but make sure it is a reliable translation and not a paraphrase.

*Additional Resources*

Like any other academic discipline, theology has developed a specific vocabulary. Some of the words will be familiar; others may be new to you and some may have a more precise meaning than you previously knew. Each chapter has identified some key terms, marked in bold in the text and listed at the end of the chapter. These terms are defined in the glossary, though you will likely find it beneficial to first define them yourself in the context of the chapter.

Each chapter also ends with some questions for review and discussion. These are starting points for your further study or for dialog with others. You will likely find ample topics for discussion or further study as you read. To aid in your further exploration, most chapters provide a brief list of additional resources that are good starting points for continued study.

*Studying with Others*

You may be reading this book by yourself as part of your personal study. This can be a helpful method of theological reflection. You may also find it helpful to discuss the book, or topics from it, with other Christians. This may occur in a classroom setting, a Bible study, with a group of fellow believers, or in conversation with your friends or family. Talk to your pastor and to other mature Christians. Discuss theological issues with them (always being anchored in the word of God). As you share your insights together, as you read and apply God's word, you will all be blessed.

*Reading as a Spiritual Discipline*

You may have picked up this book in order to understand a viewpoint (whether yours or someone else's). It may be the assigned textbook in a course. Perhaps you seek greater understanding. We are thankful for whatever caused you to start reading this book. Whatever your reason, we want you to know our purpose. Near the end of his Gospel, St. John wrote, "these [things] are written that you may believe that Jesus is the Christ, the Son of God, and that by believing you may have life in his name" (John 20:31). We do not claim inspiration for this text, but our purpose is the same. Proper theological study always directs us back to Jesus Christ and his salvation. This text may challenge you, but we pray that it will help you grow. We invite you to consider your reading as part of your life of discipleship. Pray that God uses this book to guide you in his truth. Read his word for the source of these teachings. Apply the truth of his word in your life. This is the truth that we believe, teach and confess. God bless you as you join us in exploring his truth.

## About the Writers

Korey D. Maas (S.T.M., Concordia Seminary; D.Phil., Oxford University) is Assistant Professor of Theology at Concordia University, Irvine, California.

Timothy H. Maschke (S.T.M., Concordia Seminary; D.Min., Trinity Evangelical Divinity School; Ph.D. Marquette University) is Professor of Theology and Director of Pre-Seminary Studies at Concordia University Wisconsin.

Brian M. Mosemann (S.T.M. Concordia Seminary) is tutor at Westfield House in Cambridge, England.

Steven P. Mueller (S.T.M. Concordia Theological Seminary, Ph.D. Durham University) is Professor of Theology and Dean of Christ College at Concordia University, Irvine, California.

Gregory P. Seltz (S.T.M. Concordia Seminary) is Assistant Professor of Theology and Director of the Cross-cultural Ministry Center at Concordia University, Irvine, California.

# 1

# The Task of Theology

What comes to mind when you hear the word "theology"? Some people think theology is simply an academic discipline like biology or history. Others may be suspicious, having encountered different "theologies" that may or may not reflect the truth of the Bible. Some consider it to be a dry, boring, or complicated abstraction that talks about God but may not seem to know him personally. Perhaps you think that it suggests a deep understanding, a wrestling with the riches of God's word, or a vibrant and thoughtful faith. Any of these reactions may be understandable, but what is theology? How does it go about its work? To answer these questions, this chapter will consider:

1. The Nature of Theology—*What is theology?*
2. Formal and Material Principles in Theology—*The ultimate source of information and the central teaching assist in understanding a theological position*
3. Common Sources of Theological Information—*How do people try to get information from God and about God?*
4. Some Cautions When Studying Theology—*Remembering our place before God*

## 1. The Nature of Theology

While "theology" can mean different things to different people, its essential meaning is "words about God." Christian **theology** is the study of God as he reveals himself. It includes all of his actions toward his creation and specifically his purpose, plan, and will for his children. The study of theology includes topics such as who God is, the origin of the universe, the human condition, God's gracious response in Christ, and the Christian life. It examines how God has been and ever will be involved in our past, present and future. While theology may consider ways in which mankind has responded to God, it is focused on him. Almighty God himself is the subject of true theology.

*The Purposes of Theology*

### Faith and Salvation

Christian theology seeks to understand the things that God has revealed to us and how this revelation applies in our lives and world. Therefore, its primary goal is to proclaim the Gospel of salvation in Jesus Christ faithfully. True theology points to the Savior. It is not simply a list of things God has said, a biography of Christ, or a history of the church. It certainly is not merely a record of things that people have done or said in God's name. Theology serves our Lord and his Gospel. Every teaching relates, in some way, to our salvation in Christ. St. John summarized the purpose of his Gospel, saying he wrote so that "you may believe that Jesus is the Christ, the Son of God, and that by believing you may have life in his name" (John 20:31). Likewise, this is the purpose of theology: to communicate the saving Gospel to us and to nurture us in faith.

### Growth in Knowledge and Understanding of God

A further application is seen in theology's second purpose. As we study and seek to understand God's truth, we grow in our knowledge and understanding of him and his word. We learn to read and better understand the Scriptures. We grow in understanding his will and ways. The child of God thirsts for a greater knowledge of our Lord (1 Peter 2:2-3). This is not merely knowledge of facts and information, but a deep, intimate, personal knowing. While we will learn more facts, ideas, and concepts found in the Bible, we will most importantly learn to know God better.

Part of the way we know him better is by growing in our knowledge and understanding of biblical truth. What would God have us know? What does his word teach about various topics? How are we to apply these things in our world today? All of this is part of the purpose of theology. It proclaims the whole counsel of God—his Law and his Gospel—to humanity.

*Is This Simple or Difficult?*

Christianity in general, and theology in particular, is sometimes accused of two contradictory things. Some look at the Christian faith and complain that it is too simple. There is an element of truth in this distorted judgment. The Christian faith is simple enough that a young child can proclaim its truth (while he, and even younger infants, may live in a relationship of faith with their God). A toddler may confess her faith that Jesus died and rose for her. This is Christianity. To be sure, there are more things to learn, many topics and themes to study, but at the very heart of it all is the love of God demonstrated in Christ Jesus. Christianity is simple: it is about God's relationship with people. While we never want to lose this childlike faith (Mark 10:15), at the same time we do not want to restrict our growth to this central statement alone. We are called to grow in knowledge of God (2 Corinthians 10:5). If we avoid opportunities for growth, we should not complain that we find Christianity too simple. The problem lies not with Christianity but with our ignorance of the richness of God's word. Christianity is simplistic only if we limit our study and do not hear the entirety of God's word.

On the other hand, you have probably encountered a challenging biblical passage or a particular Christian teaching and struggled to understand its

### Divisions of Theology

Like most academic disciplines, the broad field of theology can be divided into sub-disciplines. The major divisions are:

**Exegetical Theology**: the direct study of the biblical text; reading and interpreting the word.

**Systematic Theology**: arranging the content of Scripture into an organized whole; an orderly presentation of biblical doctrine by topics. (This book is an example of systematic theology).

**Historical Theology**: An examination of different theological movements, churches, groups, and people of the past and their relevance for today.

**Practical or Pastoral Theology**: the application of theology in practical ministry situations.

These four areas do not work in isolation from each other. There is significant overlap and every good theologian will do some work in every area.

meaning and application. Some biblical doctrines are challenging. When we discover a difficult teaching, our temptation is to quickly give in and complain, "it can't be this complicated!" There are challenging and complicated teachings in Scripture because God's word addresses people who live in a challenging and complicated world. We are finite human beings with limited understanding and the ways of God are beyond our full comprehension. We are described, after all, as children, and he is our Father. Furthermore, our understanding is affected by our lives of sin. If we were not sinners and if we did not live in a fallen world, we would not find these teachings so hard. But the truth is that, in this earthly life, we will struggle to understand some teachings.

Is Christianity too simple or too complex? Both of these judgments are faulty. The Christian faith is simple enough for a child to articulate, and the most learned Christian will never forsake that childlike faith and knowledge since it is sufficient for salvation (Luke 18:17). But Christianity is not simplistic. The teachings of God's word help us through even the most challenging and confusing issues of life. God has given us his word for a lifetime of Christian growth and understanding. The child of God who comes to the Scriptures in faith will not exhaust their riches (Romans 11:33). We will not run out of things to study or learn in the word of God. It has all that we need for a lifetime of discipleship in Christ.

*The Limits of Theology*

*Reliance on God's Revelation*

Theology presents the teachings of God to human beings, but we must recognize that theology has limits. It is not to invent new doctrines or modify the Scriptures. We are to confess the whole counsel of God (Acts 20:27) without adding to it or taking away from it. In fact, the final chapter of the book of Revelation sternly warns against this very temptation (Revelation 22:18-19). Changing the word may yield results that are more pleasing to the world, but it soon becomes only our word and not God's word.

The true Christian theologian confesses with St. Paul that as we read the Scriptures, we "know in part" (1 Corinthians 13:9). In his word, God reveals to us everything we *need* to know for our salvation. He has not, however, told us everything we might *want* to know about other topics. The Christian may well have questions about items that are not addressed in Scripture. If God's word is silent on an issue, we are free to speculate, to wonder, and to guess what might be, but we are never given license to answer in God's name when God himself has not told us his answer. We dare not put our fallible words in his mouth. When Scripture is truly silent, the theologian needs to have the integrity to admit, "I don't know."

To be sure, there are a number of topics that are not directly addressed in Holy Scripture. It may, however, indirectly address an issue or address elements of a question. A child of God will search the Scriptures to see if it does, in fact, address a topic in these ways. When the Scriptures speak to an issue, whether directly or indirectly, a good theologian will proclaim these truths.

## 2. Formal and Material Principles in Theology

There are, of course, many different theologies, movements and denominations in the Christian church. Part of the task of theology is to consider and evaluate these differences and the reason for the differences. Religions are complex systems of thought with many different teachings and practices that might distinguish them from other religions. How might we begin comparing disparate systems? Many things might be compared, but a good place to start is with two foundational topics that are usually called the formal principle and the material principle.

The **formal principle** is concerned with the source of information and the means of making decisions. How can one get authoritative information about a belief system? How are questions to be answered? If there is a debate among believers, how should the issue be settled? Many religions point to a sacred text as at least part of their formal principle. But, as we will see shortly, there are other sources of information that also may influence theology.

The **material principle** is the core belief or most important teaching. A well-stated material principle summarizes the essence of a belief system in one phrase. The concept sounds simple, but many people have trouble stating their faith so succinctly. And some who can state their material principle clearly find it difficult to define their formal principle. While these are not a complete presentation of a theological position, they provide a quick summary of its core principles.

## 3. Common Sources of Theological Information

The material principle is derived from the formal principle. In other words, one's source of theological information is going to affect the conclusions that are reached about God, his relationship with humanity, and other issues. So what is the source of theological information? When the theological arguments and method of various groups and religions are analyzed,

some patterns start to emerge. Five different sources of religious information are commonly used: Scripture, reason, human authority, tradition, and
experience.[1] These sources may be used individually or in combination. We
see these used in various Christian theologies. Indeed, if they are interpreted
a little more broadly, they may be seen in virtually any religion. The sources
of information employed will shape and influence the theological conclusions that are derived from them.

*Scripture*

The first major source of religious information is Scripture. Most (but
not all) religions have a written, authoritative source of some type, and most
of these consider their sacred writings to have some degree of divine authority. For Christians, of course, that source is the Bible. You may be wondering why it has taken so long to make such an obvious point. Ask a Christian
how he gets information about God, and the answer that will likely be given
is, "from the Bible." It is a common answer, but is it true? Is this really a
complete answer? Simply saying that we get our information from the Bible
raises other questions: which books belong in the Bible and which ones do
not? For example, is the **Apocrypha** to be included? This question of the
biblical **canon** divides some Christians who accept either more or fewer
books than we are expecting. Other questions are likewise significant. Is the
Bible considered to be a trustworthy source of information or is it read with
suspicion? Is it inerrant or does it contain mistakes? Is it entirely the word of
God, are only portions of it God's word, or is it simply a human document?
Is it authoritative in translation or only in its original languages? How is it to
be interpreted? All of these questions must be considered, as they will affect
the use and meaning of Scripture. (We will address these questions in detail
in chapter two of this book). Despite these further questions, Scripture is
clearly a major source of religious information for many people. Of course,
non-Christian religions may also be based on their own scriptures. These
religions have to answer the same sort of questions that Christianity does.

---

[1] The study of how one acquires information in any field is known as **epistemology**. These basic sources of information are recognized by many different theologians. There is some disagreement over which ones should be combined and which
should be distinct. For example, some systems will not list human authority as a
separate source, choosing to include it under tradition. These differences, however,
are more structural than substantial. The basic sources remain the same.

*Reason*

A second major source of religious information is reason. Some theologies encourage the unrestricted use of reason, others are cautious of its use, and a few seem to reject it. Yet every religion makes some use of reason. Even if a religion has scripture alone as its formal principle, reason is used to read that scripture, interpret, understand, organize, and present its content. Others may give human reason and logic a more decisive role. There are individuals who simply will not believe something to be true if it cannot be "proven" true (though their standards of proof may be quite different for various types of information). Some will reject teachings if they cannot make sense of them. Others will seek a combination of Scripture and reason in their theology.

Because reason can be granted different levels of authority, theologians often distinguish between a "**magisterial**" use of reason and a "**ministerial**" use of reason. This distinction comes into play whenever there appears to be a difference between the content of the Scriptures and the conclusions of reason. A magisterial use of reason places reason above the Scriptures. If there is a conflict, Scripture is generally assumed to be in error and the conclusion of reason is followed. A ministerial use of reason subjects the conclusions of reason to scriptural authority. If they are in conflict, Scripture prevails. At issue is the trustworthiness of reason. Can we trust ourselves to make correct decisions and draw logical conclusions from our mental abilities? While some put a great deal of trust in their reason, others note that reason itself is part of our fallen human nature. Our reasonable capabilities have been affected by our human sinfulness and so may not be as trustworthy as some think! Furthermore, unassisted reason may not have access to sufficient data to make theological conclusions if it is not drawing on other sources of information.

*Human Authority*

A third source of knowledge is human authority. Many people are predisposed to mistrust human authorities, tending to be suspicious of other people telling us what to think or believe. There are good reasons to be cautious, particularly if we rely on the judgment of authorities uncritically without considering their fallibility or the way in which they themselves are acquiring information. In other words, some authorities may be using the same sources that we would use, but without our awareness of the sources. On the other hand, there are times when we must be reliant on the more educated judgment of others. A person cannot be an expert in every area of life and knowledge—even in theological issues. We can learn from others who have studied particular issues more deeply than we have.

Certainly much of our early knowledge comes from human authorities. Our parents and families generally have considerable influence on us, particularly in religious matters. Pastors, teachers, writers and even friends all are used authoritatively by various people. The position of one's church is often an authority that people rely upon. We ought not dismiss these sources because they function authoritatively, but we should be wary of judgments that are made only on authority. What are the sources that lie behind their authoritative position, and is there sufficient reason to trust their authority?

*Tradition*

A fourth major source of information is tradition. Tradition allows past teachers, practices or experiences to inform and possibly influence the present and future. An awareness of history and tradition allows believers who have gone before us in time to have a voice today. It also reminds us that we are not the first Christians. Others have faced similar issues and questions before us, and they can be a resource to us. The precedent of the past often influences the way we think and act—frequently without our awareness.

Some Christians are particularly open to tradition as a source of knowledge, others are notably skeptical of tradition. If we feel ourselves bound to do something *only* because it has been done before, we are experiencing **traditionalism**. This position tends to accept actions of the past rather uncritically. In contrast, a healthy attitude towards tradition can ground us in the historic expression and practice of our faith. The collective and corporate experience of the church is remembered, honored, and may make a helpful contribution through tradition. An awareness of history and tradition may allow us to see issues from a perspective that is different from our own—thereby allowing us to see beyond our own "blind spots."

We may notice the influence of tradition most clearly when it is an unfamiliar tradition or one that we do not appreciate. We may be less than enthusiastic about a previously unknown tradition. Yet we should recognize that we all are influenced by traditions. We may see them in worship, liturgy, and prayer. Their impact may be more obvious in our commemoration of holidays or in the practice of a devotional activity. But, as with authority, we are wise to consider the rationale and justification that undergirds a tradition. Why was this first taught or practiced? Is there a good reason this tradition has been preserved? Does this practice still commend itself?

*Experience*

The final source of theological information that is often used is experience. Like it or not, our experiences influence how we think, understand, and feel. We are more likely to believe something that we have seen for ourselves, and we tend to be skeptical of things that we have not personally experienced. As with reason, experience can be used in service to other sources or seek to reign over them. Our theology can help us interpret and understand our experiences, or our experiences may shape and change our theology.

It is easy to let ourselves be affected by our experience. Consider how many people make moral decisions based not on Scripture but on their feelings. If something feels good or seems to have been effective for a friend, we may try to justify it even if our religion teaches otherwise. Our experiences are important to us, but we should remember that they are never complete. We were not present when God created the world, when Christ rose from the grave, or when the Spirit descended at Pentecost. We were not eyewitnesses to many major historical events. If our direct experiences judge these events, we may doubt them. But we do not always let our experience judge other areas of our lives. I have never flown in space, given birth to a child or visited Antarctica, yet I do not doubt that astronauts have gone into space, I know that childbirth can be painful, and I have no doubt that Antarctica exists. Our experience can mislead us if we put too much trust in it. And we must never forget that our experiences are constantly affected by our sinfulness.

Still, experience exerts an influence on our theology. The things we do and say in worship may influence and even move us to modify our theology. Whether we realize it or not, we tend to view all other times through the lens of our own times and experiences. We expect others to have the same experiences that we do. We are skeptical of things that we have not experienced ourselves. Perhaps this is why our Savior teaches us, "Blessed are those who have not seen and yet have believed" (John 20:29).

*Evaluation, Priority, and Use of the Sources*

All five of these sources can shape and inform a person's theology. In fact, each one of us feels the influence of them all, whether we admit it or not. We may realize that some of these are more helpful than others. We may see weaknesses and strengths in different sources, but all are operative in our world and exert an influence on our theology. The question that must be answered is which will constitute our formal principle? If different sources provide different information, which one will we trust and follow above all others?

Lutheran theology insists that Holy Scripture must be the source of theology and the standard by which we evaluate all theology. This is often summarized with the great Reformation principle, **_Sola Scriptura_** (Scripture alone). We thank God for our reasonable capabilities, but recognize that our reason is limited and affected by sin. When God's word and our reason are in conflict, we follow the word. God has given us various authorities, but their authority is subject to his word and truth. Tradition and experience likewise must be normed by Scripture. But having said this, we are wise to remember that we will not be free of the influence of these other sources. Our reason, experience and the rest of the sources all clamor for our attention. The question is whether we will allow them to distract us from the truth of the word, or whether we will let God's truth be our final guide.

## Knowledge of These Sources Helps Explain Divisions

We want to be aware of these influences and subject all other sources of information to the truth of God's word. At the same time, an awareness of these sources is helpful as we consider the beliefs of other religious groups. Christians are frequently perplexed by divergent beliefs of various denominations. How can these groups believe different things when we all have the same Bible? Much of the reason for such divisions and differing teachings is related to the importance of other sources of information. Not all denominations agree that Scripture is the only source and standard of doctrine. Some give equal or greater status to one or more of the other sources. Knowing this will help us understand the differences.

This does not mean that we should be satisfied with those divisions, but it gives us a starting point for dialog. When we know what others use as a foundation of knowledge, we will be better able to understand and discuss their position and our own. This is particularly important when we consider the teachings of non-Christian groups. Understanding their theological presuppositions may enable us to present the Gospel more effectively to them.

Of course divisions cannot be fully explained by considering the sources of information. False doctrine is not merely a matter of misunderstanding; it involves human sinfulness and rebellion against God. It is not only an intellectual matter but also a spiritual problem that calls for God's solution in Christ.

## 4. Some Cautions When Studying Theology

The study of theology is a wonderful thing. It is exciting to see new insights and applications, to understand things that once were confusing, or to discover a new application of God's truth. Lest our excitement distract us from the truth, we would do well to remind ourselves of a few cautions. One danger often experienced by theologians is the temptation to treat this subject only as an academic discipline. It is easy to view theology as just another intellectual pursuit and to treat God as an object to be described, discussed or even manipulated. We dare not usurp the place of God in this way. God is not a thing to be studied—he is the living God. We live in relationship to him and call him Father because he has lovingly adopted us as his children through Christ Jesus. Remembering our place before him, we undertake this study in humility and faith.

Another danger may present itself when we consider other theological views and positions. As we discussed in this chapter, different theological presuppositions and methods lie behind different movements and teachings. We can understand how people reach different theological conclusions but this does not mean that we should agree with false doctrine. God communicates his truth to us, and that truth can be known. We are called to believe, to faithfully teach and declare the word of God. While we want to be respectful of other people, we must not be over-accommodating or pluralistic and thus compromise the truth.

A third problem often manifests itself in theological students. Excited over a new insight, we may expect all others to have that same insight and feel the same zeal. Perhaps they should—but we must remember to be humble, not arrogant. St. Peter once wrote, "in your hearts regard Christ the Lord as holy, always being prepared to make a defense to anyone who asks you for a reason for the hope that is in you; yet do it with gentleness and respect, having a good conscience. . ." (1 Peter 3:15-16).

We can be faithful to the truth while still treating other people respectfully and gently. The truth and authority of the doctrine is not to be found in the forcefulness, enthusiasm, or zeal of the person who believes it. It is true if it is based on God's word.

### Getting to work

By now we have said enough about the preliminaries. There are, indeed, more topics that might be discussed, but the above method is meant to be a tool—equipping us for the study of true biblical doctrine. Our method becomes more evident in application and use. It is time to study the doctrine that we believe, teach, and confess.

---

**Key Terms**

| | |
|---|---|
| Apocrypha | Material principle |
| Canon | Ministerial use of |
| Epistemology | reason |
| Exegetical theology | Practical theology |
| Formal principle | *Sola Scriptura* |
| Historical theology | Systematic theology |
| Magisterial use of | Theology |
| reason | Traditionalism |

---

### For Review and Discussion

1.  Christianity is simple but not simplistic. Explore this distinction. Do some of the complex teachings in Christianity take away from its simplicity? What are some ways in which oversimplification can distort Christian teaching?

2.  Five basic sources of religious information are commonly used by different people to acquire religious knowledge. Since we may feel the influence of all five of these sources at times, it is vitally important that we know which source is the final authority. Explore how understanding of a theological issue is affected by the prioritization of different sources. (For example, consider how belief in the resurrection of the dead would vary if Scripture is the ultimate authority or if reason predominates).

3.  Theology can be influenced by tradition. Brainstorm at least two benefits of a healthy view of tradition, and two ways in which traditionalism might have negative consequences.

### For Further Reading

Allen, Diogenes. *Philosophy for Understanding Theology.* Atlanta: John Knox Press, 1985.

Thielicke, Helmut. *A Little Exercise for Young Theologians.* Grand Rapids: Eerdmans, 1980.

# 2

# Revelation and the Word of God

How does a person come to know God? If there is a God, can humans know him or know what he is like? What does God expect from me? Does he have a plan for my life? Questions like these have been asked by peoples of every culture, in every language throughout human history. But can they be answered? Can a person ever be sure that his or her answer is the right one? These are significant questions that need to be taken seriously, but the answers do not lie within those who ask them. True answers to these questions are found in the true God who reveals himself to us and calls us to believe. God reveals himself to humanity on his own terms. He questions us, judges us, forgives us, encourages us, and reveals himself to us with words and actions that we can understand. We will explore his revelation as we consider:

1.  Natural Knowledge of God—*What can we know about God from creation?*
2.  Revealed Knowledge of God—*What can we know about God from the Scriptures?*
3.  Jesus Christ: God Revealed—*Christ is the key to knowledge and a certain relationship with God*
4.  Attributes of Scripture—*What the Bible says about itself*
5.  External Evidence for Scripture—*Is the biblical text reliable?*
6.  Understanding the Biblical Text—*Properly reading and using the word of God*

When something is revealed it becomes known, uncovered, or brought to light. When people speak of a revelation of God, they often feel that they have "uncovered something" about God. To many, it is as if God is hiding and they have to find him. The biblical idea of **revelation** is exactly the opposite. It does not focus on humanity's search but on God's desire to communicate—to be known personally and certainly by his world. He searches for us (Luke 15:8-10). He takes the initiative. The pertinent question, then, is "How does God make himself known to the world he created?" Scripture answers that God reveals himself in two ways: natural knowledge (or general revelation) and revealed knowledge from God himself (also known as special revelation or supernatural revelation).

## 1. Natural Knowledge of God

What can be known of God if he has not spoken directly to us? When people speak about "knowing God," they often base their claims on some personal experience or overpowering feeling. They "know God" through the beauty of a sunset, the majesty of the mountain peaks or the incredible order of the universe. They "know God" through the moral order of society or the uniqueness of human reason and love. In Christian theology, this is called the **natural knowledge** of God.  It is information that is revealed through God's "fingerprints" in creation.

*Scripture's Appeal to Natural Knowledge*

The Bible identifies this knowledge clearly for what it is and does. "The heavens declare the glory of God, and the sky above proclaims his handiwork" (Psalm 19:1ff). Failing to see the hand of God behind the beauty, intricacy and order of creation is foolish, for a fool "says in his heart, 'There is no God'" (Psalm 14:1). One often hears that science, the study of nature, destroys faith. In truth, many Christians have found the opposite to be true. Probing the intricacies and majesty of creation, the heavens and the earth, leaves many in awe and wonder of God. Even as the scientist "unlocks" the power of the atom, there remains more mystery and wonder yet untapped and untamed.

The things that God has made proclaim his power and majesty.  Paul says that God's divine nature and power are demonstrably revealed in his creation. He has shown enough of himself there so that every human being can and should know there is a God, that he is holy, all-powerful and that we are accountable to him. This knowledge leaves people no excuses before God's righteous judgment (Romans 1:20). Through this natural knowledge, humans "know God's righteous decree" (Romans 1:32), and "by nature do what the Law requires. . . while their conscience also bears witness and their conflicting thoughts accuse or even excuse them" (Romans 2:14, 15). By observing the complexity and order of creation, by witnessing his continued care of creation, and even through the conscience, that inner voice that speaks of the reality of right and wrong, all people are confronted with the existence, power, and majesty of God, and humanity's total reliance upon him.

*Natural Evidence for the Existence of God*

Natural knowledge, then, is real and important. There is much to learn by examining what God has created. Some people are so confident in this knowledge that they attempt to use this information to "prove" the existence of God. Such proofs for the existence of God are really an extension of the reality of natural knowledge. It should be noted that the Bible calls this revelation self-evident but does not formulate it into proofs. God's self-revelation is ultimately not subject to our need for proof on our own terms. Instead, these proofs—the ontological, cosmological, teleological, moral, experiential, and historical arguments—are best seen as classifications of natural knowledge. Examining these arguments in detail may provide helpful insights, but the knowledge they provide about God is always incomplete.

In the **ontological argument**, God's existence is demonstrated by the fact that there is the notion of God, a "higher intelligence and power" in our thoughts and existence. It makes logical sense to conclude that there must be a being that is superior to all other beings. If so, this being is God. In its simplest forms, the ontological argument essentially claims that it makes sense to believe that there is a God.

The **cosmological argument** looks to the existence, beauty, and wonder of creation for evidence. How can this world be explained without a creator? The entire natural order suggests that there must be a God. Closely related is the **teleological argument**, which argues for God's existence from the incredible order and purpose that are observed in nature. These things are not merely random, but exhibit order and interrelated purpose. The intricacies of creation suggest that there must be someone directing and arranging reality in such a form.

The **moral argument**, that there is a "moral conscience" in individuals and communities, views the existence and nearly universal nature of moral obligations in all human societies as something coming from a divine source since it cannot be explained by naturalistic causes. If there is a fundamental law or morality that all humans experience, it stands to reason that this law comes from someone—from God.

Twenty-first century people often speak of "experiencing God," being confronted by an incredible experience of emotion, enlightenment or even amazing beauty. This is often called the **experiential argument** for God's existence. Such universal experiences of inner peace, or incredible beauty have persuaded some people that they have been in the presence of God. "Near-death experiences" convince others that they have seen evidence of heaven. They believe that they have felt God directly.

Finally, the **historical argument** attempts to demonstrate God's existence by events in history. Some argue this by noting the nearly universal awareness of a god in human historical writings. Since most human beings have concluded that there is a divine ruler guiding the affairs of the world, there must be some truth to the idea. Others believe they see evidence for the existence of God in a general triumph of good over evil in historical events. Such claims may appear particularly weak when held up against tyrannical or oppressive periods in human history.

*Evaluation of Natural Knowledge*

Some knowledge of God may be found through these and other sources, but what does it ultimately explain? There is beauty and order in the world, but there is also nature's seemingly indiscriminate destructive power. For every blessing in life there seems to be judgment and sorrow. The knowledge of God gained through observation and contemplation of the world

*How does natural knowledge affect the mission of the church?*

Natural knowledge gives humanity some indication of the existence of God and his Law. It does not, however, reveal the full identity of God nor does it reveal the Gospel. So the knowledge that it may provide is never sufficient for salvation. Christians need to remember this when they hear Christ's commission to make disciples. Natural knowledge is not enough. The Savior sends his people to proclaim the Gospel to the world. Natural knowledge might provide some common ground, but it does not negate the Great Commission.

and oneself can indicate the existence of a God, but it cannot tell us with any certainty how this God feels about us nor how we stand before him.

By means of natural knowledge, humans might conclude that there is a personal, eternal, omnipotent Divine Being, who has created and still preserves the universe. It might be concluded that this God is holy and just, demanding what is good and punishing what is evil. But because of our sinfulness and rebellion before this God, this knowledge does not and cannot produce a loving relationship with him. In fact, it has the opposite effect, resulting in further alienation. Since it reveals that we have broken God's Law, the Scriptures say that it results in nothing more than a guilty conscience (Romans 1:20; 2:15), a fear of death (Hebrews 2:15), condemnation (Galatians 3:10), and complete hopelessness (Ephesians 2:12). Natural knowledge is the basis for many "religions" that know that the "god(s) of nature" must be appeased, but natural knowledge does not say if or how this can be done.

## 2. Revealed Knowledge of God

Because human beings are constantly looking in the wrong places and listening to the wrong voices, God must speak clearly if sinners are to hear him, know him and believe. The good news is that God does speak clearly. **Revealed knowledge** is God's direct communication of himself in history and ultimately in the Scriptures. The Bible is not just a book about God. It tells of his mighty acts and saving words by which he redeems and restores a fallen humanity and creation. From Genesis to Revelation, the Bible describes the God who reveals himself in words and actions that people can understand. In the Scriptures one not only finds the reality of God, his righteous, holy character, but also his saving work and eternal purposes for sinful and lost humanity.

### *The Need for Divine Self Revelation*

Revealed knowledge is not something extra that is added on to natural knowledge; it is essential. Our understanding of God through natural knowledge leaves us to fill in the blanks of who and what God is. This partial view of God leaves us wanting and uncertain, feeling inadequate, unworthy and inept before the great questions of life. It is not sufficient to fulfill our deepest needs.

The Scriptures further explain the need for special revelation in light of the reality of human rebellion and the fall from our natural relationship with God our creator (Genesis 3). Even at our best we are untrustworthy inquisitors of God. Because of sin, the Bible speaks of human blindness and alienation from God. First Corinthians 2:14 describes spiritual blindness. We simply cannot see God as he is. Ephesians 2:1 and Colossians 1:21 speak of the root cause of man's enmity and blindness to God: the spiritual death of sin. Because of the depth and pervasiveness of sin's power, God must reveal himself clearly if humanity is to receive life and salvation.

## The Supremacy of Divine Revelation

God's mighty acts of salvation existed before there was a written word, but God also proclaims his love, his saving actions in words so that we can know him and that salvation. John says that the words of the Gospel "are written so that you may believe that Jesus is the Christ, the Son of God, and that by believing you may have life in his name" (John 20:31). Just as the voice of a loved one speaking tender words fills our hearts with joy, the writing of those same words in a letter brings that joy to the reader every time it is read. Because they are God's own words and his proclamation of love, the Scriptures are superior to natural knowledge and all other books.

Additionally, the Scriptures are superior to natural knowledge because they come directly from the most trustworthy source—God himself. Peter says, "we have something more sure, the prophetic word" (2 Peter 1:19). Jesus tells us that his words are "spirit and life" (John 6:63). He tells the apostles that the Holy Spirit will bring them the words they are to say (Luke 12:11-12). Both 2 Timothy 3:16 and 2 Peter 1:21, describe the Scriptures as "**inspired** by God," or "God-breathed": written by men who were moved by the Holy Spirit. Because it is God's inspired word, it is the only reliable source of knowledge for faith, our relationship with him.

We often evaluate the authority or accuracy of words that are spoken to us by the identity of the speaker. If the speaker is trustworthy and has the knowledge or right to speak on a topic, we can generally be confident in the information provided. God speaks in special revelation; his words are trustworthy and true. Jesus demonstrates this when he says, "Let not your hearts be troubled. Believe in God; believe also in me. In my Father's house are many dwelling rooms. If it were not so, would I have told you that I go to prepare a place for you?" (John 14:1-2). The unique character of the person and work of Jesus underlies the trustworthiness of his words even as they are written and recorded by the apostles and the prophets (Ephesians 2:19-20; 2 Peter 3:2).

The revelation of God in the words of Scripture is comforting. Reading the Bible, a person can come to know God's will and work with certainty. But this comfort also brings a limitation. Since God chose to reveal himself in this way, we are not free to search for information about God from any source. He limits us to his word. Just as Jesus told Philip that seeing him brought the true revelation of the Father (John 14:9), so the words of God in the Scriptures are our only certain and unfailing guide for questions of life and salvation. This is reflected in warnings not to add to or subtract from the word of God without his authorization. Such warnings are found in both the Old Testament (Joshua 23:6; Deuteronomy 4:2) and the New Testament (Revelation 22:18-19).

### 3. Jesus Christ: God Revealed

Underlying Christian confidence in the Bible as God's reliable self-revelation is the unique person and work of Jesus Christ. In fact, it is most appropriate to argue for the inspiration and inerrancy of the Scriptures from the certainty of Christ rather than arguing for Christ from the certainty of the Scriptures. While the result may be the same, the order is significant. The essence of special revelation centers on the person and work of Jesus Christ. He is displayed in Scripture as the One who has explained the Father (John 1:18). Hebrews 1:3 indicates Christ is the "radiance of the glory of God and the exact imprint of his nature." Jesus himself declares that both his words (John 6:63) and his works (John 5:36) reveal the Father—and both his words and his works are accurately recorded in Scripture. He is, in fact, the Word made flesh (John 1:14).

As God in human flesh, Jesus is uniquely able to reveal God. The prophets spoke the words of Christ as they were revealed to them; Jesus speaks his own divine word directly (Hebrews 1:1, 2). To know Jesus Christ is to know God himself (John 14:9). Christ claims that he is the way to the Father (John 14:6) because he himself is God (see also John 10:30). To know Jesus' words, then, is to know the words of God. To know the words of the apostles and the prophets, words that Christ himself valued and guaranteed (see John 14:26 and John 17:3-20), is to know God's Word. Jesus is the Word of God revealed, made flesh, that reveals and delivers the very presence and blessing of God to all those who receive the words of the Scripture by faith.

### 4. Attributes of Scripture

Scripture exhibits its divine character, as the word of God in human words, in various ways. An internal testimony reveals its divine character. This evidence includes its inspiration, inerrancy, clarity, coherence, authority and similar characteristics. These attributes are seen as many human writers of the Bible, who come from diverse circumstances and cultures over the span of thousands of years, all proclaim the same message of salvation by God's grace. Scripture itself points to its own unique attributes.

*The Scriptures are Inspired*

The Scriptures claim to be the word of God, not the word of men. The prophets of the Old Testament said their words were the Lord's words (for example, see Isaiah 52:3-4 or Jeremiah 4:3). Similarly, throughout the New Testament, the apostles claim that the words they speak are also the words of God (for example, see Acts 13:46; 1 Thessalonians 2:13; Revelation 1:2). The Scriptures not only tell us *that* they are God's word, they explain to us *how* this can actually be. They are divine words because these very words were inspired—"breathed" into the writers—by God himself. St. Paul says, "All Scripture is breathed out by God" (2 Timothy 3:15-16). As this translation suggests, the word for inspiration (*theopneustos*) literally means "God breathed." The only other time in the Bible when something is described as "God breathed" is when God gave Adam life (Genesis 2:7). This same idea is communicated when 2 Peter 1:21 says, "men spoke from God as they were carried along by the Holy Spirit." This divine act of inspiration establishes the fact that the Holy Scriptures, though written by men, are the word of God.

But isn't this merely arguing in a circle? Are we not saying that the Bible is divine because it is inspired, and it is inspired because it is divine? No, not really. We are indeed affirming that the divine inspiration of Scripture is self-authenticating. But, this truth does not mean that we are arguing in a circle, it merely means that the Scripture itself will demonstrate its self-proclaimed, divine nature to the person who reads it. To describe Scripture's divinely inspired nature as being beyond human reason is to root it where it belongs: in the certainty of the person and work of Jesus Christ and the self-authenticating nature of the Bible itself.

Even while acknowledging this self-authenticating nature of Scripture, it is important to remember that the Bible is not one book that gives testimony to itself. Instead, it is a collection of sixty-six books. It is not circular reasoning to assert that different books written by different authors can authenticate each other. They proclaim a common message, and jointly testify to their divine origin, but they were not written as a single book. Once it was recognized that these books (written over vast time periods by many writers, in different languages) shared a common message, they were gathered together. To deny inspiration on the basis of so-called circular reasoning is really to deny any argument for inspiration. Such a denial is not a position of logic but of unbelief.

### *Inspiration is Not Equal to Revelation*

"All Scripture is breathed out by God." In other words, God is its source. Even though it was written in human language by human authors, God controls the content of his word. However, the biblical teaching of inspiration does not mean that God miraculously revealed the entire content of a book to its human writers. Certainly some of the biblical teachings could not be known without supernatural revelation. For example, no human being was present for the creation of the world, and no human being has yet seen the second coming of Christ, yet God revealed both of these events in his inspired word. However, other portions of Scripture involve events that were witnessed by the authors. Peter says that he was an eyewitness to the majesty of Jesus (2 Peter 1:16). The Gospels repeatedly show that the disciples were present for most of Jesus' ministry. They did not need these events revealed to them again. They had seen them with their own eyes. Another example of this is St. Luke who says that he researched his Gospel with the eyewitnesses (Luke 1:1-4).

Even though portions of Scripture did not need further revelation from God for the authors to be aware of them, the Scriptures still testify that they are inspired by God. Just after saying that he was an eyewitness, Peter continues to say that the authors did not invent the stories of Scripture. Instead, "men spoke from God as they were carried along by the Holy Spirit" (2 Peter 1:21).

Likewise, this distinction reminds us that even though God may reveal himself, to a degree, in natural knowledge, we remain bound by the written words of Scripture. He limits us for our own sake. Just as God directs us to the person and work of Christ alone for the confidence and certainty of our relationship with him, so also we are directed to his word to gain authoritative knowledge of him.

### *Inspiration is the Work of the Holy Spirit*

While the Holy Trinity works together in all things, and the Bible is the word of the triune God, the inspiration of Scripture is particularly ascribed to the Holy Spirit. Peter says, "no prophecy of Scripture comes from someone's own interpretation. For no prophecy was ever produced by the will of man, but men spoke from God as they were carried along by the Holy Spirit" (2 Peter 1:20-21). Jesus teaches that the Holy Spirit would bring the apostles, the "remembrance of all I have said to you" (John 14:26). The authors wrote God's words not on their own impulse, but as they were directed by the Holy Spirit. In fact, the biblical writers regularly speak of being "compelled" to write (see 1 Corinthians 9:16 and Jeremiah 26:2. See also Deuteronomy 18:20 where strict restrictions were placed on what a person could "say for the Lord.")

The Holy Spirit, in his work of inspiration, used the unique gifts of each individual writer to convey the words and phrases he deemed necessary. Luke investigates, Paul receives direct revelation, John writes with a Hebraic style, each one's gifts are used in service to the Spirit's work of recording the word of God in human words. Though the gifts and style of each human writer comes through, the content is given and guided, even down to the words themselves, by the Holy Spirit. This teaching that all the words of Scripture are inspired (and not just the basic ideas) is known as **plenary inspiration** or **verbal inspiration**. 2 Timothy 3:15-16 teaches this clearly when it says that "*All* Scripture is breathed out by God."

In the same way, it is important to note that we speak of the inspiration of Scripture, not of the authors. Romans is inspired by God, not Paul. The Gospel of Mark is inspired, not Mark himself. The authors may have written other things (and probably did) but we only maintain that the biblical books are inspired. The words of the Scriptures are ultimately the product of the Spirit's work through the individual prophets and apostles.

To uphold this teaching in the face of skepticism, one needs to take refuge in Christ's view of the words of Scripture. He affirmed the inspiration of the entire Old Testament. In Matthew 5:17–18 Jesus states that "not an iota, not a dot, will pass from the Law"; he had come to fulfill it, not ignore it. He taught that "Scripture cannot be broken" (John 10:35), and that there was a continuity between his word and the Old Testament. In Luke 24:44 Jesus reminded the disciples that all the things written about him in the law of Moses, the prophets, and the Psalms *must* be fulfilled. He quoted verses from the Hebrew Scriptures in his rebuke of Satan (Matthew 4:4-10). Over and over again, Jesus affirms the authority and divine nature of the Old Testament and the writings of his chosen apostles that were to become the New Testament (John 14:26). Jesus, the Word of God made flesh, is our ultimate confidence then in the divine nature of the words of Scripture.

It is also important to note that Christ himself viewed the whole Scripture as God's word (John 10:35). There are no degrees or levels of inspiration. All Scripture is inspired, the words that the apostles and prophets wrote were the words compelled in them as they were moved by the Holy Spirit. Their writings are as inspired as the Gospels are. The words of Jesus himself are the inspired word of God, but so are the words written by the evangelists. In the same way the Hebrew Scriptures are just as inspired as the New Testament. A more subtle assault on the doctrine of inspiration is found among some who would restrict inspiration to its Gospel teachings. Certainly, the

Gospel is at the heart of God's revelation, but if this is taken to mean that the Law is not the inspired word of God, one has denied the biblical teaching of inspiration. The full inspiration of Scripture needs to be maintained, because it is the testimony of Scripture itself. All Scripture is inspired by God.

### Original Manuscripts and Later Copies

For accuracy's sake, it needs to be said that the original manuscripts (usually called the **autographs**) of the biblical books are the words that are the inspired, inerrant words of God. What we have in our hands today are copies of those first books, albeit very ancient copies. If such copies deviate from the original text, they deviate from the inspired character of the word. As these copies remain faithful to the words of the original texts, they too are inspired.

Some Christians are troubled by claims that the copies of biblical texts contain errors and defects. Here the science of **textual criticism** is very helpful. Careful scholarship reveals many early manuscripts showing the text of the Scriptures. Our ancestors clearly worked with great precision to ensure that a text was faithfully copied (a skill that is largely lost today). Comparison of these manuscripts provides confidence that the texts that we read today are faithful copies of the original manuscripts. They are indeed God's inspired word. There are some textual questions, but it is important to recognize that most Christians, and most Bible translations, openly acknowledge texts that might be in question. This is done so that it is clear that in most passages, there is no question whatsoever. We can be confident in the text of Scripture. [1]

It is also appropriate to note that the claim of inspiration properly refers to the original texts, not to translations of those texts. The authors said that the Scriptures were inspired, but they were not referring to the *King James Version, English Standard Version, New International Version,* or any other translation. To the extent that a translation accurately reflects the original text, it conveys God's inspired word to its readers. But an incompetent or unfaithful translator can distort the meaning of the biblical text. This is why

---

[1] There are many helpful resources to guide Christians in understanding the transmission of biblical texts and their accuracy. For example, one notable writer says, ". . .there are some five thousand manuscripts that contain texts of the New Testament documents, more than exist for any other ancient literary work. . . . In short, most New Testament scholars have concluded that we know essentially what the original writers wrote." James W. Sire, *Why Should Anyone Believe Anything at All?* (Downers Grove: InterVarsity Press, 1994), 99.

it is important that Christians read reliable translations of Scripture. We want to present the meaning of the original text accurately. This is also why we encourage individuals to learn the biblical languages. When the student of Scripture has some ability to read Hebrew or Greek, they can go directly to the original text.

### Inspired Means Inerrant

The divine nature of the Scriptures means that it contains and projects divine qualities as well. Just as God is faithful and true, his words are faithful and true. The inspired word of God is **inerrant,** that is, without error in all that it says. Inerrancy does not demand similarity in the style of the writers, nor does it mean that each writer must describe an event the same way. Rather, inerrancy simply means that the Bible is telling us the truth. Jesus says that he is "the way, and the truth, and the life" (John 14:6). That character extends to the words of Scripture. When the Bible says, "Your word is truth" (John 17:17) and the "word of the Lord is upright" (Psalm 33:4), one sees again God's character manifest in the words of the Bible. Even in the face of alleged discrepancies in the Bible, one can rest assured that when all the facts are known, the divine Scriptures will prove themselves true in everything they teach, whether that teaching has to do with doctrine, history, science, geography, geology, or other disciplines or knowledge.[2]

The word of God clearly teaches that it is inspired and inerrant. The reason this is true is that it is his own words. His character is present in the word that he speaks and reveals. Because of this, we say that the Scriptures are not only inerrant; they are also **infallible,** that is, they are perfect and cannot be in error because God is perfect and cannot err. James 1:17 says that God has no "variation or shadow due to change." He doesn't change. He is perfect in all that he says and does, in every circumstance. Psalm 18:30 says that God's "way is perfect; the word of the Lord proves true." His words cannot err; they are perfect as the Lord himself is perfect. Again, we should be careful to note that when we describe the Scriptures as infallible, we are speaking of the original manuscripts and not translations or flawed copies. Any errors that might appear in later versions are not the errors of God but the errors of humans.

The inerrancy and infallibility of Scripture are consequences of its inspiration. Because the Bible comes from him and is inspired by the Holy

---

[2]For example, there was a time early in the 20th century where people doubted that there was a historical Pontius Pilate, Peter and even Jesus himself. Such skepticism has been proven wrong through later archaeological finds in the same century.

Spirit, we can be confident in our relationship to God through his word. We can count on God; we can count on his word; we can rely on his promises. Since he is faithful, perfect and true, so are his words.

## *Consequences of Denying Inspiration*

Human reason may have difficulty accepting the biblical teaching that the Bible is God's inspired word. It may seem easier to consider the Bible as just another human book. Some even present the rejection of inspiration as a deeper act of faith, saying that they are not believing the Bible but Christ. But this is a false dichotomy. Christ and his word are not to be separated. When the unique character of Scripture is denied, the word of God is placed on a level with the fallible testimony of human beings. In fact, fallible human writings may be placed above Scripture when we deny the inspiration of God's word.

When the inspiration of Scripture is rejected, the Bible becomes merely another human book. When this happens, humans are cut off from the sure voice of God. We lose access to the Gospel, which is the power of God to salvation. The certainty of faith that comes from hearing the word of Christ (Romans 10:17) is jeopardized. Our knowledge of the uniqueness of Christ and his saving work is called into question, because this is revealed to us in the Bible. Without this revelation, we lose the certainty of the forgiveness of sin, eternal life, and salvation. Without the witness of Scripture, we lose the certainty and comfort of its many promises including the fact that God will hear our prayers (Luke 11:1-3; 1 Kings 9:3), the promise of the resurrection (John 14:19) and the promise of the comfort and encouragement of the Spirit (John 14:16). Without the Bible, we lose the effects of the word, including unity (John 17:20), freedom (John 8:31-32), confidence (John 15:7) and the reason for mission (Matthew 28:18-20). We are left only with human reason and the limited yet judging knowledge of nature that we receive through our senses alone. God assures us of the inspiration and truthfulness of Scripture to give us confidence. When we deny his word, we lose that confidence. Worst of all, we close our ears to his voice, and so fail to hear the love of our God.

## *The Authority of Scripture*

When Jesus spoke among the people, they said, "he was teaching them as one who had authority" (Matthew 7:29). Jesus, of course, was tested on this matter so in another place he asserted divine authority when he claimed the power to forgive sins (Matthew 9:6). In commissioning the disciples in Matthew 28, Jesus claims all authority in heaven and on earth. The inspired word of God speaks with such divine authority. It can only be recognized as it is confronted in our reading and hearing, just as the people who heard Jesus speak knew that Jesus was unique.

This divine authority of Scripture is absolute, just as the divine nature of the person of Christ is absolute. It is not founded on the personal character of the human writers or the testimony of the church, but on the person and work of the Holy Spirit who breathes the words into the hearts, minds, and mouths of the apostles and prophets. Scripture speaks with authority because it is inspired by God.

As such, the prophets demand obedience to their words as God's words (Leviticus 18:4; Deuteronomy 8:19). Jesus and the apostles likewise call for such obedience (John 8:31–32; Galatians 1:8). To reject the words of Scripture is to be placed under the judgment of its divine words as Christ warns, "The word that I have spoken will judge him on the last day" (John 12:48).

The authority of the Bible is seen in the obedience it demands, but it is even more evident in the faith that it creates. The divine authority of Scripture, which calls for faith in the human heart—a faith that trusts the words and teachings of Scripture for life and salvation—demonstrates its authority when people place their faith in these words as the very words of God. Saving faith is a gift (Ephesians 2:8-9), a gift that comes in and through the word (Romans 10:17).

### *The Scriptures as the Formal Principle*

Since the Scriptures are our only reliable source of the true knowledge of God, they "form" our theology. Thus the Scriptures alone, because of their divine source and authority, are the **formal principle** of theology. As the formal principle, the Scriptures are the only source and norm of our theology. What we believe and teach about God, man, redemption, salvation, and all other teachings are drawn from and held accountable to the teachings of Scripture. The words and teachings of the Bible give form to theology. Its words and teachings also "reform" theology when we deviate from it. As the only rule of faith, Scripture alone (*Sola Scriptura*) guides, directs, and corrects true Christian teaching. So 2 Timothy 3:16 says, "All Scripture is breathed out by God and profitable for teaching, for reproof, for correction, and for training in righteousness."

### *The Clarity of Scripture*

The **clarity** of Scripture refers to the Bible's clear presentation of its teachings. Psalm 119:105 says, "Your word is a lamp to my feet and a light to my path." God's word makes things clear. It speaks clearly about the realities of sin and death, life and salvation. It speaks of the realities of God as the creator and redeemer of the world. It speaks of the reality of Jesus Christ, God come into the flesh to suffer and die for the sins of the world. The clarity of Scripture means that the word of God, its presentation and proclamation, is not obscure or esoteric, but forthright and understandable to the common person who makes a reasonable effort to understand it. In other words, if we apply the same skills of reading and understanding to the Bible that we expect to apply to other books, the average reader will be able to understand its message.

This fact is not lessened if the Bible is rejected or challenged by readers. Some do find the Bible hard to understand, but this is a different matter. First Corinthians 2:14 describes this when it says, "the natural man does not accept the things of the Spirit of God, for they are folly to him, and he is not able to understand them because they are spiritually discerned." It is not clarity that is at issue here but faith and obedience (or disobedience as the case may be).

The clarity of Scripture is implied by its inspiration, but Scripture also directly teaches this attribute. It calls itself a "lamp shining in a dark place" (2 Peter 1:19) and "a lamp unto our feet and a light to our path" (Psalm 119: 105). It is clear even for the unlearned, "making wise the simple" (Psalm 19: 7). Children can also understand it, for Timothy knew the Scriptures even as an infant (2 Timothy 3:15). The writings of St. John were understood not only by the "fathers," not only by the "young men," but also by the "little children" (1 John 2:12–13). At issue, oftentimes, is not the clarity or obscurity of Scripture, but its call for simple faith.

## The Sufficiency of Scripture

All of these teachings about Scripture are revealed so that the purpose of the word is clear. The word of God is, ultimately, about the salvation of sinful humans. Scripture never claims to speak about all things in all circumstances, but it does claim to speak with authority and without error concerning the things it addresses. The Bible does not teach exhaustively about every issue pertaining to earthly life, nor does it reveal everything there is to know about God. It may not contain everything that we *want* to know, but it does teach perfectly and sufficiently all that we *need* to know for salvation and a restored relationship with our creator and redeemer. Scripture teaches perfectly whatever we need to know to obtain eternal life. It is "able to make you wise for salvation through faith in Christ Jesus" (2 Timothy 3:15). It thoroughly equips us for all good works (living in our relationship to God by faith).

*The Power of Scripture*

In order to accomplish his purpose of salvation, God has given his word power. The power of Scripture is clearly taught in Romans 1:16 and 1 Corinthians 1:18 where Paul speaks of the Gospel as "the power of God for salvation to everyone who believes." This power is often described with the word **efficacious**, which means the power to produce an effect. The word always has the power to do what God desires. In Hebrews 4:12, the word of God is described as "living and active." Only through the power of the word of God can one come to faith in Jesus Christ. "Faith comes from hearing, and hearing through the word of Christ" (Romans 10:17). This is its power.

God's word speaks of two themes inherent in its message: Law and Gospel, and thus the results of its efficacy may appear different at times in different individuals. The efficacy of the Law is the power of God's word to convict sinners of their guilt before God, to demonstrate to the human heart its utter sinfulness (Romans 3:20), while the efficacy of the Gospel is to create and strengthen faith in the person and work of Christ (John 20:31; Romans 1:16; 1 Corinthians 1:18) and to deliver the gift of his absolute forgiveness.

But why then do some who hear the message of God believe, and others not? While the Bible is the power of God for salvation, it is a resistible power. The Scripture is always efficacious—it has power to produce an effect. But it is not always **effective**. The effect does not always occur because human beings resist God's power. Jesus, incarnate as a man, came with power to forgive sins, but some resisted and rejected him. God coerces no one to believe. Yet, when a person comes to faith, it is by God's power and grace alone (John 6:29; Romans 3:24; Ephesians 2:8-10). This is a crucial teaching in Scripture. If one does not believe in Christ, it is through their own resistance and disobedience alone (Romans 3:9-20). If one comes to faith in Christ, it is through his grace and power alone.

How can this God, who created the world with his powerful word (Genesis 1, John 1) be resisted by sinful human beings? This incredible mystery should not only give us pause, it should cause us to rejoice and give thanks, for the resistible God comes gently in this means so that sinners can be forgiven. God comes in resistibility (Philippians 2:5-11) so that his power of salvation might be received by grace. To come in his raw power, unclothed in the humility of the incarnation and the rejectible yet powerful words of the Bible, is to doom sinful people to the awesome power of his righteous, holy judgment. Rather than try to unlock the clear, yet mysterious nature of this biblical truth, one should rather journey more confidently into the Scriptures as a **means of grace**, where the power of God for salvation rests for all who believe.

## 5. External Evidence for the Bible

We have been examining the internal evidence for the Bible—its self-authenticating nature. In addition to this clear testimony, there are also compelling external proofs. External testimonies are those evidences outside of the text of the Bible itself that recount the utter uniqueness of the Scriptures as compared to any other book. For instance, the Bible is uniquely anchored in history. The names and the dates of the people, places and things can be verified (see Luke 1:1-4; 1 John 1:1-5). It is as if God himself is saying, "Test me on this." His mighty acts of judgment and salvation have left their marks not only on the pages of Scripture, but in the annals of history and the record of archaeology as well.

Scripture's unique character is demonstrated externally in many ways. The Gospels' authors, and many of the other writers wrote their books soon after the events occurred. The plethora of copies of the Scriptures and the remarkable uniformity of copies, both in the original languages and in translation, speak to the care and concern for the faithful transmission of sacred documents, but also to the integrity of the Bible itself. There would have been ample opportunity to change or manipulate many of the hard sayings of the Scriptures to fit cultural sensibilities, but the manuscripts were copied and translated with remarkable care. There are literally thousands of copies of the New Testament manuscripts, making it one of the best-attested documents in history.[3]

One of the most compelling external signs of the uniqueness of the Scriptures is the changed lives of the apostles themselves. They were transformed from frightened, self-centered people who denied Christ, to fearless witnesses in the face of death. This personal transformation is a compelling sign of the unique character of Jesus and the word that the apostles taught and defended.

In light of the faithful transmission of the ancient texts, evidenced by thousands of copies, attested to by the early church fathers as early as the second century, texts that were written by eyewitnesses who gave their lives

---

[3] Other classical writings show how remarkable this is. Plutarch's *Life of Alexander*, for example, was written more than 400 years after Alexander's death. The earliest manuscripts for many works are from long after their initial composition. Julius Caesar's writings (1000 years), Plato (1200 years), and Aristotle (1400 years).

for what was recorded, one can say with certainty that the Bible is a unique
and trustworthy book. And, while we may not have the original autographs
from the pen of the apostles and prophets, the method of careful transmission, the tremendous uniformity among the copies and ubiquitous nature of
the copies throughout the Roman Empire, assure us that the text of the Old
and New Testaments are virtually identical to the autographs.

## 6. Understanding the Biblical Text

The Bible is inspired and inerrant. It is filled with God's power. It is
reliable and trustworthy. Yet Christians may still disagree about the meaning
of Scripture. It is, therefore, important to consider the text of Scripture and
proper methods of biblical interpretation.

### *The Canon of Scripture*

Canonicity describes the process that has resulted in the books of the
Bible that constitute the Holy Scriptures. Scripture's composition and its
being gathered together are unique in human history. While other so called
"holy" books allegedly were revealed to or authenticated by one person, the
canon of Scripture bears the mark of divine, self-authenticity. No human
person decided what was to be in the Bible. The books that make up the Old
and New Testaments demonstrated their authority and authenticity in history
so clearly that the church was compelled to recognize (canonize) what was
already authoritative.

At the time of the apostles, the Old Testament canon was already recognized. Jesus and the apostles bore witness to that fact in how they viewed
and used the Old Testament as Scripture. In fact, 2 Timothy 3:16, in speaking of "all" Scripture, is first and foremost speaking of the Old Testament
which was already recognized and used by the early church.

The canonization of the New Testament documents is a lesson in the
actual process of self-authenticity unfolding in history. **Canon** means "a
standard or rule." To be canonical, a book must be inspired, written by an
apostle or prophet, contain the divine mysteries in Hebrew or Greek, enjoy
the recognition of the early church (or faithful Jews in the case of the Old
Testament), and have been in use in the ancient, apostolic church. But these
were not imposed standards, they were merely ways that the church recognized writings that had authenticated themselves among the church and
those that did not.

*Interpreting Scripture*

Of course, agreeing on which books belong in the biblical canon does not necessarily mean that Christians will agree about their meaning. Like any other book, the Bible is meant to be read. Its words need to be understood and rightly interpreted. But this is not a matter of personal opinion; there are fundamental principles of interpretation that should be used when reading. **Hermeneutics** is the art of applying such principles to a text, to interpret what it means and to appropriately communicate its message to others

The reader of any book that claims to be true should be concerned with the intent of the author. What was this writer trying to say through this book? To truly understand a text, it may be necessary to exert tremendous effort in understanding the historical and grammatical context and issues surrounding a given text. What was the context of the writer and his readers? What issues were they facing? What did the words used in a text mean at the time they were written? How would the first readers have understood them? How does the language of a text and the structure of its grammar affect the meaning? This method of interpretation, known as the **historical-grammatical method**, is designed to help the modern reader understand how the text was understood when first written. One first must understand "what it meant" before one can apply "what it means to us today."

As the interpreter seeks to understand the language, grammar, and context of a writing, he must try to understand what the writer was attempting to say. An author has a meaning in mind in writing a text. A true text (especially one that is God's truth) is communicating information. The interpreter must ask, "What was the author trying to say?" Ordinarily, the literal sense of the author's words will clearly communicate the intended meaning. At times, however, an author will use metaphors, illustrations, examples, or other figures of speech. The reader should have good evidence that a text was not intended to be understood literally before saying that a text is metaphorical.

Another important principle of interpretation is that a book is its own first interpreter. When we read in the context of a book, we first look at the place of a passage in its paragraph or chapter. How does this sentence fit in relation to the rest of the book? This allows the interpreter to read a book as the author intended. In biblical interpretation, this point is often summarized as "let Scripture interpret Scripture." Since the Bible is a unity, we interpret it in the context of the rest of the book. If a passage seems difficult to understand, we do not change it to make it fit our presuppositions. Instead, we look to other passages. In fact, it is a general principle of interpretation that the reader should begin with clear passages before moving on to the more challenging. For example, a biblical interpreter who reads Revelation without the rest of the Bible may quickly grow confused. One who starts with the Gospels and other sections of Scripture and then proceeds to Revelation will find the last book of the Bible much clearer!

While we have used some biblical examples, every principle mentioned so far is used in reading and understanding any text—biblical or non-biblical. Because the Bible is God's word, divinely inspired, powerful and trustworthy, it demands and deserves a certain perspective from its interpreters. Christians should also recognize some important truths when reading the Bible. Understanding will be enhanced when we remember the objective nature of the Scriptures' truth: namely that it is God's word for all people. Recognizing that it is God's word means that we will pay greater attention to its message.

Furthermore, Christians recognize that Scripture should always be interpreted in light of Christ and its central message of salvation through him. Christ is the heart of the Scriptures. Whatever Scripture says relates, in some way, to Jesus and his saving work. The christocentricity of the Bible is a hermeneutical principle that applies to the Old Testament as well as the New. Paul says in 2 Corinthians 1:20, "all the promises of God find their Yes in him [Jesus Christ]." On the day of Jesus' resurrection, he walked to Emmaus with two of his confused and doubting disciples. Luke tells us that on the way, he explained the christocentricity of Scripture. "And beginning with Moses and all the Prophets, he interpreted to them in all the Scriptures the things concerning himself" (Luke 24:27). The Savior is at the heart of the Scriptures.

Interpretation is the result of applying proper hermeneutical principles so that the ancient text speaks faithfully to the contemporary hearer. It is a process that requires prayer, humility and ultimately faith and confidence in God's word. It is not merely a human process, as the Holy Spirit confronts the one who reads the text. God has a stake in whether people understand and believe in his word. With such confidence one approaches the Scriptures, expecting to hear God and to fellowship with him on every page.

### Scripture and the Church

The Holy Spirit works through the word to create believers. He calls each reader to faith through the Gospel. But God is not content to leave us as individuals. His word ultimately creates the body of Christ, the community of saints, gathered around Christ in worship and bonded to each other in service. Scripture is the word of God for the family of God, and in this sense, always draws people together as it draws people to Christ.

Modern culture generally emphasizes the rights of an individual over the responsibilities of the individual to a community, family, or church. This radical individualism tends to be isolationistic and selfish. As long as the individual has a Bible and a "personal" relationship with Jesus, everything seems to be fine. While God does bless us as we read and study his word, this individualism easily colors one's interpretation of Scripture. The central message of the Bible—that God has freely given himself for the salvation of others, is easily lost in such an attitude.

The word of God calls us out of isolation and into community. There is value in reading the word of God with the people of God, and not just as an individual. Our experience of the word is deepened as we hear it read and proclaimed in worship and as we discuss it with other faithful believers. In Scripture, the voice of God comforts and allays our individual fears and sins and reconstitutes our families and our communities through the forgiveness of sin shared and received. Scripture is for the individual and for the community as it rebuilds both by grace.

*Rightly Using Scripture*

God reveals himself and his word because he wants humanity to know him and to receive his gifts. He even reveals his purpose in giving the word to his people. John admitted that he could have written more about Jesus' life. What he did write was enough, however. It was written so that its readers "may believe that Jesus is the Christ, the Son of God, and that by believing you may have life in his name" (John 20:31). Similarly, John wrote his first epistle so that his readers "may know that you have eternal life" (1 John 5:13). Paul says that "from childhood you have been acquainted with the sacred writings, which are able to make you wise for salvation through faith in Christ Jesus" (2 Timothy 3:15). The purpose of the Scriptures is to bring fallen sinners to salvation. They do this by acquainting sinners with Christ Jesus and cultivating in them God's gift of faith. They convey the Gospel of Jesus Christ. In so doing they function as God's power in the lives of believers (Romans 1:16).

Alongside this central purpose of making believers "wise for salvation," the inspired Scriptures also are useful "for teaching, for reproof, for correction, and for training in righteousness" (2 Timothy 3:16). Believers use the Bible to learn more of God's gracious will and wondrous ways. They use them to rebuke and correct false ideas, which inevitably interfere with a proper understanding of God's word. They use them to grow in the practice of a godly life. The goal of the church's use of the Scriptures is that believers may enjoy the fullest renewal of their humanity possible—that they may become complete or mature—and thus be equipped for every good work (2 Timothy 3:17).

As the biblical message comes to believers through apostles, prophets, evangelists, pastors, and teachers, the saints are equipped for service in Christ's kingdom. They are edified so that they might become one in their faith, in their knowledge of God's Son, and that they might grow in maturity of faith. The Scriptures will prevent them from being tossed to and fro with every wind of cunning, crafty, deceitful view of life. Instead, they will be maturing in Christ, and they will speak God's truth to one another in love. They will be joined together in Christ's body, which he supplies with the power of his word in order to make sure that his body continues to grow (Ephesians 4:11–16).

## Key Terms

| | |
|---|---|
| Autographs | Inerrant |
| Canon | Infallible |
| Clarity | Inspired |
| Cosmological | Means of grace |
| argument | Moral argument |
| Effective | Natural knowledge |
| Efficacious | Ontological argument |
| Experiential argument | Plenary inspiration |
| Formal principle | Revealed knowledge |
| Hermeneutics | Revelation |
| Historical argument | Teleological argu- |
| Historical- | ment |
| grammatical | Textual criticism |
| method | Verbal inspiration |

**For Review and Discussion**

1.  Compare the natural knowledge and revealed knowledge of God. What can these two methods of God's revelation teach us? What are the limitations of natural knowledge? Is it of any use to Christians today?

2.  This chapter briefly discussed the evidence supporting the authenticity and reliability of the biblical text. Research this topic further. How does the Bible compare to other ancient books? How does this help to support the Christian faith?

3.  One of the attributes of Scripture is clarity. How does this attribute relate to challenging passages?

4.  There are many Bible translations available to Christians today. Why is it important that Christians have an accurate and reliable translation of Scripture? Why is it important that this translation be readable?

5.  After reading a biblical text, a participant in a Bible class says, "to me, it means…" How does this common statement bypass good principles of biblical interpretation? How might other participants ensure that the Scriptures are being read correctly without reducing the enthusiasm and interest of this person?

**For Further Reading**

Bruce, F. F. *The New Testament Documents: Are They Reliable?* Grand Rapids: Eerdmans, 2003.

Engelder, Theodore. *The Scriptures Cannot be Broken: Six Objections to Verbal Inspiration Examined in the Light of Scripture*. St. Louis: Concordia Publishing House, 1944.

*Gospel and Scripture*. A report of the Commission on Theology and Church Relations of the Lutheran Church—Missouri Synod. St. Louis, Missouri: The Lutheran Church—Missouri Synod, 1972.

*The Inspiration of Scripture*. A report of the Commission on Theology and Church Relations of the Lutheran Church—Missouri Synod. St. Louis, Missouri: The Lutheran Church—Missouri Synod, 1975.

# 3

# Law and Gospel

It is finals week and you have just finished your exams. Unexpectedly, the professor of your hardest class comes over to you and says, "May I have a word with you?" A request like this can send shivers of fear down a student's spine. In a different context, a kind word whispered in one's ear can bring feelings of joy, happiness or comfort. Human speech can have many different effects on people just by using different words. The words, the identity of the speaker, and the context in which they are spoken can all affect us. Particularly when one is under someone's authority, words can have great impact. A critical or judging word from an authority can truly deflate or even destroy a person. But a word of encouragement from that same person can uplift your spirits and strengthen your resolve. Words—even mere human words—can be powerful.

As powerful as human words are, they pale in contrast to the word of God. In dealing with the power of God's word in our lives, God speaks first. The Word became flesh and dwelt among sinful humans (John 1:14), while we were still sinners (Romans 5:8). He speaks with power. God's word does not merely talk about justice and mercy, it actually judges and forgives, condemns and heals. God speaks words of judgment and grace: words that are Law and Gospel. This chapter will examine these biblical themes by examining:

1. Definitions of Law and Gospel—*God's own powerful words*
2. The Law of God—*God's strong, crushing word of command*
3. The Gospel—*God's liberating promise*
4. Distinguishing and Confusing Law and Gospel—*Rightly understanding God's word*

## 1. Definitions of Law and Gospel

Before one can fully appreciate the impact of these crucial themes of the word of God, these words must be defined. Both Law and Gospel are God's word, yet each has an absolutely different content, purpose and effect in the lives of people. They are as different as "yes" and "no."

The **Law** is the word of God that commands people to do what is right according to God's standards. It tells us what God demands, what a person must do, what blessings are promised to those who fulfill it, and what curses await those who fail to keep it. Fulfillment of the Law is judged by God's perfection, not our best effort. The Law reflects the character of God to the world, calling all people to perfectly reflect that character in every aspect of their lives. Because it reflects his holiness, the Law is good (Romans 7:12). However, as it reveals God's perfection, the Law also reveals our status before God. It demonstrates the truth that, on our own, we have not lived up to God's standard.

There are many examples of Law in Scripture. The Ten Commandments provide a concise summary. A shorter summary is found in Jesus' words, "You shall love the Lord your God with all your heart and with all your soul and with all your strength and with all your mind, and your neighbor as yourself" (Luke 10:27). Notice Jesus' emphasis on the word "all." His summary of the Law demands total obedience. Such words challenge people to be perfectly holy (Leviticus 19:2).

The **Gospel** on the other hand is exactly the opposite of the Law. It reveals the actions of God alone to save those who are "dead in their trespasses and sins" (Ephesians 2:1). The Gospel always declares what God graciously does to forgive. It is his gift: completely unmerited. The Gospel makes no demands on people whatsoever. It offers what God alone has earned. It is life and salvation freely given in accord with God's character and action. He alone pays the penalty for sin. He alone offers righteousness, salvation and peace on his merciful terms.

*Wide and Narrow Senses*

While Law and Gospel are as different as night and day, there are times in the Bible when they are used in both a **narrow** or **proper sense** and other times in a **wide sense** or more general sense. The Law is most properly understood as a demanding, commanding word proclaimed to humanity. There are times, however, when the word, **Torah**, which is often translated as the "Law," is used to describe the complete revelation of God's actions to save (see Isaiah 2:3). When the Bible speaks of the Torah of Moses, it frequently means the whole revelation of God, both God's Law (in the narrow sense) and his promise of salvation by grace.

The Gospel in its narrow and primary sense encompasses the words and actions of God alone to redeem and restore sinful humanity. In this proper sense, the Gospel makes no demands of human beings. It excludes all human actions and works. Yet there are times when the word Gospel is used in a wider sense that encompasses the whole of divine revelation. The first four books of the New Testament are called Gospels (in the wide sense) even though they contain both Law and Gospel (in the narrow sense). The context of these words will help one in making the distinction needed between wide and narrow senses. While recognizing the validity of using Law and Gospel in this wide sense, we would do well to keep the wide and narrow senses of these words distinct. This will aid understanding of the power and purpose of both the Law and the Gospel.

*What the Law and the Gospel Have in Common*

It is important to recognize the proper distinction between Law and Gospel, yet both of these doctrines have some common features. While they are opposites in content, power and purpose, both are still God's word. Both are true and trustworthy, though to different ends. God himself will cause them to accomplish the tasks he intends.

Since both are God's word, both Law and Gospel ultimately apply to all people. The Law "levels" all people before an almighty, holy God. In this regard, no sociological, socio-economic, cultural or ethnic divisions account for anything with regards to one's position before God (1 Corinthians 1:26-31, Galatians 3:28). Romans 3:23 says it well, "all have sinned and fall short of the glory of God. . . ." Likewise, the Gospel concerns all people. When Christ Jesus died on the cross to redeem and restore all humanity (2 Corinthians 5:17-20), all people were redeemed. He has objectively paid the price of salvation for all. When Jesus sent the apostles out to evangelize the world, he told them to go to "all nations" (Matthew 28:19). The Gospel is meant for all.

As God's word to all people, both Law and Gospel are spoken out of his love for sinners. Such a statement challenges our limited sensibilities. People are often very comfortable with the message that God's love is for all. However, the biblical message that God's love is earned by Christ alone and given as a gift is more challenging. The biblical message that we do not deserve such gracious love and must completely "die to self" offends human pride. Surely God must mean "real sinners" and not "good people" like us. Yet even this crushing message of the Law gives evidence of God's love for sinners. He must kill our confidence in our own righteousness so that we might trust in his righteousness alone. Any notion that our efforts can bridge the chasm that sin has caused between us and our creator must be destroyed so that our trust more certainly and more surely centers in Christ alone. We need to see the reality of sin and grace from God's point of view. Both Law and Gospel are spoken to sinners because God loves them.

*The Distinction between Law and Gospel*

These general similarities move to the background when one seeks to understand the unique power and purpose of the Law and the Gospel in human lives. They are absolute opposites; their content and purpose are antithetical. One kills and destroys; the other gives life and restores. One causes despair; the other provides real hope. One demands and judges; the other promises and fulfills.

Maintaining the absolute distinction of Law and Gospel in the proper sense is vital. Paul instructs Timothy to rightly divide the word of truth (2 Timothy 2:15) because the very life and salvation of people before God is at stake. The proper distinction of Law and Gospel enables us to rightly hear God's truth. It is ultimately about the certainty of salvation and one's eternal relationship with God. When the Law causes us to despair of our own works as a cause of a right relationship with God, we are driven to look to God alone for hope and salvation. The comfort of the Gospel is precisely that it brings real forgiveness, hope and life where there was only despair. The Law commands us to look at ourselves and to "get it right," while the Gospel invites us to look to Christ alone and to receive what he alone gives. Before examining the right distinction between Law and Gospel, it will help if we look more closely at the uniqueness of each.

## 2. The Law

Everyone in the world is familiar with the Law of God in some manner. They may not be consciously aware that it is *God's* Law, but it is present in their lives nonetheless. It is written on the hearts of all people (Romans 2: 14-15). Whether from the internal voice of the conscience, from the governing authorities, or from the rules that guide our interpersonal relationships, people are constantly confronted by issues of right and wrong, or rewards and punishments. The Law indeed confronts people in a variety of ways. Even without the Scripture's testimony concerning the Law, people have a sense of what is right and wrong.

The Law of God is not only manifested in the conscience; it is shadowed in the legal systems of governments and partially reflected in the taboos and behavioral norms of cultures. The voices of the reality of right and wrong are all around us. For things to be good, they must be right. If things are wrong there must be evil. Do right: receive blessings. Do wrong: be punished. Such knowledge of right and wrong is written in human hearts so that there is at least a rudimentary understanding of what is good and right.

While human beings may describe the law as requiring their best effort, Scripture repeatedly calls for perfection. When it makes this demand (in the Ten Commandments or the Sermon on the Mount, for example), it can be argued that it is merely clarifying something that deep down one already knows is true. The content of the Law includes all the things that one must do and not do to get right with a holy God. "Do this, and you will live" (Luke 10:28).

*Dimensions or Types of the Law*

Scripture contains many different laws and regulations. In order to properly understand and apply the Law, it is important to recognize that there are three different types or dimensions of the Law in the Bible. All of these laws were commanded by God, but not all are commanded of all people. Consequently, not all of these laws govern us today.

The first of these is the **civil-political law**. These laws govern the outward actions of a nation's citizens. God gives governments the responsibility to enforce certain standards of behavior and to encourage appropriate conduct (Genesis 9:5-6;1 Romans 13:1-5). Through such regulations, civil order is maintained. Human beings are to follow the laws of their society as long as these laws do not require them to violate God's Law (Acts 5:29). At the same time, citizens are not required to obey the laws of another country (unless they are in that country). Some of the laws and regulations in Scripture are civil laws of ancient Israel. These were God's word to this theocracy, and were binding on that nation. These are not binding on citizens of other countries unless their countries adopt them as their own laws. Nonetheless, many of these laws may provide useful examples of civil laws to modern governments.

The Old Testament also provides examples of **ceremonial law**, which addresses such things as the manner, meaning and purpose of sacrifices, the Sabbath, and the Temple. These laws foreshadowed what was to come in all its fullness in the person and work of Jesus (Colossians 2:16-17), and identified Israel as a chosen people, set apart for God's service. The New Testament depicts the fulfillment, embodiment, and transformation of these laws in the person and work of Jesus. He is the Sabbath rest of which Israel's worship was the shadow (Hebrews 4:9). He is the Temple foreshadowed by Israel's Temple (John 1:14; 2:21). He is the ultimate sacrificial Lamb that takes away the sin of the world (John 1:29, 36). God's people are now free from the obligation to follow dietary laws and regulations of ceremonial purity (Acts 10:9-16). Likewise, we are no longer bound to keep the Sabbath in the way that Israel did, nor to observe other Jewish festivals (Colossians 2:16-17). It is vital to remember that Christians do not ignore these laws because of the laws themselves or because of personal preference. We are able to ignore them precisely because they have been fulfilled by Christ. A Christian may voluntarily choose to follow some of the ceremonial laws, such as keeping a kosher diet, as long as this is not seen as a holier diet than any other, and as long as no special merit is assigned to it. But some aspects of the ceremonial law are forbidden to us today. We may not reinstitute the sacrifice of animals, for example, since Christ has offered the final sacrifice (Hebrews 8:13).

The most overarching and penetrating aspect of the Law is its moral dimension. **Moral law** is a description of those standards expected by God of all human beings. Scripture teaches that this Law is written in the hearts of all people (Romans 2:13-16), but sinful, selfish hearts often blunt or mute its message. Because of this, God reveals the full extent of this Law in direct revelation, outside of our sinful hearts. The clearest presentation of the moral law is the Ten Commandments (Exodus 20:1-17; Deuteronomy 5:1-22). The moral dimension of the Law not only calls people to righteous outward behavior, but to inner holiness and perfection (see Matthew 5:48). It penetrates beyond mere actions and words, challenging humanity at the level of thoughts and motives. Unlike the civil-political laws and the ceremonial laws, moral law remains in effect. However, it is essential to remember that this law was also fulfilled by Jesus Christ. We cannot be saved by the Law, only by the Savior.

*Three Functions of the Law*

The Bible speaks about the purpose and power of the Law in several ways. It describes different **functions** (or uses) **of the Law** along with their different effects. The Law impacts people in a variety of ways, due more to the conscience, situation, and character of the person hearing it than the character of the Law itself. While the Law merely reflects God's holiness and righteousness, its general impact on people is a result of mankind's sinfulness. The Bible declares that "none is righteous, no not one" (Romans 3: 10; Psalm 143:2). When God's Law confronts the lives of sinners, it impacts people externally and internally. It affects people externally as a "curb" and internally as a "mirror." These are the main functions of the Law of God, as Paul describes it in Romans 3:20. The so-called "**third use** of the Law" is the reality that the Law still impacts a believer, one who is saved by grace alone apart from any works of the Law. After conversion, the Law can guide the believer to know and do God's will (though a sinful person will never be able to do this fully). It gives direction to the grateful response of faith that is looking for ways to thank God and to serve others in God's name.

## *The First Function of the Law: Curbing Evil*

In the area of external actions, the Law functions as a "curb." Curbs have two purposes. First, curbs warn us of impending danger, shocking us back onto the right path. A tired driver who drifts to the side of the road and strikes a curb is instantly aware of his error. He may take immediate steps to correct his car's direction. Curbs also prevent carnage. The greater the speed of a vehicle, the more impenetrable the curb must be. The "curbs" on highways are often concrete dividers. Here the protection exists so that if one loses control of a car, the vehicle is prevented from entering oncoming traffic and an accident is often of lesser severity. Of course, there are times when drivers deliberately violate curbs, or when their speed is so great that the curbs do not stop their recklessness, but curbs often perform their function of keeping cars where they belong.

The Law as a **curb** functions to restrain the outward manifestation of sin and evil. The threat of punishment may cause individuals not to perform an illegal or sinful act. Fear of consequences may urge them to do what is right to avoid unpleasant consequences. The promise of a reward for good behavior might also lead them to external obedience. Doing good things at this outward level does maintain a certain amount of peace and tranquility. It is better to live among good neighbors or good citizens than bad. (Some may object that doing the right thing for the wrong reason is hypocritical. This is true, but doing the wrong thing for the wrong reason is even worse.) The main external function of the Law is not to define the depth of righteousness and goodness but to curb the depth and destructiveness of unrighteousness. A person who refrains from breaking into someone's house only from fear of being caught is motivated by the wrong thing. Still, the homeowner is happy that her possessions have not been stolen. Most people would prefer that their fellow citizens follow the law as a curb than that they do whatever evil they desire.

### *The Second Function of the Law: Revealing Sinfulness*

The restraint of outward evil and the compulsion to outward good is a function of the law, but it pales in comparison to its second and primary function. The Law is a **mirror** to sinful people. While the law as a curb only controls external behavior, this function penetrates the outward veneer and exposes the heart. This great function of the Law exposes sinful people to God's reality; through the Law, we see ourselves as God sees us. His Law shows us how we measure up to divine standards. The answer is always distressing. This "mirror" functions as a theological and moral X-ray machine, exposing us to reveal the greatness of our sin and our great need of God's forgiveness. It calls all people to account before the righteousness of God. It promises rewards to those who are truly holy in thought, word and deed, according to God's standard of perfection and it promises righteous punishment to those who

> Paul Speratus (1484-1551) vividly captured the second function of the Law in his hymn, "Salvation unto Us Has Come":
>
> It was a false, misleading dream
> That God his Law had given
> That sinners could themselves
>    redeem
> And by their works gain heaven
> The Law is but a mirror bright
> To bring the inbred sin to light
> That lurks within our nature.

transgress. Since no sinful human ever lives up to God's standard, the Law as a mirror always shows our sinfulness, crushes our pride and self-reliance, and demonstrates our inability to save ourselves. This use of the law shows our desperate need for Christ.

## *The Third Function of the Law: a Rule*

Even after conversion, Christians continue to need the Law. While it still applies to us in its first and second functions, Christians also discover a third function or use of the Law. This function is quite different from the first two. It only applies to those who are God's people through Christ's grace. Christians who live in the grace and forgiveness of Christ can now use the law as a guide or standard of life (often called a "**rule**" in the sense of a measure). The forgiven child of God who desires to serve and please God sees the Law as an account of things that are pleasing in his sight. It provides direction to thankful hearts, redeemed and restored by God's grace alone. It gives content to the uncoerced, willing obedience that exists in the hearts of those reconciled fully to God by the person and work of Jesus alone. It continues to reveal what is truly good and right in the eyes of God even to the Christian who knows the certainty of the love of God by faith in Jesus.

This does not mean, however, that Christians will be able to obey the Law completely. Indeed, they may approach the Law as a guide, but when they attempt to follow it, they repeatedly fail. The third use of the Law inevitably transforms into the second use. It reveals sinfulness and shows our continuing need for God's grace. The faithful child of God recognizes this, repents, and receives Christ's forgiveness anew.

In summary, the main purpose of the Law is to show the full extent of sin in the human heart. Romans 7:13 tells us that while the Law is good, its purpose was that "sin might be shown to be sin" in us. Romans 3:20 similarly says, "through the Law comes knowledge of sin." In fact, one really does not know the full extent of sin until one's life is compared to the holy character of God, through the Law. Consequently, the chief purpose of the Law is to destroy sinners' confidence in themselves and any idea that they are righteous by their works. It levels all humanity as sinners before a righteous, judging God (Romans 3:19). It calls all to account, offering salvation only to those who are perfect, holy and righteous in thought, word and deed. God desires that human beings are saved, but the Law does not bring this salvation to sinners. It is true, but does not bring hope and forgiveness. Instead, it causes despair in any human activity outside of God's grace through faith. Because of this, the law is sometimes called God's "**alien work**." It is holy and necessary, but, it cannot save human beings. Its purpose is to reveal our need for the Gospel. Galatians describes this purpose another way when it says that the Law drives us to Christ (Galatians 3:24).

## 3. The Gospel

In the narrow or proper sense, the Gospel could not be any more different from the Law. "Gospel" literally means "good news," and no news could be better than this. It is the work of God to redeem and restore sinful humanity to himself. It differs from the Law in content, power and purpose. The content of the Gospel includes all the things that God did and does in and through Jesus Christ to save sinful humanity. It is the work and offer of God alone. The Gospel is most clearly seen in the life, death and resurrection of Jesus Christ in the New Testament. Yet, even in the Old Testament, one can see clearly the Gospel as the promise of the Christ who was to come. Such a word could only be revealed to us, since nothing in the heart of a sinful human would be able to imagine it.

The Gospel also differs from the Law in its purpose. Where the Law demands and coerces obedience, the Gospel offers and delivers the gracious forgiveness of God to sinful people. While the Law describes a righteousness that comes by a person's good works (Luke 10:28), it also punishes such "righteousness" when it inevitably fails to meet the absolute standard of God's holiness. The Gospel on the other hand describes and offers a righteousness that comes as a gift, the righteousness of another that covers the reality of our sin and death (Romans 3:21-25).

The Gospel not only describes and proclaims what God has done, it actually offers the merits of God's work in Christ to all who believe (Luke 24: 47; Romans 1:17). The message imparts the blessings of the message. The Gospel has power to create and sustain faith in hearts that were dead in their trespasses and sins (Ephesians 2:4-6). The proclamation that Christ died so that the world might be redeemed and reconciled to God, delivers the forgiveness, life and salvation that he has earned. Romans 10:17 tells us that "faith comes from hearing, and hearing through the word of Christ." This is the Gospel. Hearing this good news delivers what it describes.

## 4. Distinguishing and Confusing Law and Gospel

Though both are powerful words of God, the Law and the Gospel serve different purposes in the lives of sinful humans. One condemns, the other forgives. One is known, in part, by reason and conscience, the other is a message that can only be revealed as God's special revelation. One crushes and kills, the other gives life. One breaks the pride and selfish will of sinful man before God, the other covers guilt and fills the repentant with the mind of Christ (Philippians 2:5ff). One causes sorrow for sin, the other creates and sustains faith in the human heart. The Law demands perfect love and yet curses and kills when its commands are not obeyed (Romans 7:11), the Gospel offers love and life to that which is dead in trespasses and sins (Ephesians 2:1ff).

There are other ways to describe the clear distinction between the Law and the Gospel in the Bible. Both offer life and salvation. The Law promises life upon the condition of perfection before God. The Gospel offers the grace of God, life and salvation unconditionally because of the work of Jesus alone. Both impact humans. The Law exposes a person's utter sinfulness, while the Gospel proclaims one's total salvation in Jesus alone.

The Law and Gospel are often described as God's alien work and God's proper work. Ezekiel 33:11 says that God takes "no pleasure in the death of the wicked, but that the wicked turn from his way and live." The "alien" work of God, bringing sorrow for sin, guilt and remorse into our lives, is the exact opposite of his life-giving Gospel. Yet, both are God's actions in the lives of sinners. The Law kills; the Gospel makes alive.

*Dangers of Confusing Law and Gospel*

In 2 Timothy 2:15, Timothy is admonished to correctly handle or divide the word of truth. Paul makes such "correct handling" clear when he says, "by the works of the law no human being will be justified in his sight, since through the Law comes knowledge of sin" (Romans 3:20). In contrast, the Gospel is God's pure gift of his righteousness which covers our sins (Philippians 3:9; Romans 3:21-22). To falsely teach, or to misapply these two great themes of the Bible can have disastrous results in human lives.

To confuse Law and Gospel breeds either false confidence or despair. Galatians 2:21 reminds us that if people could obtain righteousness before God on the basis of their works, Christ died for nothing. Weakening or diminishing the demands of the Law, to make it appear as if people could actually fulfill them, breeds false confidence that cannot withstand the righteous judgment of God. It is like convincing a person that he can fly, and then letting him step off a ten story building. He is unprepared for the reality of his actions. Others try to mix Law and Gospel by claiming that we must receive the Gospel "properly." This inserts a human work into the reception of God's gift and does nothing but make us doubt if we are truly receiving the Gospel. The confidence and assurance that we are indeed part of God's eternal plan are destroyed in this confusion. When the Gospel, no matter to what degree, is made into something that we must do, pride or despair can be the only result.

On the other hand, correctly maintaining their absolute distinction roots forgiveness, life, salvation, joy and peace in the person and work of Jesus

> Rightly distinguishing the Law and the Gospel is the most difficult and the highest art of Christians in general and of theologians in particular. It is taught only by the Holy Spirit in the school of experience.
>
> C. F. W. Walther
> *The Proper Distinction between Law and Gospel*, Thesis Three.

Christ alone. This breeds confidence in the grace and promises of God. Knowing that we are forgiven, we are enabled to live life boldly in Christ for others. It is this certainty in relationship to God in Christ that empowers Christian service to others in God's name.

Confusing Law and Gospel also isolates a person from the resources, strength, and power of God by directing us to look to ourselves and our own strength. Any religion that speaks of "getting right with God" based on works in reality cuts one off from God. It rejects his powerful Gospel and grace in favor of our sinful works. Only he has the power to recreate us and to transform our hearts and minds. He is the only source of love, life and salvation that is able to live in believers through faith, and can empower believers to truly serve others. These things cannot truly be found apart from him.

Confusing or co-mingling Law and Gospel removes each from its rightful context, and distorts God's word. Without the crushing message of the Law, a person has no need for the forgiveness and salvation of Christ. The Gospel seems irrelevant and pointless to one who does not acknowledge this profound need. Without the healing word of the Gospel, a despairing sinner has no hope.

The distinction of Law and Gospel is ultimately about the knowledge that we are loved and redeemed by Christ. It shows us that it is impossible for sinful people to change their hearts, but that miraculously, in and through Christ alone, the heart of God has changed towards sinners. Only as one looks away from oneself and looks to the work of Jesus on the cross is there real certainty about one's eternal life in God. As such, the proper distinction challenges us to apply the Law to those who are comfortable in their trespasses and sins and to apply only the Gospel to those who are remorseful of and terrified by their sin and the righteous judgment that will be theirs without Christ. Certainty of our standing and relationship to God, and real love to serve our neighbor: what more reason does one need to properly divide the word of life?

## 5. The Christian and the Law

While Christians are free from the Law's demands because of Christ (see Romans 6:14-15; Galatians 5:18), we are still subject to the Law according to our sinful human natures. Paul speaks about the war of these two natures within us, namely the sinful nature (or "old Adam" which is corrupt and spiritually dead), and the new nature (Christ within us, alive to God by faith). Even though covered completely by the righteousness of Christ, our sinful nature often rises up to challenge grace and to instill pride in ourselves and not Christ. The Law, in all its severity, must be continually applied to such sinful feelings, compulsions and actions. In this sense, the Law continues to curb and mirror the Christian. Our sinful nature needs the Law's rebuke and judgment. The mirror of the Law continues to drive us daily back to Christ alone. Since Christians have these two natures working within them (until Christ returns), the Law must be preached to those who know Christ, not just to unbelievers. The Law always convicts and drives the sinful nature to despair. The Gospel then answers and heals this despair, continually rooting confidence in the person of Christ alone. Thus the Christian continues to need both Law and Gospel.

While it serves a vastly different purpose, the Christian also makes use of the whole counsel of God—both Law and Gospel—in the life of sanctification. The third use of the Law, discussed above, is an important use of this word. Only Christians can truly use the Law as a guide and, even then, they will fail; the Law will again transform into the second use.

The Law has no role to play as a coercive guide in the life of one redeemed by Christ. The Bible clearly teaches that there is "no condemnation for those who are in Christ Jesus" (Romans 8:1). The Law still exists as an accurate reflection of God's holiness and righteousness, even to those who are not condemned by it. Therefore, it can still guide the Christian who wants to express thankfulness in a life of faith. It can also provide direction and understanding about what pleases God and what truly serves one's neighbor. To be redeemed from being under the Law is to be empowered to serve as the Law describes without compulsion or guilt. Even Ephesians 2:8-9, the great "saved by grace passage," concludes with the knowledge in verse 10 that "we are his workmanship, created in Christ Jesus for good works, which God prepared beforehand, that we should walk in them." The new person in Christ is freed from the Law's coercive demands to be holy before God (Romans 8:1-2), and is freed for the joyful opportunity to love God and serve our neighbors (Galatians 6:2).

Controversies have always troubled the church when people totally dismiss the Law of God in the life of the Christian. This false teaching is called **antinomianism** (literally "against law"). Antinomianism distorts the biblical teaching on the Law and, because of this, it also distorts the Gospel (see Paul's answer to that in Romans 6). The opposite error, called **legalism**, is just as bad. Here the church turns the Gospel, or customs and traditions that are not mandated by Scripture, into new laws. This reliance on the tools of the Law only leads to mistrust and despair. Both of these errors, though opposite, distort both the Law and the Gospel. The teaching that people are 100% sinners and 100% saints (Romans 7 and 8), as well as the proper understanding and application of Law and Gospel, helps us apply God's judgment when judgment is needed, and apply God's complete forgiveness rightly.

### 6. Adiaphora

The proper distinction between Law and Gospel also helps the church properly deal with issues that are not directly addressed in Scripture. "**Adiaphora**" refers to issues that the Bible neither commands nor forbids. Issues such as the time or style of worship, the clothes one should wear to church, what hymns are to be sung, what specific prayers are to be offered are usually (though not always) adiaphora. If God does not address these things, they are in the arena of Christian freedom (1 Corinthians 9). If God has left an issue open, we are not to compel other people to act in a certain way. We are not authorized to "fill in the gaps" of Scripture with our own laws and regulations. We are never to speak our own word while pretending that it is the word of God himself.

Decisions regarding adiaphora are ordinarily simple matters, but when controversy or dispute arises, the discussion should focus not on the action, but on the motive that compels the action. Paul says, "whatever you do, do all to the glory of God" (1 Corinthians 10:31). He also tells us, "let no one pass judgment on you in questions of food and drink, or with regard to a festival or new moon or a Sabbath" (Colossians 2:16). Christians have freedom in areas of adiaphora, but we should never use this selfishly. We should not say, "Since it is adiaphora, I get to do what I want." Rather, the key to all discussions should be, "Since it is adiaphora, neither commanded nor forbidden by God, which action or tradition best serves the cause of the Gospel?" In all things, even those areas of Christian freedom, one's concern is how best to glorify God and to serve one's neighbor. In this regard, all things done out of faith towards God and fervent love for others are works that are good, even if not specifically commanded. And when there are differences of opinion on such matters, it is appropriate to remind ourselves to be kind to one another, to respect one another and to seek to do what is best for all out of reverence for Christ.

## The Center of Scripture

The center of the Scripture is Christ and the two vital themes to show our need for Christ and deliver him to us are the Law and the Gospel. The Law makes a person ask the right questions before God. The Gospel answers those vital questions concerning sin and grace, judgment and forgiveness, righteous wrath and undeserved mercy. Understanding the content, power and purpose of the Law and Gospel message of Scripture is not an abstract theological point. It is appropriating words whose ultimate goal is the eternal life of sinners. Both Law and Gospel are words from God whose function is, ultimately, to create faith in hearts that were dead in sin. The Law kills, the Gospel makes alive. The Law humbles, the Gospel exalts. The Law produces shame, fear or pride which ultimately leads to death, so that sinners might look outside themselves for a real answer to the evil that plagues us. Ultimately, the Law helps us understand the need for the cross of Christ, showing the full extent of God's righteous wrath so that the Gospel can show us the abundance of his gracious mercy and forgiveness. Law and Gospel describe life as it is. They are not merely words on a page; they are words empowered by God for the tasks he desires. They are words that call us to life on God's terms alone.

| Key Terms | |
| --- | --- |
| Adiaphora | Legalism |
| Alien work | Mirror |
| Antinomianism | Moral law |
| Ceremonial law | Narrow sense |
| Civil-political law | Proper sense |
| Curb | Rule |
| Functions (uses) | Third use of the law |
| of the law | Torah |
| Gospel | Wide sense |
| Law | |

## For Review and Discussion

1.  Is the "Gospel Reading" in a worship service referring to "Gospel" in the wide or narrow sense? Why is this important?

2.  It is possible to present the death of Jesus as either Law or Gospel. How might this be done? What can we learn from this?

3.  How does putting conditions into Gospel statements (for example, "if you are truly sorry, God will forgive you") confuse Law and Gospel?

4.  While it is important to properly distinguish Law and Gospel, the Gospel should dominate, since it is God's "proper work." Does your use of the Scriptures properly distinguish Law and Gospel? Is the Gospel the dominant teaching?

## For Further Reading

Giertz, Bo. *The Hammer of God: A Novel about the Cure of Souls*. Minneapolis: Augsburg Press, 1960.

Walther, C. F. W. *God's No and God's Yes: The Proper Distinction Between Law and Gospel*. Condensed by Walter C. Pieper. St. Louis: Concordia Publishing House, 1973.

_____. *The Proper Distinction Between Law and Gospel*. Translated by W. H. T. Dau. St. Louis: Concordia Publishing House, 1986.

# 4

# The Triune God

If a group of people was asked to define "religion," they would likely suggest a wide variety of answers. It is probable that most of these definitions would make some reference to "God." But what is a god? An answer might be sought by examining the religious life of human beings. Approximately four percent of the people in our world today identify themselves as **atheists**. They are willing to say no God exists. Another sixteen percent call themselves nonreligious or **agnostic**. They are unwilling or unable to acknowledge or deny the existence of a god, or they do not identify themselves with any particular religion. The other 80 percent see themselves as a part of a religion or they say they believe in one or more gods. Though the majority of human beings believe in the existence of God or gods, they have very different conceptions about the divine. Some identify their deities with specific names, others simply call them "god." Sadly, many people follow false gods. So what is a god? This chapter will explore the one true God's revelation of himself as we consider:

1. The Nature of "God"—*What is a god?*
2. Knowing God—*How can human beings know and understand God?*
3. The Triune God—*God's self-revelation*
4. The Necessity of the Doctrine of the Trinity—*Is this doctrine really necessary?*
5. Trinitarian Heresies—*Simplifying God's revelation leads away from him*
6. Characteristics of the Triune God—*Some key attributes of the living God*

## 1. The Nature of "God"

Human beings call on many different gods, but what is a god? Martin Luther wrote, "A 'god' is the term for that to which we are to look for all good and in which we are to find refuge in all need. Therefore, to have a god is nothing else than to trust and believe in that one with your whole heart" (*Large Catechism* I, 2). He says the same thing even more simply as he explains the first commandment: a god is whoever or whatever we "fear, love, and trust above all things" (*Small Catechism* I,1). Luther's explanations show what it means for a person to have a god. Whatever is most important in your life, whatever you rely on for your most profound needs, is your god. By this definition, everyone has a god. Some trust in themselves, in money, in friends, or in other people. Some rely on idols or false gods. Some believe in the God who reveals himself in the Bible. People give God's place and honor to many different things, but only the true God is worthy of this honor, and only the true God can help us.

Like us, St. Paul lived in a world where many people trusted in false gods. Seeing others worship false gods, the apostle responded:

> we know that "an idol has no real existence," and that "there is no God but one." ⁵For although there may be so-called gods in heaven or on earth—as indeed there are many "gods" and many "lords"— ⁶yet for us there is one God, the Father, from whom are all things and for whom we exist, and one Lord, Jesus Christ, through whom are all things and through whom we exist. (1 Corinthians 8:4b-6)

Paul did not argue about what to call these other deities. He simply told the truth: there is only one God. He also reminds his readers who that God really is. Other so-called "gods" and "lords" are nothing. Some are idols made of wood, stone, or precious metals; they do not have any power or real existence (Deuteronomy 4:28; Revelation 9:20). Some exist only in the human imagination, and so are powerless. Many things are called "gods," but there is only one true and living God.

## 2. Knowing God

How, then, can God be known? If God exists, it is important to know this God, but no one wants to be deceived or to worship a false God. There is no point to believing in a powerless "god" that can offer no real help. But which one is the true God? Can he be known? God is far greater than human beings or anything in creation. We are limited in space, in time, and in understanding, but God has no limits. Finite human beings can only know him when he chooses to reveal himself. If God chose to remain hidden, we would never know him. But God does not hide. The true God is seen in his actions and his self-revelation. In other words, God is revealed in his work and in his word.

God's work among us shows us who he is. Some knowledge of God is evident by his work of creation, by the way that he made us, by our conscience, and by his daily work in our lives. Yet this natural knowledge of God does not provide a complete or adequate picture of who God is. More direct and accurate knowledge of God comes as he chooses to tell human beings about himself. Hebrews says, "Long ago, at many times and in many ways, God spoke to our fathers by the prophets, but in these last days he has spoken to us by his Son. . ." (Hebrews 1:1-2a). God himself speaks in the Scriptures through the prophets and the apostles. Yet his clearest revelation comes in the person and work of Jesus Christ (John 1:18). Jesus is the key to God's self-revelation. In Christ, the work and the revelation of God are brought together in one person. Jesus is God and he reveals the true God to us.

*A Personal God*

God's self-revelation of himself consistently describes himself as a personal God. Since the words "person" and "personal" are often used imprecisely, it is important to define them carefully. This is especially vital when they are used in reference to God. To call God a person does not mean that he is essentially a human being or is a physical being (though it is true that God became human in the incarnation). Nor do we mean "personal" in the sense of "my own property." A **person** is a living individual who has a specific identity. It is someone (not something) who exists, is self-conscious, can think, will to do things, act, and feel. A person is distinct and recognizable from other persons. Asserting that God is personal means that he is not an object or a "thing" that we can manipulate or control. He is not a vague force or formless power. God is an identifiable and relational being.

This personal character is confessed when Christians address God with definite, personal pronouns. God is not an "it" but "he." A person is designated with proper names (Father, Son, Holy Spirit, Yahweh, Jesus) or titles (Lord, Creator, Comforter). One of the most significant attributes of persons is that they can and do relate to other persons. Objects are used or manipulated, but persons exist in relationship. They communicate with other persons. They can love, support, and help other persons. They can be known by other persons. God reveals himself to us as personal: someone who comes to us, who loves us, and who wants us to know and love him.

## 3. The Triune God

Of course, Christianity is not the only religion to proclaim a personal God. It is not enough to acknowledge that God is personal without knowing him. Thankfully, God personally reveals himself to humanity. When he does this, it is soon evident that God is much greater and more complex than his creatures would have imagined. God's nature and existence can seem confusing when human beings try to fit him into their own experience of what it means to be a person or to exist. Yet God graciously reveals his true nature so that his people may know him.

God reveals two paradoxical (but not contradictory) truths about his nature: there is only one God, but that one God exists in three persons: the Father, the Son, and the Holy Spirit. This truth, known as the doctrine of the Holy **Trinity**, summarizes a great deal of biblical teaching. As the basis for this doctrine is considered, it is important to remember that we want to know God as he reveals himself. What does he communicate about himself? When this knowledge is sought, some challenging teachings may be encountered, but they are God's challenging teachings and not human fabrications.

The doctrine of the Trinity is a fundamental Christian teaching, since it articulates the very nature of God. It is important to remember, however, that this is something we are called to believe, even if it is not something that we are able to understand completely. As the children of God, we recognize that while human understanding is limited, we can be faithful to what God has revealed. Christians believe the doctrine of the Trinity because God has

### Is faith unique to religion?

People often think that trusting something without completely understanding it is unique to religion. This is not true. Every day we use things that we do not understand. You may use a computer without understanding how it works or how its components function. A person may fly in an airplane without understanding the physics involved. A meal can be delicious and nourishing even when eaten by someone who cannot cook, or who does not know what ingredients are being eaten. We may not understand all of these things, but we trust that they work. Similarly, while we will not fully understand the doctrine of the Trinity, we can trust God and his word.

revealed it. His word reveals two truths: there is only one God, and that one God exists in three persons.

## The Unity of God

The testimony of Holy Scripture is clear. While the peoples of the world worship many gods, there is only one true, living God. Both the Old and New Testaments directly proclaim this truth. Isaiah writes, "Thus says the LORD, the King of Israel and his Redeemer, the LORD of hosts: I am the first and I am the last; beside me there is no god" (Isaiah 44:6). There is no God other than the one true God. When one of the teachers of the Law asked Jesus which of the commandments was the most important, he answered, ". . .Hear, O Israel: the Lord our God, the Lord is one" (Mark 12:29). He was quoting Deuteronomy 6:4, showing again that both testaments unanimously confess the existence of only one God. Genuine Christianity is a purely monotheistic religion. There is only one true God. There is no other being to compete with him and no appeal beyond him. Those who know that they are loved by this God have all that they need, since "if God is for us, who can be against us?" (Romans 8:31).

## Three Divine Persons

The challenge of the doctrine of the Trinity appears when this one God describes himself. Jesus Christ comes to this earth and teaches that there is only one God. Jesus calls his Father God and prays to him as God. At the same time, Jesus himself also claims to be God. Further complexity is added when Scripture speaks of the deity of the Holy Spirit. All three persons are specifically called God, yet the Bible still proclaims that there is only one God.

### The Father

The first person of the Trinity identifies himself as the Father. Scripture specifically calls the Father God. For example, Ephesians 4:6 says that there is ". . .one God and Father of all, who is over all and through all and in all." The New Testament is filled with greetings and benedictions which speak of the Father's deity. "Grace to you and peace from God our Father and the Lord Jesus Christ" (Romans 1:7). For many people, the deity of the Father is so obvious that it hardly needs to be mentioned. Indeed, while the word "God" is properly used of all three persons of the Trinity, many Christians use it more as a synonym for the Father. The Bible itself often refers to the Father simply as "God." The Father is truly God.

### The Son

The conception of the one God grows more complex, however, when the person and work of Jesus is considered. The Scriptures call Jesus ". . .God over all, blessed forever" (Romans 9:5). When others identify him as God, Jesus does not rebuke them, but calls them blessed (Matthew 16:16-17). When, at his trial, Jesus was asked if he was "the Christ, the Son of God," he agreed (Matthew 26:63). Jesus claimed to be the one God, yet he also spoke of his Father, who is God, and of the Holy Spirit who is also God.

### The Holy Spirit

The Holy Spirit is present throughout the Scriptures, from Genesis to Revelation. Like the Father and the Son, the Holy Spirit is also identified as God. According to 1 Corinthians 3:16, the church is "God's temple." The temple is the place where God dwells. This passage teaches that the Spirit lives in us, and that we are God's temple. In other words, since God the Holy Spirit lives in us, we are God's temple.

Acts 5:3-4 records an event in the early church in which a couple sold some property and claimed to give the proceeds to the church. In truth, they held some of the money back. The problem was not that they kept the money, which they were free to do, but that they lied about their actions. Peter confronted the deceiver,

> . . .why has Satan filled your heart to *lie to the Holy Spirit* and to keep back for yourself part of the proceeds of the land? ⁴While it remained unsold, did it not remain your own? And after it was sold, was it not at your disposal? Why is it that you have contrived this deed in your heart? *You have not lied to men but to God.* (Acts 5: 3-4)

Ananias had lied to the Holy Spirit who is God. Like the Father and the Son, the Spirit is also God, but he is not identical with the Father or the Son.

### The Triune God

While consistently maintaining that there is only one God, the Bible repeatedly refers to the Father, Son, and Holy Spirit as that one true God. Each person of the Trinity is fully and completely God. Each does work that only

God can do. Each person is eternal, and was not created or made by another person. Each person is rightly acknowledged as the almighty God, and as Lord of all. Each person of the Trinity is rightly worshipped and honored by his creation.

If one wishes to be faithful to the entire revelation of Scripture, and therefore to summarize God's self-revelation accurately, these two paradoxical biblical truths must be acknowledged: there is only one God who is the Father, the Son, and the Holy Spirit. This is the mystery of the triune (or three-in-one) God that he has revealed in his word.

### The Trinity is Revealed in Both the Old and New Testaments

The Trinity is a challenging, and possibly confusing, doctrine. Yet it is a teaching that permeates the Scriptures. Again and again, the Bible shows us the complexity of God's triune existence. A few examples will demonstrate the prevalence of this teaching. For instance, the Trinity is seen in the very first chapter of the Bible.

> In the beginning, God created the heavens and the earth. ²The earth was without form and void, and darkness was over the face of the deep. And the Spirit of God was hovering over the face of the waters. . . . ²⁶Then God said, "Let us make man in our image, after our likeness. . . . (Genesis 1:1-2, 26)

God refers to himself with plural pronouns: "let *us* make man in *our* image." Both "God" and "the Spirit of God" are recognized. God is present, but the Spirit of God is also present. Other passages make it clear that the Son was involved in creation as well (John 1:3; Colossians 1:16). Creation shows the existence and the work of the Trinity. Another reflection is found in the words of the Messiah recorded in Isaiah 48:16. The coming Messiah says, "the Lord GOD has sent me, and his Spirit." God sends the Messiah, who is God, with his Spirit.

The Gospels record the baptism of Jesus, providing a revelation of the Trinity. "When Jesus was baptized, immediately he went up from the water, and behold, the heavens were opened to him, and he saw the Spirit of God descending like a dove and coming to rest on him; and behold, a voice from heaven said, 'This is my beloved Son, with whom I am well pleased' (Matthew 3:16-17). The entire Trinity was revealed at the Jordan that day. Rising from the water, the Son is identified as God by the other two persons of the Trinity. The Father is manifest in his voice from heaven, and the Spirit is seen descending as a dove. As the earthly ministry of Jesus continues, he reveals the triune nature of God. He speaks of the Father and the Spirit, but also of the unity that he has with them both (John 14:16, 26; John 15:26).

Before ascending to heaven, Jesus commissions his disciples to "make disciples of all nations, baptizing them in the name of the Father and of the Son and of the Holy Spirit" (Matthew 28:19. Notice also that the three persons are described as one "name.")

Other New Testament books are also filled with references to the Trinity. This trinitarian content may be overlooked as readers focus on other elements in these texts, but it is important to see God's self-revelation. For example, 1 Corinthians reveals the Trinity as it discusses spiritual gifts. "Now there are varieties of gifts, but the *same Spirit*; and there are varieties of service, but the *same Lord*; and there are varieties of activities, but it is the *same God* who empowers them all in everyone" (1 Corinthians 12:4-6).

The many benedictions and greetings found in the Epistles also testify to the Trinity. For instance, 2 Corinthians 13:14 says, "The grace of the Lord Jesus Christ and the love of God and the fellowship of the Holy Spirit be with you all." These are just a few examples of the many accounts of the Trinity found in both the Old and New Testaments.[1] Such references are common because they are depictions of God's own identity—and he wants all people to know him.

*Trinitarian Vocabulary*

The doctrine of the Trinity permeates the Scriptures and is an accurate summary of what the Bible teaches. The data permeates the Old and New Testaments, but can this complex doctrine be summarized concisely? For generations, Christians have summarized this teaching with some standard terms. While the words themselves are not biblical, they summarize the content of Scripture. The word "trinity" cannot be found in a biblical concordance, but the doctrine of the Trinity is taught throughout Scripture. Once vocabulary is defined, it can be used to communicate more efficiently with other Christians. Other words could serve the same purpose, but they would still require definition for clarity. Furthermore, these new words would not be shared with other Christians. It is far easier to use the terminology that Christians have historically used to discuss this doctrine. Yet it is important

---

[1] Some Christians think that the strongest reference to the Trinity is found in 1 John 5:7 where the King James Version contains some words that are not found in other translations: "For there are three that bear record in heaven, the Father, the Word, and the Holy Ghost: and these three are one." These words are not found in any Greek manuscripts of the New Testament prior to the 16th century, and appear to be a much later addition to the biblical text. Because of the doubtfulness of this verse, it is not suitable to use in forming doctrinal statements

to remember that the doctrine is not based on the words themselves, but on the biblical data that they summarize.

While orthodox Christianity has always believed in the Trinity, it took some time before the entire Christian church was using the same words in the same way. Much of the reason for this is that the early church had two major languages: Latin and Greek. Some of the earliest debates were really over which words in each language best expressed the biblical truth. Eventually, a general consensus emerged about what the words meant when used theologically. This theological vocabulary was used in the Creeds and in subsequent theological writings.

## Describing the Oneness of God

The biblical teaching that there is only one God is usually summarized by the word **substance**. (The word **essence** may used in place of substance.) Substance *is* deity; it means to be God. Substance is what the three persons are in common, and what no one else is. It is the manner in which God is one. God is one in substance. There is no division of God. The Father is not 1/3 God or part of God; the Father *is* God. The same is true of the Son and the Spirit. All three persons share in the divine substance. They are equally and fully God. So the Nicene Creed says that Jesus is "of one substance with the Father." They are both fully and truly God. The same is also true of the Holy Spirit. There is one God, one divine substance.

## Describing the Three-ness of God

The "three-ness" of the Trinity is described with the word "person." Each person is a distinct, identifiable, self-conscious, relational individual, as discussed above. These two concepts together summarize the biblical teaching: there is one God (one divine substance) in three persons.

Though the three persons are one in essence and each is fully God, the three persons are distinct from each other. Human beings know only those details of the Trinity that God has revealed to us. He has chosen to reveal some of the distinctions as the three persons relate to each other. These "internal works of the Trinity" show us how the three persons relate to each other and are summarized in the Creeds.

The Father is the source of the other two persons of the Trinity. He was not created by anyone, nor is he **begotten** by anyone. The Father is the origin. The Son owes his existence to the Father. He was not created by anyone, including the Father, yet he is eternally begotten by the Father. We beget things that are of the same nature as ourselves; we make things that do not share our nature. So a human being can beget human children, but make things that are not human. Saying that the Father begets the Son means, in part, that the Son is true God and not part of creation. His existence derives from the Father, and he is of the same substance as the Father. Yet since the triune God is eternal, this all happens without reference to time.

Since God is infinite, he is independent of the linear constraints of time. Finite creatures have trouble conceiving of how anything can exist outside of the temporal framework of this life. This can impede human understanding of the interaction of the persons of the Trinity. We tend to force their actions into chronological sequence when, in fact, they occur outside of time, and consequently without respect to linear sequence. There never was a time when the Son was not begotten from the Father. The Holy Spirit was not created by anyone, nor is he begotten of the Father (like the Son). Instead, the Holy Spirit **proceeds** from the Father and the Son.

All three persons are fully God, but they are not identical. They have a relationship with the other two persons. While the three persons are distinct and have a unique relationship with the other persons, all three share one divine substance. There is only one God. As the Trinity interacts with us, the three persons are all involved and active. These external works are trinitarian works. So while the Father is the source and origin of the Trinity, all three persons were present and involved in the work of creation. While the Son makes atonement for sins by sacrificing himself on the cross, he was sent by the Father and offers that sacrifice to the Father, and the Spirit conveys those benefits to his children. All three persons are involved in redemption and salvation, and Christians gratefully respond to the entire Trinity. When we worship the triune God, we do not need to keep track of how many times we address each person. The triune persons do not get jealous of each other. We rightly worship the one God who is three persons.

*Analogies of the Trinity*

Christians can summarize the biblical data on the Trinity, provide specialized vocabulary to discuss it, and explore the relationship of the three persons (to the extent that God has revealed it to us). But the fact is that humans will never fully understand the substance or persons of the Trinity in this life. God is greater than his creation. He is beyond our full comprehension. We believe the doctrine of the Trinity, and confess the biblical truths,

| Father | Uncreated Eternal Fully God | Begets the Son | Sends the Spirit |
|--------|------------------------------|----------------|------------------|
| Son | Uncreated Eternal Fully God | Eternally begotten of the Father | Sends the Spirit |
| Holy Spirit | Uncreated Eternal Fully God | Neither begets nor begotten | Eternally proceeds from the Father and Son |

but this doctrine will always remain mysterious and paradoxical because there is nothing else in our experience that is truly like the Trinity. There is only one Holy Trinity.

Nonetheless, many Christians have found that their understanding is assisted by certain illustrations of the Trinity. These illustrations show, to a degree, how something can be both one and more than one at the same time. While these may be helpful, it must be remembered that they are only illustrations. All of them fall short of the doctrine of the Trinity. In fact, if you press any one of them far enough, the illustration will end up describing a trinitarian heresy. Still, these may be useful tools to reflect on the Trinity.

St. Augustine described the Trinity in terms of a relationship of love. If God is love, he needs someone to love. So he thought of the Father as the lover, the Son as the one being loved, and the Holy Spirit is love. Tertullian compared God to a river system. The Father is like a spring: the source of water. The Son is the river that flows from that spring to other places. The Spirit is like irrigation canals that carry the water from the river to thirsty people. St. Patrick compared the Trinity to a shamrock. It is one plant, but has three leaves. These are just a few of the many illustrations that Christians have used to illustrate the Trinity. Ultimately, however, Christians confess the Trinity not because of the illustrations, but because this is how God has described himself to us.

## 4. The Necessity of the Doctrine of the Trinity

Is all of this really necessary? Why must Christians struggle with such a complex and difficult doctrine? Isn't it enough that we love God? While we don't want to become bogged down in theological or philosophical explanations of the Trinity, this is a vitally important doctrine. God has revealed himself as the triune God. Since he loves us, we are moved to want to know him better—to know him as he reveals himself to us. For that reason alone, the doctrine of the Trinity must be taken seriously. In addition, there are also other things that the doctrine of the Trinity can help us understand.

The most important thing is salvation. Jesus Christ was crucified as a sacrifice for our sins. His death has brought us peace with God. These biblical statements are virtually incomprehensible without the Trinity. Who received the sacrifice of Jesus? The Father did. The Son died to reconcile us to the Father (Ephesians 2:16). The Spirit works faith in human hearts so that we receive these benefits (1 Corinthians 12:3). The entire Trinity is involved with our salvation. We see other reflections of the Trinity as we pray and worship. We pray to the Father through Jesus (John 15:16) in the Holy Spirit (Romans 8:26-27).

The doctrine of the Trinity also reminds us that the one true God exists in relationship. Whether we use St. Augustine's illustration of the Trinity as love or not, Scripture says that God is love (1 John 4:8) and speaks of the love of the persons of the Trinity for each other (John 14:31; John 15:9), a love which overflows to all. From eternity, God is love, beginning with the love the three Persons share. In the same way, humans, who are created in the image of God, find their own being in the call to live in loving relationships with God and others. These relationships are to be filled with God's love.

## 5. Trinitarian Heresies

Sadly, many people are not content to confess the biblical doctrine of the Trinity. Instead of believing God's self-description, they see the paradox of one God in three persons as an illogical doctrine or a stumbling block. From the very beginning of Christianity until today, some have chosen to ignore or change part of the biblical teaching in order to make it more palatable to their own reason or logic. When the divine revelation is modified, doctrines that seem more logical may result, but they are no longer God's truth. Fallen minds have instead taken dominion over the word of God. Biblical data is quickly oversimplified. When this happens to the doctrine of the Trinity, a number of heresies emerge. While these false teachings were all known by the early church, they are not ancient history. Every one of these is taught by cults, sects, and false religions even today.

### Unitarian Heresies

One category of trinitarian heresies removes the paradox by denying the three persons of the Trinity. These are called **unitarian** heresies, because

*Error or Heresy?*

Errors and heresies are both false teaching, but the distinction is important. A heresy is a persistent error relating to a central Christian doctrine. When confronted with biblical evidence, a heretic refuses correction. Heresies undermine the true Christian faith and, for this reason, place one's salvation in jeopardy.

they deny God's three-ness while holding to his unity. Some do this by denying the deity of the Son and the Holy Spirit. God then is only one person. This is the error of modern Judaism and Islam: they accept the oneness of God, but deny the deity of Christ and the Spirit. The same thing is done by many modern Unitarians. While they say they believe in one God, it is not the God of Scripture.

### Modalism

A sophisticated variation of this heresy is called modalism. **Modalism** accepts the names and roles of the three persons, but denies their distinctness. It teaches that there is only one God and one person, but this one God interacts with creation in different ways. At times he takes on the role of the Father, other times the role of the Son, and still other times the role of the Spirit. Yet, modalism claims, these are not three distinct persons, but only three roles. While this appears to be a logical explanation of the Trinity, it does not do justice to the trinitarian teaching revealed in Scripture. By removing the distinction among the persons, it affects the plan of salvation. Against all Unitarian heresies, we emphasize the three persons of God as the Scriptures reveal them.

### Hierarchical Heresies

While modalists deny the persons of God, the hierarchical heresies deny the oneness of God. They make the persons unequal and so affect our understanding of all three persons and of the divine substance. There are a number of ways that heretics have made the Trinity into a hierarchy.

*Adoptionism*

**Adoptionism** attacks the Trinity by reducing the deity of Christ. While there are many variations of this heresy, adoptionism usually sees the Father alone as the one true God. Wanting to save the world, the Father sought someone to redeem humanity. He found Jesus—an exceptional human being, but not God. When the Father saw that this man Jesus could accomplish the work of salvation, the Father "adopted" Jesus as his "Son" and gave him a status and role above that of other people. (Many adoptionists think that this happened at the baptism of Jesus.) Adoptionism says that Jesus was a good man who did wonderful things by the power of God, but Jesus himself was not God. Yet the Gospels clearly show us that Jesus claimed to be more than a human being. He claimed deity. Adoptionism endangers our salvation by denying that our Savior is God.

*Subordinationism*

**Subordinationism**, on the other hand, does not make Jesus a mere human being. It recognizes that the biblical evidence asserts the deity of Christ. Yet subordinationism cannot accept the full deity of Christ or his equality with the Father. They maintain that the Father is uniquely and supremely God, so the Son and the Holy Spirit must be lesser deities of some sort. In fact, most of the subordinationists thought that the Father created the Son and the Holy Spirit. They are greater than other creatures, but they are not on the same level as the Father. They are not fully or truly God; the three persons are unequal. Like adoptionism, this heresy has to overlook Jesus' claims to real and full deity and thus affects salvation.

*Polytheism*

One final trinitarian heresy is **polytheism** or **tritheism**, which rationalizes the Trinity by denying God's unity. It makes the three persons into three independent gods that may or may not work together. This denies the many biblical references to the unity of God. While there are many polytheistic religions in the world, Christianity proclaims the oneness of God.

*Responding to Heresies*

Each of these heresies substitutes human reason or speculation for the biblical data. Each of their explanations is simpler than the biblical account and easier to explain, but each distorts or even rejects the biblical teaching on the Trinity. Faithful Christian teaching proclaims what God has revealed without changing it to conform to our own fallen intellect. These false teachings must be answered with the truth of God's word.

## 6. Characteristics of the Triune God

The doctrine of the Trinity describes the nature of God as he reveals himself in Scripture. It summarizes the biblical teaching accurately, but the Bible also offers further descriptions of God. He is not only known in his self-revelation as the Trinity, but also in his actions toward humanity. When the biblical writers depict the things that God has done, and when they lead his people in adoration and worship of the Trinity, they often describe him. Since God is a personal God, he can be known and described. Just as you can describe yourself or a friend, so God is describable. These biblically based attributes of God are depictions of who he is and what he is like.

When describing God, humans beings may be prone to **anthropomorphism** (viewing God—or anything else—in human terms). For example, it is anthropomorphic to depict God the Father as an old man with a white beard. Since he does not have a human body, this is not an accurate portrayal of what the Father is really like. It is a natural tendency to think of God in such human-centered description, but it is important to maintain that God is not a deified human being or a super-human. In fact, Scripture clearly teaches that God, in his essence, is not human. "God is **spirit**" (John 4:24). Of course, the issue of anthropomorphism changes when the incarnation of the Son of God is considered. We may, and should, speak of the humanity of Christ, for he truly became human. God became man in Christ, but the Father and the Holy Spirit do not have a human nature as Christ now does. God is spirit.

Furthermore, anthropomorphism may allow human experiences to shape our conception of God. We tend to project our own emotions and experiences on God, but this can lead away from his revelation. The nature and attributes of God cannot be determined by examining the characteristics of his creatures. Nor should his attributes and character be defined on the basis of speculation or philosophy. The true theologian will recognize the attributes of God that are revealed in Scripture. These are not a complete description of God, yet they are an accurate depiction of who he is. Many books, papers, and Bible studies have been written about various divine attributes. This book will not attempt to discuss every divine attribute. Instead, it will address some key attributes of God, while remembering that many other divine characteristics are revealed in Holy Scripture.

Some of the divine attributes have already been examined in this chapter. God is living, personal, one, and triune. Furthermore, he is uncreated or self-existing. No one made God or gave him life. Rather, God has life in himself (John 5:26). Where did God come from? Though it stretches our imagination, the answer is simply "God is." He exists of himself. But what is this self-existing God like? "Whatever the LORD pleases, he does" (Psalm 135:6). He is not subject to human limitations. This is not a philosophical abstraction, but part of his own revelation. He is able to do things that humans cannot because he is God.

God is **eternal**. As part of God's creation, human lives take place within time, but God is not bound by this constraint. His earthly creatures experience one day after another in sequence, but God is free from the limits of time. Humans tend to conceive of eternity as an existence that never ends, but God's eternity has no beginning either. "From everlasting to everlasting you are God" (Psalm 90:2). Christ calls himself "the Alpha and the Omega, the first and the last, the beginning and the end" (Revelation 22:13). God transcends all time. In fact, when he reveals his name to Moses, he calls himself "I AM" (Exodus 3:14).

As God is not limited by time, so he is not limited by space or by matter. God is **omnipresent**. He is able to be present simultaneously in every place. "'Do I not fill heaven and earth?' declares the LORD" (Jeremiah 23:24). There is no place a person can go to escape God. No one can hide from him and nobody is ever out of his care. When King David thought about the presence of God, he asked,

> Where shall I go from your Spirit? Or where shall I flee from your presence? [8]If I ascend to heaven, you are there! If I make my bed in Sheol, you are there! [9]If I take the wings of the morning and dwell in the uttermost parts of the sea, [10]even there your hand shall lead me, and your right hand shall hold me. [11]If I say, "Surely the darkness shall cover me, and the light about me be night," [12]even the darkness is not dark to you; the night is bright as the day, for darkness is as light with you. (Psalm 139:7-12)

God is always present. This is a great comfort to the child of God who knows his love.

In a similar way, there are no limits on God's knowledge. He is **omniscient** (1 John 3:20). He has complete and perfect knowledge of everything that exists, since he created everything. Human knowledge is always incomplete, but God knows all. His knowledge is not simply a listing of facts, but it is coupled with perfect wisdom, the ability to use and apply knowledge in the best way (Romans 11:33; 1 Corinthians 1:30).

Furthermore, God has the power and ability to do what he pleases. In other words, he is **omnipotent** or almighty. God can do anything—more than anyone else could ask or imagine. Nothing is beyond God's ability to do (Ephesians 3:20). "Nothing will be impossible with God" (Luke 1: 37). God can use this power in any way that pleases him. He could use his limitless power to compel our obedience or our action. Yet God frequently uses his power in a way that is more gentle and accommodating of human weakness. He allows a degree of external freedom as human beings live the lives that he has given to us.

An odd puzzle of human logic often arises as people discuss the power of God. It asks, "Could God create a rock so big that he could not lift it?" This is ultimately a silly question. The question itself is logically invalid, nullifying itself by creating a contradiction—one that could never occur in reality. Any such question is invalid even when the subject is God. Almighty God can do anything he pleases, but why would it please him to limit his power in such a way? This question is only a puzzle of logic, not a theological statement.

*Attributes of Moral Character*

Most of the attributes already discussed show that God is not constrained by human limitations in existence, time, place, or power. Other major attributes describe his moral character or the way he consistently chooses to act towards other persons. One of the most common biblical descriptions of God notes that he is **holy**. Holiness is absolute perfection. God is acclaimed as the One who is "holy, holy, holy" (Isaiah 6:3) and is "majestic in holiness" (Exodus 15:11). He is uniquely holy (Revelation 15:4), and therefore he demands holiness from his creatures (Leviticus 19:2). Even though all have failed to keep that standard, he declares us holy because of the work of Christ (Romans 3:22).

Closely related to the perfection of holiness is justice. God is perfectly **just** and **righteous**. "His work is perfect, for all his ways are justice" (Deuteronomy 32:4). Justice means that God is perfectly consistent and fair in how he applies his will. He does not randomly make decrees or demands, but is consistent and deliberate in all that he does. Because God is just, he decrees his standard of holiness and demands that it be met. He establishes penalties for breaking his Law and he enforces those penalties. God's Law is never ignored; it must be satisfied because God is just and righteous.

If righteousness and holiness were God's only moral attributes, there would be no hope, for all people fail to keep that standard. Thankfully, God is also merciful. **Mercy** does not give a person what is deserved but rather blessings that are not deserved. Mercy looks upon human sinfulness and desires to forgive. Mercy is God's will to save sinners who deserve to be damned. It is the antithesis of justice. This is closely related to **grace** (Joel 2:13). God gives us not what we deserve, but what Christ has earned. There is a biblical tension between God's justice and God's mercy. As a just God, he rightly condemns and punishes sins. As a merciful God, he desires to forgive. These two attributes seem to work against each other, but find glorious reconciliation in Christ. In Christ, God is perfectly just by punishing human sinfulness, yet he is merciful to his people through Christ's obedience and righteousness. He now declares us righteous for Christ's sake.

God is also good. A human being can be perfectly consistent and yet work consistently towards evil ends. Not so with God. "The LORD is good to all; and his mercy is over all that he has made" (Psalm 145:9). He knows what is in the best interest of his creatures. When he created the world, he declared it good. He allows the sun to shine and the rain to fall on both the righteous and the unrighteous (Matthew 5:45). He has a good purpose in all that he does. Yet his creation is not always satisfied with goodness. We do not always see just how something is meant for our good, but the Bible reminds us that "we know that for those who love God all things work together for good, for those who are called according to his purpose" (Romans 8:28).

Another attribute of God's moral character is his patience. God is patient with his creation, giving the gift of time so that more humans may be saved. St. Peter shows this when he talks about the timing of Jesus' return. Why is the Savior waiting so long? Peter answers, "The Lord is not slow to fulfill his promise as some count slowness, but is patient toward you, not wishing that any should perish, but that all should reach repentance" (2 Peter 3:9). Thank God that he is so patient!

There are many other attributes that could be considered. Scripture is filled with descriptions of the character and actions of God towards his creation. The child of God has ample material to know God better. Furthermore, each chapter of this book examines more of the attributes and character of the triune God. One final attribute really unites the rest: "God is love" (1 John 4:8). He has lavished his love on us (1 John 3:1). The persons of the Trinity love each other, and the triune God acts in wonderful love towards humanity. This perfect, self-giving love motivates God to create and redeem us, establishes us in relationship with God, and fills our lives with joy and meaning.

How do we describe the triune God? Words fail us. Our descriptions are inadequate. Our images fall short of the wonder of God. Our thoughts cannot contain him or fully describe him. But he reveals himself to us. He tells us who he is, what his purpose is for us, and how he loves us. We know him when we receive his love and grace, and we respond to him in worship and adoration. The Holy Trinity is the God of love and grace: the only true God, our Lord and God.

**For Review and Discussion**

1.  Martin Luther defined a "god" as whatever you fear, love, and trust above all things. In light of this definition, are people today prone to idolatry? What are some of the gods of this age? How is this also a danger for Christians?

2.  This chapter discussed some of God's attributes. Look again at these characteristics of God. Are these attributes Law or Gospel? Why?

3.  Cults often reject and attack the doctrine of the Trinity. Why do you think this doctrine is such an attractive target? How can we better present and defend the faith in the face of such denial?

4.  There are many illustrations that are used to help describe the Trinity (for example, St. Patrick used the shamrock). Choose one or more illustrations. What aspect of the Trinity does it describe? What are the strengths and shortcomings of this illustration? Is it biblically accurate? Is it helpful?

---

### Key Terms

| | |
|---|---|
| Adoptionism | Omnipresent |
| Agnostic | Omniscient |
| Anthropomorphism | Person |
| Atheist | Polytheism |
| Begotten | Proceeds |
| Essence | Righteous |
| Eternal | Spirit |
| Grace | Subordinationism |
| Holy | Substance |
| Just | Trinity |
| Mercy | Tritheism |
| Modalism | Unitarianism |
| Omnipotent | |

## For Further Reading

Augustine. *The Trinity*. Brooklyn, NY: New City Press, 1991.

Lewis, C. S. "Beyond Personality: Or First Steps in the Doctrine of the Trinity," book four of *Mere Christianity*. San Francisco: HarperSanFrancisco, 2001.

McGrath, Alister, ed. *Understanding the Trinity*. Grand Rapids: Academie Books, 1988.

Watson, Philip S. *Let God be God!: An Interpretation of the Theology of Martin Luther*. Eugene, OR: Wipf and Stock, 2001.

# 5

# Creation

It has been suggested that modern individuals find few Christian teachings as offensive as the doctrine of creation. Familiar with popular scientific worldviews, many non-Christians, and even some Christians, consider divine creation an absurdly anti-intellectual concept. Because of this, they may refuse to give Christianity any serious attention. Christians struggling to synthesize modern evolutionary theories with a belief in creation may give up in despair, abandoning the biblical account as outdated mythology. Scientific theories are not the only stumbling blocks to an acceptance of the biblical doctrine of creation. Philosophical objections might also be raised. For example, some consider it absurd to believe that God created a perfect world when famine, disease, and the horrors of war are now so common.

Such questions and objections deserve to be considered seriously. Indeed, since they may dissuade many people from investigating Christianity—and persuade others to forsake it—they must be treated very seriously by all who believe the Christian faith to be the only path to salvation. Because this doctrine so often proves controversial, and because it is intimately related to the central article of salvation, it is worth examining:

1. Creation *Ex Nihilo*—*The manner and means of the world's origin*
2. Biblical Affirmations of Genesis—*Old and New Testament confirmation of Genesis*
3. What Scripture Does and Does Not Teach—*Some unanswered questions about creation*
4. Evolution—*Do Scripture and Science Conflict?*
5. Hybrid Teachings—*Attempts to combine Scripture and reason to explain the world's origin*

## 1. Creation *Ex Nihilo*

Christianity is not unique in discussing **cosmology** (the study of the universe and its origins) in terms of divine creation. In fact, until relatively recently, almost all religious and philosophical worldviews made room for a creator god of one sort or another. As one might expect, however, the Old and New Testaments reveal certain emphases that distinguish the Christian understanding of creation from others. A logical starting point for the examination of the Christian doctrine is its particular emphasis on creation *ex nihilo*, that is, from nothing. Many ancient cosmologies held that the world was formed or assembled from pre-existing material. In this view, creation was not a matter of calling something new into being, but rather of giving shape to that which already existed. (This was the view, for example, of the influential Greek philosopher, Plato.)

In contrast, the biblical authors speak of *all* things, even matter itself, being created by God. St. Paul includes everything "in heaven and on earth, visible and invisible," specifically noting that God existed "before all things" (Colossians 1:16-17). John's Gospel makes the same point (John 1:3), while the author of Hebrews speaks even more explicitly: "what is seen was not made out of things that are visible" (Hebrews 11:3; see also Romans 4:17). But common sense (as well as good science and philosophy) indicates that something cannot naturally come from nothing. We must therefore take a more detailed look at what Scripture says about the way in which the universe was created.

### The Mechanism of Creation Ex Nihilo

The author of creation, of course, is the Lord himself. The Hebrew word for "created" in Genesis 1 (*bara*) is only used in the Old Testament as an action of God. Only God creates. The same thing is true of its Greek equivalent in the New Testament (*ktizo*). In fact, Paul argues, the natural world itself gives such clear evidence of a divine creator that there is no valid excuse for failing to acknowledge him (Romans 1:20). But our examination and contemplation of the natural world cannot tell us precisely how or by what means God created it. Analogies might be borrowed from areas of human creativity—painting, for example—but these ultimately fail for the simple reason that humans "create" with materials that already exist. Another analogy which has sometimes been employed to explain God's creative method is that of emanation. As light radiates from the sun or heat from a fire, so too did creation emanate from its source, the Creator. But this description also has problems; not only might it imply that creation was an involuntary act, but also that the Creator is an impersonal God. Another logical conclusion of creation by emanation would be that the created world is itself God or a part of God.[1] Throughout Scripture, however, all of these conclusions are rejected.

The creation account contained in the first chapter of Genesis is explicit and repetitive in its identification of the mechanism of divine creation. Over and again one reads the phrase, "And God said." Most famous is its first occurrence: "And God said, 'Let there be light,' and there was light" (Genesis 1:3). God spoke. It was. The word of God caused it to be. The New Testament description of the divine word as "living and active" (Hebrews 4:12) sheds important light on its nature and power. It indicates that this word not only *is* something; it *does* something. It not only has descriptive power as all words do, but, being God's own word, it has creative force. Thus the author of Hebrews categorically states that "the universe was created by the word of God" (Hebrews 11:3). As will be seen in a later chapter, the creative properties of the divine word also have considerable significance for a proper understanding of re-creation, or conversion.

## *The Order of Creation*

A close reading of the Bible's opening chapter reveals that the Lord's work was itself carried out in an orderly fashion. He not only created; he imposed order on his creation. He separated light from darkness, water from sky, and land from sea. Day was separated from night, and order was given to the succession of days, seasons, and years. Plants and animals were distinguished according to their various kinds. In short, order was given to that which had first been "without form and void" (Genesis 1:2). When speaking of this process of ordering and organizing, it becomes possible to employ analogies which were previously found unhelpful. Creative analogies such as building or painting, which proved inadequate to describe creation *ex*

---

[1] The believe that everything is God and God is everything is known as **pantheism**. The related view that God is *in* everything is known as **panentheism**.

*nihilo*, might indeed be useful in discussing God's ordering of that which he first called into being from nothing. In fact, Scripture often employs such analogies, describing the Creator, for example, as a craftsman or a potter (see Proverbs 8:30; Isaiah 29:16). The latter analogy is particularly fitting in light of the manner in which the first man was created from the dust (see Genesis 2:7).

However, the order of creation is not limited to God's actions. Genesis also reveals that the actions or functions of creation itself have been given a particular order. Nothing in creation exists by or for itself. Instead, all of God's creatures are related by the order imposed at creation. The heavenly bodies, for instance, exist to give light to the earth (Genesis 1:15, 17). Plants were created, in part, to provide food for both man and animals (Genesis 1: 29-30). Human beings, uniquely created in the image of God, inhabit a special place in the order of creation; they have been placed over the rest of the created world both to tend it and to rule it (Genesis 1:26; 2:15).

Rather intriguingly, the author of Genesis has highlighted the orderliness of creation not only by describing it, but even by the manner in which his description is presented. The account itself is carefully ordered and organized. The description of each day's events begins with the same words—"And God said"—and also ends with the same phrase: "and there was evening and there was morning." Such parallelism or repetition is a common feature in Hebrew poetry. Here it provides a formal, ordered structure for the author's narrative. There is also a more subtle parallelism in the text. When the first three days of creation are compared with the second three, the ordered nature of God's work becomes even more striking. On day one, light and darkness are distinguished while on day four, the celestial bodies are put in place to govern day and night. On day two, the water and sky are separated while on day five, the fish and birds which inhabit water and sky are created. On day three, dry land appears and on day six, the land

| First Day<br>Light & darkness separated | Fourth Day<br>Celestial bodies put in place<br>sun, moon, stars |
|---|---|
| Second Day<br>Water & sky separated | Fifth Day<br>Fish & birds created |
| Third Day<br>Land and water separated | Sixth Day<br>Land animals created |

animals come into being. There is a poetically balanced order within the six days of creation.

## 2. Biblical Affirmations of Genesis

Strangely, because the creation account appears to be formally and poetically ordered, some have argued that it should not be read literally. As justification for this conclusion, it is typically noted that one reads poetry much differently than one reads history: history is read for facts; poetry is read for beauty. This is an unwarranted oversimplification; there is no literary rule prohibiting poetry from being true, just as there is none demanding that historical writing be ugly. But more critically, the dismissal of the Genesis account as poetic fiction ignores the manner in which it is interpreted throughout the rest of Scripture and by Christ. It is therefore necessary to compare briefly what other portions of Scripture have to say about the time, manner, and scope of creation.

*Old Testament Affirmations*

Throughout the Old Testament it is evident that Israel firmly believed that creation was a divine work of God. Furthermore, this was held to be a foundational truth for other important assertions about God, the world, and the place and role of humanity within the created order. The authors of the Old Testament—whether they are writing poetry (Psalm 121:2), prophecy (Zechariah 12:1), or history (2 Kings 19:15)—unanimously credit the Lord with having created the heavens and earth. In confirmation of the Genesis account, emphasis is placed on the fact that he *alone* is responsible for bringing the universe into being (Isaiah 44:24). What was earlier said about the mechanism of creation being God's spoken word is also clearly affirmed outside of the Bible's opening chapter (Psalm 33:6; 148:5). Consistent with what Genesis reveals about the orderly relations between the world and its inhabitants, Isaiah notes that the earth was formed to be inhabited (Isaiah 45:18). The people of Israel confessed that not only the heavens and earth themselves were created by God, but also all of the living creatures which fill them (Nehemiah 9:6). Moreover, even outside of Genesis, the Old Testament testifies to a period of six days in which this creative work was carried out (Exodus 20:11). So fundamental was this proposition that it could even serve as the basis for a central point of Israelite law, a point so important that transgression of this law was punishable by death (see Exodus 31:15-17). Even this cursory survey reveals that God's Old Testament people unmistakably interpreted Genesis in a literal, historical manner. In accordance with its account of creation they affirmed that God alone is the creator, that he created the heavens, earth, and all living creatures, that he did so in a period of six days, and that he did so by the power of his divine word.

## New Testament Affirmations

The New Testament likewise drew the same conclusion. The prayers of the earliest Christians opened with the confession that God "made the heaven and the earth and the sea and everything in them" (Acts 4:24). This was emphasized in the preaching of the apostles (Acts 14:15). The apologetic proclamation of St. Paul is even more specific. In public debate with the philosophers of Athens he asserted that the God who created the universe also created man. More to the point, he affirmed Genesis as historically factual by expressly stating that God created one man, Adam, from whom all people have descended (Acts 17:24-26). Paul's interpretation of Genesis is perhaps particularly noteworthy in light of the fact that his study of Old Testament history and theology had taken place under Gamaliel, the most learned Jewish theologian of his day (see Acts 22:3).

More noteworthy, of course, is the authoritative testimony of Jesus himself. Like Paul, he too appealed to a literal, historical understanding of Genesis in order to answer disputed theological questions. And like Paul after him, he did so by specifically confirming the divine creation of human beings (Matthew 19:4). And once again, the authors of the New Testament, like those of the Old Testament, maintained with the first chapter of Genesis that the mechanism by which God initially created was none other than his word (Hebrews 11:3). Not only on its own merit, but also on the basis of the consistent testimony of the entire Bible, Genesis is presented as a true account of the origins of the universe and of life. The specific details of those origins—from means to purpose to amount of time involved—are frequently reiterated and reaffirmed throughout Scripture. Quite often, these affirmations also act as interpretations. As such, they further indicate that the earliest account of creation is meant to be read literally and historically. There is thus little warrant for dismissing the early chapters of Genesis as poetic myth. But to say that the biblical witness to creation is clear is not the same as saying that it is comprehensive. Scripture does not explicitly answer all of the questions one might have about creation, even as it is described in Genesis. For this reason particular attention must now be given to some disputed points which regularly cause confusion and even controversy.

### 3. What Scripture Does and Does Not Teach

Scripture reveals everything that we need to know regarding our salvation and our lives as God's children in this world. But his word does not necessarily tell us everything that we might want to know about certain topics. Consequently, one must be wary of making dogmatic assertions where the biblical authors themselves make none. Conversely, however, lack of a definitive answer does not necessarily mean that Scripture is completely silent on an issue or that any one answer is as good as another. It will be helpful to keep both of these points in mind while investigating some of the long-debated questions which arise from a reading of the first chapter of Genesis.

*The Meaning of "Day"*

Scripture describes God's creative work as having taken place over a span of six consecutive days. As in English, so also in Hebrew, the word "day" (*yom*) has more than one fixed meaning. While English speakers recognize a twenty-four hour cycle as one day, we also refer to a shorter interval within these twenty-four hours—the time during which the sun shines—as day. Speaking colloquially, we might also refer to periods longer than twenty-four hours by the same term. (For example, Hebrews 3:8 refers to Israel's 40 years in the wilderness as "the day of testing," and many biblical passages refer to the "day of the Lord.) This same variety of meanings can also be found in Scripture. In fact, a close reading of even the first two chapters of Genesis reveals three different uses of "day." (Compare the two uses in Genesis 1:5 with that in Genesis 2:4.) So, while the confession of a six-day creation may be relatively uncontroversial among Christians, defining the length of those days often proves contentious.

Two possible definitions are the most common. The first conclusion is simply that each day of creation was roughly the same as a twenty-four hour "solar day." Against this straightforward, literal reading, others have suggested that the days of creation be understood as lengthy ages or epochs. This view is often referred to as the **day-age theory**. Though a non-literal reading might seem counter-intuitive, proponents can indeed cite some biblical warrant for questioning the necessity of solar days. It might be pointed out, for example, that the sun itself was not made until the fourth day (Genesis 1:14-19). And of course, as has already been mentioned, even within the creation account the word "day" is used in reference to a duration of longer than twenty-four hours (Genesis 2:4). In fact, elsewhere in the Old and New Testaments, authors compare a day to a thousand years (Psalm 90:4; 2 Peter 3:8).

Although a non-literal reading is thus possible, the real question is whether it is the most probable. A standard rule of interpretation is that the literal or common reading should be assumed unless compelling evidence indicates otherwise. When defining "day" in the context of creation, the most compelling evidence in fact seems to support the understanding of a twenty-four-hour length of time. The description of creation by God's word ("God said. . . and it was. . .") implies an immediacy that is not wholly consistent with a longer period. Furthermore, in all other instances where the Old Testament uses "day" with a definite number, it is clear that a regular solar day is intended. The parallel between regular twenty-four-hour days and those of creation is specifically highlighted in the mandates regarding the Sabbath (Exodus 20:9-11; 31:15-17). But perhaps most importantly, the consistent references to evening and morning seem to identify the periods mentioned in the first chapter of Genesis. This is seen most clearly in a very literal translation of the second half of Genesis 1:5—"There was *an* evening and there was *a* morning: one day."

*The Age of the World*

If indeed the days of Genesis are to be regarded as twenty-four hours rather than unspecified and perhaps incredibly protracted periods, some conclude that it would be fairly easy to calculate the age of the world itself. The seventeenth-century Irish Archbishop James Ussher certainly thought so, dating the world's beginning to the year 4004 BC. (The claim that he was even more specific—narrowing the time to 9:00 am, October 23rd, 4004 BC—is false and has often been repeated for no purpose other than uncharitable ridicule.) Unfortunately, dating the origin of the world on the basis of Scripture is not nearly so simple. Archbishop Ussher's conclusion was based upon biblical genealogies and the available information regarding the number of years specific individuals lived. For those who take the biblical record seriously, it appears to be a logical method. But it is fundamentally flawed. Although the Bible includes a great number of genealogies, and although these do demonstrate an orderly progression from the time of Adam to that of Christ, it is not altogether evident that these genealogies are complete. To the contrary, there is much evidence which indicates that they are not comprehensive and were not meant to be. Lists of descendants were frequently telescoped or compressed; a lineal descent is portrayed, but some generations are passed over without mention. (Compare, for example, 1 Chronicles 6:3-7 with Ezra 7:3, and Genesis 11:10-26 with Luke 3:34-36). Likewise, we are not always told how old some of the people were when their children were born. It is therefore impossible to say with any certainty precisely how many years or generations have passed since the creation of the first man and woman.

It is worth recalling what was mentioned above, however. While Scripture does not provide a precise age of the world, this does not mean that any answer is as good as another. This bears repeating since controversy concerning the age of the earth most typically flares in debate over evolutionary theories which posit a world which has existed for billions of years. Even allowing for the possibility of a large number of gaps in biblical genealogy, a duration of billions—or even millions—of years cannot easily be harmonized with the chronology of Scripture.

One particularly popular attempt to effect such a harmonization has become known as the **gap theory**. This theory, popularized in the *Scofield Reference Bible*, postulates an extended period of time between Genesis 1:1 and 1:2. Some proponents of this theory believe that, during this time, an angelic world was created (complete with dinosaurs and other long-extinct species), which was later destroyed when Satan and his followers rebelled. Only after this great period of time did God begin the creation outlined in the rest of the chapter. Though this hypothesis perhaps has some allure for those hoping to reconcile biblical chronology with that suggested by modern scientific dating, it suffers two fatal flaws. Not only is there no real scriptural support for such an assumption, but in fact the evidence of Scripture mitigates strongly against it. For example, God's designation of all that he had made as "very good" does not sit comfortably with the proposal that rebellion, sin, death, and destruction had already entered the created order. Furthermore, even Christ himself refers to the creation of human beings as having taken place "from the beginning" (Mark 10:6, clearly meant to parallel Genesis 1:1), rather than after a prolonged gap of innumerable years.

*The Meaning of "Kind"*

Questions about the definition of "day" and the age of the earth often arise in the context of debates concerning the modern theory of evolution, particularly when it conflicts with the biblical doctrine of creation. Another question is frequently raised in the same context. Do new species gradually come into existence with the accumulation of genetic mutations, as supposed by evolutionary theory or, as the author of Genesis asserts, did God create all things "according to their kinds"? This question has prompted a number of long-running and sometimes rather heated debates. The question itself, though, poses more problems than necessary. At the heart of the confusion, once again, is the matter of definition.

To begin with, the term "species" is an ambiguous and ultimately arbitrary label. It is meant to denote a distinguishable group of organisms which resemble one another. But the exact criteria for determining resemblance is one of the perennial feuds of taxonomy. Many scientists have no commonly shared concept of species. Confusing matters further are assumptions that, however "species" is defined, the biblical word "kind" (Hebrew: *min*) must be synonymous. Yet there is nothing in Scripture that requires such a definition. The word "kind" certainly denotes distinct divisions between, as well as similarities within, the divided groups; but how close the similarities and how narrow the divisions is left unanswered. It would therefore be unwise to make any dogmatic assertions about the possibility and scope of variations within the created kinds.

## 4. Evolution

All of this shows, once again, that we must be wary of speaking where Scripture is silent. But this should not cause us to hesitate or to remain silent where Scripture does speak. And it speaks quite clearly in its rejection of some views of creation and God's relation to it. There are, of course, an almost infinite number of opinions which might contradict the biblical doctrine of creation. But evolution and its popular understanding deserves special comment.[2]

Since evolution has different meanings and presentations (some being more incompatible with the Christian faith than others), it is important to carefully define what is meant in a particular instance. In its most basic presentation, **evolution** is simply defined as a gradual process of change from one form to another. In ordinary discussion, this usually refers to biological evolution: the combination of genetic mutations and natural selection which leads gradually to the development of new and distinct physical characteristics. In this basic form, neither of these ideas necessarily conflicts with the biblical data concerning creation. Why, then, are evolution and creation so often considered contradictory points of view?

One answer is that the most commonly defended theory of evolution is that which may be called **atheistic evolution**. The descriptive term "atheistic" does not here refer to the individuals who hold this theory, but only to the theory itself. That is, it is a theory of evolution which dismisses the pos-

---

[2]It is often quite important to distinguish scientific theories of evolution from the popular presentation of these theories. Popular presentations of evolution sometimes have little to do with the work of scientists (just as popular expressions of Christianity are sometimes inaccurate).

sibility of God acting in, with, or through what are deemed wholly natural processes (while not necessarily rejecting the idea of God's existence). For this reason the theory is also described as naturalistic or materialistic evolution, evolution driven solely by the natural properties of the material world. The implicit but nonetheless logical conclusion of such a scheme is that the world, being guided by no divine mind and toward no purposeful end, is fundamentally random and meaningless. Scripture, however, clearly declares the opposite. It proclaims that the universe was created with wisdom and understanding (Psalm 104:24; 136:5). It asserts that all things were not only created *by* God but also *for* him (Colossians 1:16) and that he therefore works in and through them for his own ends and purposes (Proverbs 16:4; Philippians 2:13). Moreover, an atheistic rejection of God's working in and with the natural world clearly cannot be harmonized with the creation account itself, where the Lord not only calls matter into being, but himself shapes it, forms it, and gives it life in various forms (see especially Genesis 2:7 and 2:19).

This biblical description of God creating life in various forms also highlights a related problem in any attempt to accommodate both materialistic evolution and divine creation. It is the materialist presupposition that mutation and natural selection account for *all* biological development. All living beings, it is asserted, trace their descent to a common biological ancestor. (On this basis, it is sometimes further concluded that one can make no moral or essential distinction between the species.) Scripture, however, not only proclaims that humans were created by a special, divine act of God; it also proclaims that they were distinguished from the rest of creation by being made in the image of God himself (Genesis 1:27). Consequently, atheistic evolution must be rejected by those who confess the Christian doctrine of creation.

### 5. Hybrid Teachings

Even if one rejects atheistic evolution as incompatible with the biblical explanation of the origins and development of life, is it necessary to completely dismiss evolution? Is it possible to speak of evolutionary theory without the atheistic adjective, thereby making it more amenable to Christian doctrine? Many people, consciously or unconsciously, have attempted to synthesize the evidence forwarded in support of evolution with belief in a divine Creator who remains active in his creation. In contrast to the atheistic theory already mentioned, this hybrid teaching is usually referred to as theistic evolution.

*Theistic Evolution*

As was noted above, a belief in evolution itself is not necessarily incompatible with a belief in divine creation. There is therefore no need for the Christian to reject out of hand any talk of evolutionary theory. To the contrary, it would be more appropriate to admit that evolution is an observable scientific fact. (For instance, various forms of "**micro-evolution**" can be plainly seen at any dog show or flower shop, where selective breeding has resulted in the development of distinct physical variations. The real questions are: what kind of evolution and to what degree?

In a previous comparison of the biblical term "kind" with the scientific term "species," it was noted that the biblical vocabulary does not necessarily imply that one of every single species was created over a six-day period. While certain distinctions and demarcations are clearly indicated in the Genesis account, subsequent variation within each kind remains highly probable. This is not to suggest that a special divine creation was followed by a solely materialistic evolution. As will be discussed in more detail under the topic of divine providence, God remains present and actively involved in all worldly events, including those which seem completely natural. Therefore *any* biological evolution can quite properly be defined as theistic evolution.

In reality, however, most proponents of **theistic evolution** mean something more than this. What is typically meant is that evolution occurred in the manner described by the materialist theory, and on the same time scale, with the only substantial difference being the theistic belief that it was directed by God rather than by random and purposeless forces of nature. But this is a very tenuous position both scientifically and theologically. Science cannot prove God's existence or involvement. Theologically, this line of thinking posits divine involvement, but its conclusions suggest a god far different from that described in the opening chapters of Genesis. It does not allow for the God who became *directly* involved by shaping beings from the dust of the earth, breathing life into a fully formed man, or creating woman from the flesh and bone of that man. In the end, such attempts do not really harmonize evolution and creation. Instead they affirm evolution by radically reinterpreting creation. (This is further seen in the common theistic approval of billion-year time scales, which, as indicated above, are difficult to synchronize with a straightforward reading of Genesis.)

## 6. Doctrines Affected by a Denial of Creation

Clearly, many people object to the Christian doctrine of creation. As a result, various modifications or even outright rejections of this doctrine have become increasingly common, even among otherwise orthodox Christians. But the belief that creation can be rejected without consequence to other doctrines is dangerously naive. The coherence of the Christian faith does not allow for a "pick-and-choose" approach to individual doctrines. Denying the biblical creation account inevitably leads to drastic consequences for several related doctrines.

### *The Inspiration of Scripture*

Perhaps most obviously, skepticism about the biblical account of creation implies an equally skeptical view of the Bible itself. Only by being logically inconsistent can one believe that God has divinely inspired the whole of Scripture while at the same time hold that certain scriptural propositions are false. This is especially noteworthy with regard to the account of creation, which is set at the beginning of Scripture and therefore informs all that follows.

But even if the creation account did not hold this place, the assumption that it is false would raise great difficulties for attempts to interpret *any* portion of Scripture properly. For instance, if Scripture is in error in its opening chapters, on what basis does one with any confidence say that other chapters are true? Nor can this problem be avoided by claiming that Genesis is not false *per se*, but that it is simply ambiguous. As demonstrated above, the Genesis record of creation, even in its details, is amply confirmed throughout both the Old and New Testaments. If the opening chapters of Genesis are to be dismissed, it follows that large portions of other biblical books must also be rejected. In short, a denial of the doctrine of creation leads inevitably to a denial of the doctrine of inspiration.

### *The Nature of Sin*

The same is true with regard to sin. The Christian doctrine of sin does not exist in a vacuum; to the contrary, it is very closely tied to the doctrine of creation. The first chapter of Genesis asserts that the world was created without sin; it was "very good." Sin was only introduced when one of God's creatures transgressed a divine command. Moreover, the biblical authors point to this historical transgression as the origin of all subsequent sin (for example, Romans 5:12). To reject the historicity of Genesis 1-3 therefore necessitates an alternative explanation for the existence of sin and its nature. (And, while they might sometimes prefer to give it another name, even the most ardent secularists will admit that sin is a reality.) But the very fact that the Genesis account of sin's origin and nature is confirmed by other biblical writers again raises the issue of the inspiration and authority of Scripture as a whole. Once again, the integral nature of the doctrine of creation becomes evident.

*Death and New Life*

A similar situation exists when we consider what Scripture has to say about death: it entered creation with the first sin. That is, contrary to evolutionary assumptions, death is not natural, necessary, nor in any way "good." It is a curse laid upon creation as a result of the fall into sin. And once again, this fact is deduced not only from Genesis itself, but is highlighted even by New Testament writers. In explaining the nature and origins of death, St. Paul, for example, turns immediately to the creation account as his primary reference point (Romans 5:12-19). But Paul's real concern, as he makes plain, is not death itself; it is the ultimate abolishment of death in the crucifixion and resurrection of Christ. His concern is the central Christian doctrine of salvation. Paul's proclamation of new and eternal life is predicated on the truth of an historical Adam once inhabiting a sinless creation in which death did not exist. To reject this confession—the confession of Genesis 1-3—therefore not only affects the Christian estimate of death; it undermines the central tenet of Christianity itself.

*Creation and Christian Life*

A final point can be made concerning the integral nature of the doctrine of creation. The denial of divine creation not only touches upon Christian doctrine, it also affects Christian practice. To confess that the world and all within it was created by God is to confess that creation is good. Like humanity itself, the world was created perfect, and will one day be redeemed from the consequences of sin (Romans 8:19-22; Colossians 1:15-20). Christians thus reject all forms of **Gnosticism**, which holds that the material world is essentially evil and therefore to be shunned. A confession of the biblical doctrine of creation encourages a world-affirming spirituality, which has implications extending beyond theology into other important areas of life and thought.

It has long been acknowledged, for instance, that the rise of modern science received its major impetus from a biblical view of creation. The assumption that "laws of nature" not only exist, but that they are discernible by the human mind, was derivative of the Christian belief in a rational God who created and preserves an orderly world. The world-affirming outlook of Christianity, including a belief in humanity created in God's image, also continues to provide an important foundation for addressing social and political issues of ecology, bioethics, and human rights, to name only a few of the most prominent. In this light it becomes increasingly evident that the article of creation can neither be disassociated from other Christian doctrines nor be ignored when contemplating many of the pressing non-theological issues with which Christians and others are daily confronted.

## 7. The Creator's Care

In contrast to all of these philosophies and worldviews, the Christian faith offers a simple account. Almighty God made the universe and all that is in it by the power of his word. In his wisdom, he made his creation in such a way that it is able to adapt to changing situations and stimuli, and to be able to thrive in many circumstances. Christianity does not need to reject any possibility of evolutionary change; indeed, we should expect that God's creation should work so smoothly. This is not in conflict with the biblical evidence.

But God is not a remote power who once created and then left his creation to tend to itself. He remains active and involved in his creation. He sustains creation by his powerful word (Hebrews 1:3), and holds all things together (Colossians 1:17). As St. Paul says, "in him we live and move and have our being" (Acts 17:28). How blessed we are that our God has made us and all that exists, and that he still cares for and sustains us. Even when while we seek greater understanding of creation, Christians rejoice, seeing creation as a wonderful gift from our gracious God.

## Key Terms

| | |
|---|---|
| Cosmology | Gap theory |
| Day-age theory | Gnosticism |
| Evolution | Micro-evolution |
| Evolution, Atheistic | Panentheism |
| Evolution, Theistic | Pantheism |
| *Ex nihilo* | |

### For Review and Discussion

1. The day-age theory suggests that creation and macro-evolution can be easily combined by lengthening the days of Genesis into epochs or ages. Look at the order of creation found in Genesis 1. Would this order still make sense if the time in question was a lengthy period of time instead of a day?

2. Several consequences that follow a rejection of creation were presented. Can you think of any other doctrines that might be affected by a rejection of creation? Would this same problem occur if one rejected other biblical doctrines?

3. Creation is often viewed as a "problem" or a "challenging doctrine." Does this status cause us to overlook the wonder and joy of God's creation? How should the child of God best respond to God's creation?

# 6

# Humanity

What does it mean to be human? It is probably safe to say that most people are confident that they know what a human being is. Yet a week rarely passes without some reminder that the answer to this question is not as obvious as we might assume. When does an individual human life begin? What is the value of a human life? Do identifiable and irrevocable human rights exist and, if they do, on what are they founded? These are just a few of the questions frequently debated in hospitals, courtrooms, legislatures, and media outlets throughout the world. Such issues are contentious and confusing because there is a fundamental disagreement about what it means to be human. For the Christian wrestling with this important question of **anthropology** (the study of humanity), the primary source for answers will be the word of the One who first shaped life and gave it to humanity. This chapter will explore that source as we examine:

1. The Crown of Creation—*Man and woman as the culmination of God's creation*
2. The Image of God—*Humanity was created in the likeness of God himself*
3. The Nature of Humanity—*Our existence as physical and spiritual beings*
4. Creation and Human Relations—*The implications of creation for our relationships with each other and with the world around us*

## 1. The Crown of Creation

Many of the questions raised in the previous chapter's examination of the doctrine of creation are contentious, not simply because they relate to the origins of the universe, but because they relate more specifically to the origins of humanity. They do not merely deal with theoretical issues of space, time, matter, and energy, but also with the very personal and practical issues of human identity and worth. As we now turn our attention from creation in general to the creation of humanity in particular, these issues can be addressed in more detail.

It is important to remember the clear biblical assertion that the first man and woman were part of God's creation. In addition to placing human origins "in the beginning" with the rest of God's creation, the author of Genesis explicitly underscores their divine creation with a triple-parallelism:

> So God *created* man in his own image,
> in the image of God he *created* him;
> male and female he *created* them. (Genesis 1:27)

The author emphasizes the fact of creation while accentuating the exceptional significance of human beings among God's creatures. In fact, the opening chapters of Genesis devote more verses to God's creation of man and woman and his interaction with them than to the rest of creation combined. But the author also testifies to a special human status in other more explicit ways.

One notes, for instance, that it was on the sixth day, as the culmination of God's creative work, that man and woman were brought into being. And while the Lord had labeled each work of his hand "good," only with the appearance of humanity is the created world finally called "very good" (Genesis 1:31). Why should this be? One clue is found in the intended relationship between humanity and the rest of the created order. Man and woman were to be the "crown" of God's creation; they were to "have dominion over the fish of the sea and over the birds of the heavens and over the livestock and over all the earth and over every creeping thing that creeps on the earth" (Genesis 1:26; see also verse 28).

This relationship of rule over and responsibility for the rest of creation is further seen when God places the man in the garden of Eden as its caretaker and assigns him the responsibility to name the animals (Genesis 2:15, 19-20). This assignment is especially noteworthy as it becomes increasingly common to label the belief that humans are of greater worth than other creatures as speciesism, and to denounce this belief as no different from racism or other bigoted views. While the Scriptures are undoubtedly clear that we are to treat even the least of God's creatures with respect, it also unmistakably testifies that humans are qualitatively different from the rest of creation and that God has placed humans in a position over it.

Further support for this biblical concept is seen in the unique method of humanity's creation. While God simply spoke the world and its elements into existence, he became intimately involved with the creation of humanity. Rather than merely saying "let there be humans," the Creator shaped the first man from the dust (or elements) of the ground (Genesis 2:7). Involved no less intimately in the creation of woman, he formed her from the substance of man (Genesis 2:22). It is true that other living creatures were, like Adam, formed from the earth (see Genesis 2:19); but Scripture says something particular about man's creation that is mentioned in no other context. He was given life when God "breathed into his nostrils the breath of life" (Genesis 2:7). The means by which God brought humanity to life strongly emphasizes his closeness and familiarity.

The intimacy and familiarity seen in the creation of man is not an illusion. It is reality, reflecting the fact that God has a special relationship with humanity and he has given humans a special status among his creatures. The reason for this is that, unlike the rest of God's creation, humanity was made in the image of God himself.

## 2. The Image of God

Because God in himself is both invisible and incomprehensible, a certain caution is in order when we define and discuss the **image of God**. As God does not have a limited, corporeal body as do humans, his image is not to be understood as a physical or visible likeness. Some have described the image as a relational likeness, others in terms of an intellectual similarity or one of will. Some have drawn an analogy between the creative powers of God and human creativity, while yet others have emphasized a moral likeness. The greatest danger, perhaps, arises when one insists on only a single definition. The relevant biblical data contains several strands of thought.

### The Nature and Implications of the Divine Image

Not surprisingly, the first mention of God's image is found in the creation account. The triune God said, "Let us make man in our image, after our likeness" (Genesis 1:26). The words "image" and "likeness" are used synonymously, indicating God's intention to make man somehow *like* himself. Indeed, the next verse says that he did this; but it is not immediately clear in exactly what sense man was created to be like God. However, the following verses and chapters paint a portrait of humanity in its **primeval** or perfect and unfallen state. By comparing this picture of man with what Scripture says about God and his attributes, some small steps can be taken toward understanding the nature and implications of the image of God that he imparted to humanity.

Genesis reveals that the first man was created as an intelligent and a moral being. He spoke, made decisions, and displayed an understanding of right and wrong (see, for example, Genesis 2:17, 23). It is also evident that he was not created to be alone, but was meant to live relationally with others (Genesis 2:18). Furthermore, this life he lived would be without death (Genesis 2:17). Each of these characteristics, which by no means comprise an exhaustive list, partially reflects attributes of a God who is himself intelligent, moral, relational, and immortal. It is therefore reasonable to assume that these attributes are related to the image of God. Some theologians place particular stress upon the first two of these, arguing that intelligence and morality particularly distinguish human beings from the rest of creation. While these explanations account for part of the biblical evidence, they do not do full justice to Scripture's portrait of the first man.

When one looks at the attributes of intelligence, morality, relationality, and immortality, it becomes obvious that one of these no longer applies to us. Humans are unquestionably mortal. As will be discussed in more detail below, the loss of immortality is inextricably tied to the loss of God's image. Paul teaches that sin brought death to man (Romans 5:12; 6:23); but God is not sinful and Adam was not created in sin. In this light it becomes increasingly apparent that the nature of the divine image is not simply morality, but *faultless* and *sinless* morality—pure holiness and righteousness. Likewise man as first created in God's image was not only granted knowledge, but holy knowledge: both of God and of his world. Additionally, man's relationships with God and his creation were perfect. The need for this emphasis on perfection as an essential aspect of the image of God will become more apparent when we consider the loss of God's image.

*Man and Woman in God's Image*

If the previous paragraphs seem concerned almost solely with the image of God as imparted to "man," it should not be assumed that "woman" was not included in this image. The language simply reflects that of Genesis itself, which speaks of God creating both man and woman, and that when he had done so he "named *them* man" (Genesis 5:2). Because the inclusive use of this term can often be confusing if not contentious, it is important to highlight the fact that the first woman was also created in God's image. This is implied by the attributes noted above, which she shared with Adam. It is also explicitly stated by the author of Genesis. Just before the verse in which he expressly includes male and female under the title of "man," he writes, "When God created man, he made him in the likeness of God" (Genesis 5:1). Even more explicit in relating the image of God to both man and woman is the triple-parallelism quoted earlier:

> So God created man in his own image,
> in the image of God he created him;
> *male and female* he created them. (Genesis 1:27)

While Scripture clearly teaches that Eve shared the divine image with which Adam was first created, it is equally clear that woman, as well as man, forfeited this image with the fall into sin.

### *The Loss of God's Image*

Various interpretations of the image of God have made this topic quite controversial. This is partially due to the difficulty of precisely defining God's image; but it is no less due to disagreement arising over the question of whether this image was lost or retained when humans fell into sin. In fact, these two difficulties are related, for the loss or retention of God's image bears heavily on its definition. For instance, if one concludes that the image of God was not lost with the first sin, then immortality and perfect righteousness are obviously not part of the divine image. Conversely, if one believes that God's image was lost, then intellect and morality cannot be the sum of its essence, for even sinners continue to think and to make moral decisions.

The question at hand, though seemingly straightforward, does not elicit a simple answer from Scripture. This is not to say that the Bible is silent on the issue; the dilemma is in interpreting biblical evidence which might, at first, appear contradictory. Even in the early chapters of the Bible it is implied that the image in which our first parents were created was not passed on to their offspring. After reminding us that Adam was made in the image and likeness of God, the author of Genesis goes on to explain that, after his fall into sin, Adam bore a son "in his own likeness, after his image" (Genesis 5:3). This distinction between the image of God and the image of sinful man is further confirmed in the New Testament. Paul, for example, contrasts "the image of the man of dust" with a future, restored "image of the man from heaven" (1 Corinthians 15:49). That this image or likeness—which Adam had possessed in the past—will be fully restored only in the future seems quite clearly to suggest that it has been lost. Paul does indicate that it is even now beginning to be restored in those who have come to faith in Christ; he speaks of a "new self" which is being renewed and recreated "after the likeness of God" and "in the image of its creator" (Ephesians 4:24; Colossians 3:10). Nevertheless, by speaking of a renewal and a recreation of this "new self," even these passages testify to the image of God being absent from men and women as they now come into the world.

And yet both the Old and New Testaments continue to speak as if men and women retain God's image after the fall. Murder is forbidden, "for God made man in his own image" (Genesis 9:6). James offers a similar denouncement of cursing men; and again the reason is that they have been "made in the likeness of God" (James 3:9).

How are these apparently contradictory conclusions to be understood? The answer, as is often the case when attempting to define theological vocabulary, lies in making a distinction between the image of God in a narrow (or proper) sense and in a wide sense.[1] This image in its wide sense may be described as that which sets humans apart from animals. (So, for example, the prohibition against taking human life in Genesis 9 is located in the same context as God's permission to take animal life.) Some examples of such characteristics have been previously noted: intelligence, moral capacity, and dominion (the ability and responsibility for rule on earth). These attributes were clearly not completely lost with Adam's fall into sin, and human beings continue to exhibit them today.

What sinful humanity does not and cannot exhibit is the perfection of these attributes as they existed at the creation. Human intellect, especially its knowledge of God, has been darkened. Thus when Paul speaks of the Christian being renewed in the image of the Creator, he specifically mentions being "renewed in knowledge" (Colossians 3:10). Man's rule of the earth has likewise been compromised (see Genesis 3:17-19). And the human moral capacity can only be described as depraved. These consequences are the result of the loss of God's image in its narrow sense, which constitutes not only these characteristics, but also the crowning attribute of perfect

---

[1]As we have already seen in other topics (such as Law and Gospel), distinguishing between the narrow and wide sense of a term is as necessary in theology as it is in common speech. Relevant to the topic at hand, for instance, one daily distinguishes between "man" in its wide sense, meaning the whole of humanity, and in its narrow sense, meaning specifically a male of the human species (or even more narrowly yet, signifying only an adult male). The evidence made available by context will determine which is the correct definition in any given instance.

holiness or righteousness. When the first man sinned, and thereby forfeited righteousness, he consequently forfeited God's holy image. This proper understanding of the image of God is reflected in St. Paul's claim that the Christian is being recreated "after the likeness of God in true righteousness and holiness" (Ephesians 4:24). Just as God's image was lost when humans abandoned righteousness, so also will true holiness be fully restored with the restoration of the divine image.

### 3. The Nature of Humanity

The status of man and woman before the fall (known as **prelapsarian** humanity) differs radically from their (and our) **postlapsarian** (after the fall) status. This simple yet profound fact raises important questions about the fundamental nature of humanity. Is human nature defined by the image of God? If it is, are we now less than human since we are no longer holy or righteous? Conversely, if God's image is not itself the essence of humanity, does this mean that it was not a part of human nature at all? Could it even be said that we are "more human" without it? Because the answers to such questions have wide-ranging implications one must be particularly cautious about saying more than Scripture reveals.

God called his final and perfectly good creation "man." The Bible demonstrates that this name applies both before and after the fall. Adam and Eve neither lost nor gained their humanity in the fall. Yet Scripture is also clear that man was *made* in the image of God; this image was part of the created human nature. (That is, it was not added later, as is officially held for example by Roman Catholic theologians.) Pulling together these two strands of evidence enables us to summarize the biblical data by saying that the image of God was a part of human nature, but not its sum. Practically speaking, this means that our distinctly human nature was retained in the fall; but this nature, though no less human, is now corrupted. This subtle distinction might be clarified by analogy. Using an anatomical description, one might note that humans are four-limbed bipeds. If an individual were to lose his or her legs in an accident, he or she would not be any less human. A distinct human characteristic has been lost, but human nature has not been lost with it.

We previously noted that two distinctly human characteristics that have been retained in the fall are intellect and morality (though they are quite different after the fall). Also retained, according to Scripture, is our personal existence as a unity of body and **soul** together. As a brief working definition, then, we may describe a human being as an intelligent and moral being, consisting of a body and a soul, which are united in one complete person. Because the distinctive intellectual and moral capacities of humanity have received some attention above, an examination of humans as body and soul now deserves some special attention.

## The Human Body

One of the most fundamental biblical teachings about humanity is that we are part of God's creation. Our first parents were created on the sixth day of creation—the same day as the land animals. Human creation is specifically described in more detail than any other creature (Genesis 1:26-2:25), but we are still created beings. God formed Adam from the dust and brought him to life (Genesis 2:7). Human beings have bodies. Whether gestating in the womb, growing as a child, or living as an adult, humans have a physical existence. Even though this body has been corrupted by the fall into sin, it remains part of our existence. Nor is human physicality limited to this world alone, we will have bodies for all eternity. The biblical teaching of the resurrection means that human beings will always have bodies (Daniel 12: 2). Granted, they may be somewhat different in eternity (1 Corinthians 15: 40), yet they will still be physical bodies. Those who deny the human body either in this life (as, for example, in the Christian Science sect) or in the life to come are denying a clear biblical truth.

## The Human Soul

Along with the biblical teaching that human beings have bodies is a related teaching. We are not merely bodies, but much more. Human beings also have a soul or a spirit. Despite clichés about eyes being "windows to the soul," the existence of the soul remains beyond the reach of our five senses. For this reason some people have argued that it does not exist. A crude **reductionism**, which denies the existence of anything immaterial, will make this conclusion inevitable. (Although, rather naively, some have attempted to establish the existence of the soul by the scientific method. One such attempt involved comparing the weights of a body immediately before and after death.) Scripture was not written with such materialistic presuppositions. Not only do its authors testify to the reality of the soul, but Jesus himself emphasizes its importance (see Matthew 10:28 and 16:25-26). But what is the soul and where does it come from?

### The Nature of the Soul

The Bible repeatedly uses "soul" and "**spirit**" in parallel phrases (for example, 1 Samuel 1:15; Job 7:11; Isaiah 26:9; Luke 1:46-47), indicating that they are often meant synonymously. These words indicate that the essence of the soul is spiritual rather than material. Spirits, for instance, do not have flesh and bones (Luke 24:39), even though the human soul resides within a fleshly, material body (1 Corinthians 2:11). The spirit returns to God at death, though the body is buried (Ecclesiastes 12:7). This fact raises intriguing questions about the interaction of body and soul, perhaps comparable to those raised by the so-called "mind/body problem" in psychology and philosophy. (This may be an opportune time to point out that *psyche* is the word for "soul" in the Greek New Testament.) But contrary to some psychological models, which hold that the immaterial "mind" is controlled solely by the material body (the brain), Scripture asserts something like the opposite: the immaterial soul animates the material body. The evidence for this is seen first in the creation account (Genesis 2:7). But it is also affirmed when the biblical writers describe death not simply as the cessation of bodily functions, but as the departure of the spirit from the body (for example, see Matthew 27:50 and James 2:26).

The soul's departure at death raises further questions concerning its existence afterwards. Is the soul immortal? If so, where does it go when it leaves the body? The author of Ecclesiastes describes both body and soul as returning to the places from which they first originated: the body returning to the dust of the ground and the spirit to God (Ecclesiastes 12:7; see also Genesis 2:7). From there, Scripture asserts that departed souls begin already to experience the consequences of the final judgment (see Luke 23:43 and Revelation 6:10 with 1 Peter 3:19. Also see Luke 16:19-31). Since the soul does not die with the body, it is described as immortal.

However, the immortality of the soul should not lead one to conclude that the soul by itself constitutes the essence of humanity. Properly speaking, human beings consist of soul and body together. Scripture not only rejects **materialism**, which denies the existence of the spiritual, but it also repudiates all forms of **Gnosticism**, the ancient (though still popular) heresy which denigrates all matter as corrupt and sinful. Gnostics generally define a human being not as a united soul and body, but essentially as a soul, which only happens to inhabit a non-essential body. More pointedly, Gnosticism often describes the soul as "imprisoned" within the body. This false view of humanity quickly leads to heresy in the doctrine of salvation. To cite just one implication, the gnostic goal of salvation is one's release from the bonds of a material body to enjoy a purely spiritual existence. But the Bible clearly and frequently asserts that the final result of salvation will be the reuniting of the soul with the resurrected body. The body created by God will also be raised by God; it is not something to be despised.

## 4. Creation and Human Relations

The biblical evidence on these topics tells us quite a lot about what it means to be human. It means we are created beings, made in the image of God. It means we are intelligent and moral beings. It means we consist of body and soul. But to know our origins and our nature is not to know the whole story; the Bible also has much to say about humanity's purpose. Scripture tells us what humans are *in* themselves, but it also makes clear that humans are not meant to be *by* themselves. This examination of biblical anthropology, then, must conclude with a brief look at humanity's relation to the rest of creation

### Man, Woman, and Marriage

That relationships are fundamental to God's designs for humanity is immediately evident in the account of man's creation. The Lord looked upon Adam and declared, "It is not good that the man should be alone" (Genesis 2: 18). Because he saw that this was not good, God presented Adam with a partner: a woman made of the man's own flesh and, like him, created in God's image. In our day especially, there is no lack of controversy arising from the word with which Genesis describes this first woman—"helper"—and from its interpretations and resulting implications (both correct and incorrect). In order to understand properly what Scripture has to say about men, women, and their relationships, some careful distinctions must therefore be made.

Man and woman stand on equal terms in their relationships with God. Both were created in the image of God (Genesis 1:26-27). With regard to redemption, Paul specifically asserts that there is neither "male nor female" in Christ (Galatians 3:28). As individuals before God, there are no significant distinctions to be made between the sexes. However, as Paul also notes, we do not live alone as individuals in the world: "woman is not independent of man, nor man of woman" (1 Corinthians 11:11). Thus we must look not only at the relationships they have with God, but also at those which they have with each other.

Here some attention must be given to the description of the first woman as man's "helper." By itself, the use of this word certainly cannot be construed as attributing to the woman a lesser status; in fact, quite frequently throughout the Old Testament God himself is described as man's "helper" (see Exodus 18:4; Deuteronomy 33:29; Hosea 13:9). But when reflecting on the order of creation, Paul does note that "man was not made from woman, but woman from man. Neither was man created for woman, but woman for man" (1 Corinthians 11:8-9). Such reasoning from the order of creation occurs more than once in Paul's writings. The same is found, for instance, when he addresses issues of authority within the church (1 Timothy 2:13). The point Paul makes in both instances is that the order in which man and woman were first created is of fundamental importance for right relationships between the sexes even today. This is seen most clearly in what Scripture has to say about the most intimate male-female relationship: marriage.

The biblical model for the male-female relationship in marriage is perhaps most memorably summarized in Ephesians 5:21 ff.:

> . . .submitting to one another out of reverence for Christ. [22]Wives, submit to your own husbands, as to the Lord. [23]For the husband is the head of the wife even as Christ is the head of the church, his body, and is himself its Savior. [24]Now as the church submits to Christ, so also wives should submit in everything to their husbands. [25]Husbands, love your wives, as Christ loved the church and gave himself up for her, [26]that he might sanctify her, having cleansed her by the washing of water with the word, [27]so that he might present the church to himself in splendor, without spot or wrinkle or any such thing, that she might be holy and without blemish. [28]In the same way husbands should love their wives as their own bodies. He who loves his wife loves himself. [29]For no one ever hated his own flesh, but nourishes and cherishes it, just as Christ does the church. . .

Paul wrote these instructions because he was all too aware that this model is seldom imitated. The fall into sin was not without consequences even for marital relationships (Genesis 3:16). But Paul and other biblical writers clearly maintain that, even after the fall, the Christian will view the relationship between man and woman as one of mutual love and service (see Colossians 3:18-19; 1 Peter 3:1-7).

*The Unity of Humanity*

The implications of divine creation for human relationships go beyond those for man and woman; they extend to the whole of humanity. Perhaps most obviously, the confession that God created the first man and woman also implies that all human beings have subsequently descended from these first parents. All people are united by their common humanity and a common parentage. This point is made most explicitly in the Old Testament, where it is noted that Eve will be "the mother of all living" (Genesis 3:20). But the same conclusion is reached also in the New Testament, for example, when the universality of sin is attributed to a shared ancestry (Romans 5: 12-21).

On account of Scripture's teaching about the essential unity of human-ity, the Christian faith makes no allowance for distinctions that ascribe lesser worth to particular groups of human beings. Racism, for example, finds no support in Scripture. (The nonsensical suggestion that the origin of the black race is to be found in the so-called "curse of Ham" (Genesis 9:22, 25) has no merit whatsoever.) In fact, racism is strongly condemned. In the parable of the Good Samaritan Jesus dramatically makes the point that all people are equally to be loved as neighbors (Luke 10:25-37). Even more bluntly, James outrightly condemns all favoritism as sin (James 2:9). This teaching also has highly significant implications for such practices as abortion and euthanasia. In both of these, human worth is judged on the basis of age, health, or even convenience. Against any attempt to marginalize or exploit certain human beings as "less than human," it is the Christian confession that all people are created in the image of God; they therefore have inherent dignity and worth, and consequently are to be loved and respected.

*Our Place in the World*

While Scripture makes clear that respect is to be a part of all human relationships, it also goes further. Respect for God's creatures encompasses the whole of the created order. Therefore we now return to the topic with which this chapter began—man and woman as the crown of creation—and take up the type of relationship such a designation implies.

As the use of the term "crown" is meant to indicate, human beings were placed by God at the head of his created world. They received a divine mandate to rule over the other creatures (Genesis 1:28). Taking their cue from the word found in the Latin translation of this command, theologians describe humans as having **dominion** over creation. Some people are un-comfortable with this word, fearing that it actually means domination and implies exploitation. Images of strip-mined wastelands, devastating oil spills, or smoldering slash-and-burn forest clearings come quickly to mind as consequences of such an understanding. A literal translation of dominion as "lordship" might do little to calm such fears. But it is the theologian's task to interpret particular passages of Scripture with reference to other passages; therefore we must ask what Scripture says elsewhere about how Christian lordship is to be understood and exercised.

The obvious place to begin is with the Lord himself. Jesus rather explic-itly addressed the issue of dominion when speaking to his disciples:

> You know that those who are considered rulers of the Gentiles lord it over
> them, and their great ones exercise authority over them. [43]But it shall not

be so among you. But whoever would be great among you must be your servant, [44]and whoever would be first among you must be slave of all. [45]For even the Son of Man came not to be served but to serve, and to give his life as a ransom for many." (Mark 10:42-45; see also Philippians 2:5-7)

The implication of Jesus' teaching is unmistakable. Exploitative domination has no part in dominion properly understood. If even *the* Lord acts as a servant, then Christian lordship will likewise be characterized as service. And indeed this is precisely what one sees in the garden of Eden. Adam was placed in the garden both to work and to care for it (Genesis 2:15). This notion of caretaking, or **stewardship**, is decisive for understanding the relationship between humanity and the rest of the Lord's creation. It is God's world; he created it. It is ours only insofar as it is a gift held in trust. Our dominion over it is both a great blessing and a great responsibility.

Sadly, this harmonious relationship between humanity and the rest of creation did not last long. Like the relationships between man and woman and between man and God, the relationship between man and nature was drastically altered with the first sin (Genesis 3:17-19). And human relationships are not all that was affected; human nature itself has been affected. Thus, to more fully understand what Scripture says about anthropology and the human condition, we must now turn our attention to a fuller examination of sin and its consequences.

## Key Terms

| | |
|---|---|
| Anthropology | Prelapsarian |
| Dominion | Primeval |
| Gnosticism | Reductionism |
| Image of God | Soul |
| Materialism | Spirit |
| Postlapsarian | Stewardship |

## For Review and Discussion

1.   What does it mean to be human? This chapter provided a definition based on God's word. How does this definition compare to other definitions commonly used in our society? How would you evaluate these other definitions?

2.   The relationship between the sexes has often been contentious. How have the Scriptures been distorted to allow for false distinctions of value between the sexes? How have human beings minimized or distorted the differences between the sexes in ways that go against the Bible?

3.   Carefully read Genesis 1-2. How does this description of humanity's first existence compare with our lives today?

4.   This chapter related the image of God to issues such as abortion, euthanasia and racism. How can the Christian make a positive impact in society in defense of biblical principles?

5.   Christians have sometimes tried to exploit their role as stewards of God's creation. How can we exercise dominion over creation in ways that show that we are grateful and respectful caretakers of his gift?

## For Further Reading

Kantonen, Taito Almar. *Man in the Eyes of God: Human Existence in the Light of the Lutheran Confessions.* Lima, OH: C.S.S. Publishing Company, 1972.

Chemnitz, Martin, and John Gerhard. *The Doctrine of Man in Classical Lutheran Theology.* Edited by Herman A. Preus and Edmund Smits. Translated by Mario Colacci et al. Minneapolis: Augsburg Publishing House, 1962.

Delitzsch, Franz. *A System of Biblical Psychology.* Translated by Robert Ernest Wallis. Eugene, OR: Wipf and Stock, 2003.

McDonald, H. D. *The Christian View of Man.* Wheaton: Crossway, 1980.

*Racism and the Church.* A report of the Commission on Theology and Church Relations of the Lutheran Church—Missouri Synod. St. Louis, Missouri: The Lutheran Church—Missouri Synod, 1994.

# 7

# Sin

"Polite society" often avoids the term. Some might speak of mistakes, others of poor choices, and a few might be so bold as to distinguish wrong from right. But the word "sin" has many connotations and it makes many extremely apprehensive.

It is quite possible that the doctrine of sin is the most uncomfortably controversial subject addressed by Christian theology. Any number of doctrines can stir heated debate, but many might sometimes seem rather abstract. With sin, however, things become both concrete and personal. Given the level of discomfort that this doctrine naturally causes, wouldn't it perhaps be best to pass over it in silence or perhaps even to deny the existence of sin? Indeed, some religions do. But since the essence of Christianity is the *forgiveness* of sin, we cannot afford to ignore or deny sin's reality. Without a proper grasp of sin, a true understanding of the Gospel is impossible. In order to enrich our knowledge and appreciation of the Gospel, we will investigate:

1. The Fall into Sin—*How sin first entered a perfectly created world*
2. Original Sin—*The nature and consequences of the first sin*
3. Actual Sin—*The daily results of a fallen human nature*
4. The Cause of Sin—*External and internal sources of human sin*

## 1. The Fall into Sin

The origin of sin has been one of the most perplexing questions in the history of Christian thought. How did sin first enter an absolutely sinless and perfect creation? One single Bible verse informs us that the whole of the cosmos, including humanity, was "very good" (Genesis 1:31). Shortly thereafter we read that sin has reared its ugly head and that all creation, including humanity, has fallen under a curse (Genesis 3:14-19). How did this happen? And why? The verses found between Genesis 1:31 and 3:19, which chronicle the events referred to as the **fall**, answer both questions. Along with Genesis, the whole of Scripture reiterates and further supports this account of the fall's cause, nature, and tragic consequences.

*The Cause of the Fall*

Perhaps unsurprisingly, the first question often raised is that which is typically asked whenever something goes wrong: "Who is to blame?" Seeing that few individuals were present at the time, arriving at an answer would appear to pose little difficulty. The Genesis account records that the first man and woman were forbidden from eating the fruit of a particular tree; no other prohibition was laid on God's first human creation. But we soon read that the woman, seeing that the fruit was good, "took of its fruit and ate." Her husband also ate some of this fruit (Genesis 3:6). This act of rebellion was one of free will: uncoerced human choice. It cannot be denied, then, that the man and woman bear responsibility for the fall and its introduction of sin (see also Romans 5:12).

However, while Adam and Eve acted without coercion, they did not do so without having been tempted. Eve complained, "the serpent deceived me" (Genesis 3:13); and indeed he did. The serpent (clearly identified as the devil in Revelation 12:9) sowed seeds of doubt by misrepresenting the nature and purpose of God's commandment (Genesis 3:1-5). In doing so, he too is judged responsible for sin's introduction into the world. This is made especially evident in the punishments soon pronounced by God; not only was the serpent cursed, but his condemnation and ultimate destruction was first announced (Genesis 3:14-15).

The Genesis record, together with the whole of Scripture, testifies to a shared accountability for the fall into sin. But it also asserts unambiguously that God shares no responsibility in this matter. This point needs special attention, as it has often been questioned even by prominent theologians. The influential Protestant reformer John Calvin, for instance, put such a strong emphasis on God's sovereign control of all events that he would even argue that humanity's fall into sin was the result of God's ordained decree (*Institutes*, 3.23.8.). This may be a logical conclusion if one begins with Calvin's presuppositions, but it finds no biblical support. It is evident from Scripture that God created humanity with the ability to sin. Being omniscient, he surely would have anticipated our use of this ability. It might even be said that, since he did not prevent the serpent's deception, he *allowed* the fall to happen. None of this, however, makes God responsible for *causing* the fall into sin. Not only does Scripture make clear that God himself is wholly without sin; it also records his utter hatred of sin (Deuteronomy 32:4; Psalm 5:4-6; Zechariah 8:17). In his long-suffering patience, the Lord may permit sin; but he neither causes nor condones it.

*A Fall Down, Not Up*

Because sin clearly is not God's will and the fall into sin took place against his will, it must be acknowledged that the fall was not a good thing. The fall did not "improve" upon God's creation either by making humans autonomous beings or by affirming, in some sense, their right to make their own moral decisions. As the word "fall" implies, it involved a downward motion, a descent of humanity from the state in which God intended us to live. Humanity gained nothing in the fall, but rather suffered terrible losses: the loss of innocence, the loss of God's own image, and eventually the loss of life itself. In order to make this point more readily understandable, the consequences of the fall—the exchange of original righteousness for original sin—must be explored in some detail.

## 2. Original Sin

If some people consider sin to be an unpleasant topic, many more are troubled by original sin. As the adjective suggests, **original sin** refers to sin rooted in our origins, our beginnings. For this reason it is sometimes also described as **hereditary sin**, the sinfulness inherited in our own conception and birth. But, as with other hereditary traits, the ultimate origin of our sinful condition can be traced back beyond our own parents; it goes as far back as those first parents in the garden of Eden.

*The Nature of the First Sin*

Though we have already touched on the fall into sin and its cause, it is worth continuing briefly in order to examine the nature of the sin which started it all. We earlier implied that the first sin was Eve's eating of the fruit that she had been commanded to avoid. This is certainly a fair reading of Genesis; but a closer reading also reveals something a bit more subtle going on. The serpent does not simply appear on the scene telling the woman to eat. Instead, he begins with a question: "Did God *really* say. . . ?" Before she tasted the first bite—indeed, making that first bite possible—Eve succumbed to doubt (see Genesis 3:1-6). She doubted God's words and doubted his motives. Put another way, she had lost faith in her God.

Paul says, "whatever does not proceed from faith is sin" (Romans 14:23). Our first parents sinned, not only by acting against the words of God, but even before this, by doubting his word, by lacking faith in them and their speaker. The Genesis account of the fall, together with Paul's definition of sin, highlights an extremely important fact. Sin is not simply an action; it is also a condition. It is a condition in which God is not loved and trusted above all things. Tragically, like many fatal diseases, it is an inherited condition.

### Inherited Sin and Its Results

Because of this hereditary sin, none of Adam's descendants, with the exception of Christ, is without it. We would remain sinners even if we never *actively* sinned (which, in any case, is impossible). Paul summarizes this when he states, "by the one man's disobedience the many were made sinners" (Romans 5:19). That "the many" indeed means "all" is made evident not only in the context of Paul's letter, but also by other biblical authors, such as the Psalmist who emphasizes, "there is none who does good, not even one" (Psalm 14:3).

Even in the face of such clear evidence, many are tempted to look for exceptions, most commonly in the apparent innocence of infants. But Scripture leaves no door open for such exemptions. When the Lord himself described the state of man he noted that "the intention of man's heart is evil from his youth" (Genesis 8:21). This is so, the Psalmist confirms, because we are born in sin; in fact, he writes, we are sinful from the very moment of conception (Psalm 51:5). As with an inherited disease, the fact of our inherited sinfulness means we also suffer the effects and symptoms of our condition.

### Guilt and Shame

Two immediate effects of sin, evident even at the fall, are guilt and shame. Though closely related, it is important that each be properly distinguished and defined. **Guilt** is an objective state, a status in which one exists, the opposite of innocence. A stress on the objective nature of guilt is neces-sary because it is entirely possible to *be* guilty even though one does not *feel* guilty. (Note the relatively few displays of remorse in a typical courtroom. A defendant may not feel any guilt, yet still may be rightly convicted of a crime.) Scripture is clear that one cannot commit sins without incurring guilt (Leviticus 6:4). Since we are born sinful, we also inherit guilt. It is for this reason that Paul argues so forcefully that all people are "*by nature* children of wrath" (Ephesians 2:3). All are sinful; all are therefore guilty. Because of this, every person deserves divine punishment.

Although it is possible to be guilty without feeling guilty, a sense of guilt is also intimately related to human sin and sinfulness. **Shame**, the self-conscious awareness of our guilt, not only arises from sin, but also serves to make us aware of our sinfulness. Consider Adam and Eve: before the fall they were "naked, and were not ashamed;" immediately afterward they took great pains both to clothe themselves and to hide (Genesis 2:25; 3:7, 10). Shame thus became an integral part of human existence. Now all people have some innate sense of shame, so that the conscience accuses even those who are unfamiliar with the demands of God's revealed law (Romans 2:15).

## Depravity

The effects of original sin make us shamefully aware of our guilty sta-tus before God. Our sin also prevents us from doing anything about it. The sinful nature we have inherited from Adam is one of **depravity**. This innate corruption receives several names in the pages of Scripture: Paul refers to it as one's "flesh" (Romans 8:13), the "old Adam" or "old self" (Ephesians 4:22), and a "law waging war" against us (Romans 7:23).

As the biblical writers comment on this "law," they make two very important points clear. The first is that human depravity prevents one from approaching God or pleasing him. The sinful mind is described as funda-mentally and, by itself, irreversibly hostile to God: "It does not submit to God's law, indeed it cannot" (Romans 8:7). This was something Paul had learned not only from Scripture, but also from his own experience.

> Nothing good dwells in me, that is, in my flesh. For I have the desire to do what is right, but not the ability to carry it out. [19]For I do not do the good I want, but the evil I do not want is what I keep on doing. (Romans 7:18-19)

Paul's lament not only highlights our inability to do what is good; it also points to the fact that we inevitably do what is evil. This is the second, and an extremely important, point which Scripture clarifies concerning human depravity. Not only does being afflicted with original sin mean that we now lack the ability to pursue what is good; it also means that we *necessarily* pursue what is evil. We are predisposed to sin. Theologians often refer to this inescapable inclination toward evil as **concupiscence**. There is no morally neutral state of human existence. God's Old Testament estimation of man has already been noted, that, "the intention of man's heart is evil from his youth" (Genesis 8:21). Nothing in the New Testament indicates that this has changed. Since Adam's fall from righteousness, our flesh naturally desires what is contrary to the will of God (Galatians 5:17; Romans 8:5).

## Mortality

Sadly, a final result of original sin is that we receive something else contrary to the will of God: death. Death, which had no place in God's original plan for creation, is the ultimate consequence of sin; it is what is familiarly called "the wages of sin" (Romans 6:23). Both the Old and New Testaments clearly relate the origins of death to sin and the fall. God had commanded Adam to avoid the forbidden fruit, warning, "in the day that you eat of it you shall surely die" (Genesis 2:17). Because Adam violated this command, "sin came into the world through one man, and death through sin, and so death spread to all men because all sinned" (Romans 5:12). Our mortality is thus a constant reminder of the reality of sin in our lives.

In addition to the temporal, physical death which all people must now face, Scripture accents the relation between sin and death when it speaks of both spiritual death and eternal death. Emphasizing the depraved state of sinful humanity, for example, Paul describes those who have not been converted by the Gospel as "dead" in their sins (Ephesians 2:1). And those who have not been raised by the grace of Christ from this spiritual death will at the time of judgment face what St. John calls the "second death" (Revelation 20:14). In this eternal death will be found the final and everlasting punishment for all sins, unrepentant sinners, and the devil who first introduced sin (see Matthew 25:41-46). It is not a pleasant prospect, and not one which can be wished on anybody, but it emphasizes like nothing else (except the innocent death of God's own Son) the utmost seriousness with which God considers the sin which came uninvited into his perfect creation.

## Holistic Consequences

All of this shows that the effects of original sin touch our entire existence. Physically, our bodies suffer pain, suffering, and finally death. The human will is also affected, having lost the freedom to approach or please God on our own. It has turned stubbornly in the opposite direction. Feelings of shame offer evidence that original sin acts upon our emotions. And Scripture asserts that the human intellect is darkened as a result of the fall (Ephesians 4:18; 1 Corinthians 2:14). In short, there is no human faculty which escapes the holistic consequences of sin. As will be seen in greater detail in a later chapter, this has extremely important implications for the doctrine of salvation by Christ and by his grace alone. The total corruption of our human nature makes it impossible for us to save ourselves.

### 3. Actual Sin

The doctrine of original sin is unquestionably of central importance to the whole of Christian faith and theology. It is not, however, important only for its relation to other doctrines of the faith; it also sheds significant light on various aspects of the doctrine of sin itself. This will become clearer as we turn our attention to the topic of actual sin. As its name implies, **actual sin** has to do with sinful *acts*; therefore it is to be distinguished from the sinful *state* or sinful *nature* described under the heading of original sin. To distinguish between original and actual sin, though, is not to disassociate them. In fact, they are very intimately related. Paul makes this evident in his Letter to the Galatians, where he prefaces a list of sins by calling them works of the sinful nature (Galatians 5:19). Actual sins are a product of original sin; sinful actions are the natural fruit of sinful people just as bad apples are the natural produce of a diseased tree. As we define sin more precisely, we will see that it relates not only to our internal and fallen nature, but also to an objective external standard.

### *Definition of Sin*

Scripture is rich in its vocabulary of sin. In the Hebrew of the Old Testament, we find variously nuanced synonyms such as "transgression" or "rebellion" (*pesha*), "iniquity" (*awon*), and "missing the mark" (*chata't*). The Greek word most commonly used in the New Testament (*hamartia*) is simply translated with the familiar "sin." But what exactly does it mean? The apostle John provides a concise and readily grasped definition: "sin is lawlessness" (1 John 3:4). Not only is this definition concise and understandable; it has a refreshing objectivity. For according to this biblical definition sins are not, as is so often assumed in popular debate, merely "deeds which harm other people" (a definition which not only dismisses the possibility of sinful *thoughts*, but which also raises the impossibly subjective question of what constitutes "harm"). Understanding the definition of sin to be inextricably linked to an objective code of law (see also Romans 7:7), Scripture speaks consistently of sins as "lawless deeds" (2 Peter 2:8) and sinners as "workers of lawlessness" (Matthew 7:23).

The law to which the biblical writers refer is, of course, the divine law of God, which is most clearly revealed in Scripture. But the Bible is not the only place in which the law makes its existence and authority known. The apostle Paul asserts quite clearly that even those unfamiliar with the Bible have some understanding of the divine law and therefore also of sin. This is so, he explains, because "the work of the law is written on their hearts" (Romans 2:15). Paul's turn of phrase highlights a striking parallel between the law written on human hearts and that of the Decalog, written on tablets of stone (see Exodus 31:18). And this is precisely the point: human consciences, even those of unbelievers, have been marked with the same law that God has openly revealed to his people. The experience of a guilty conscience is the effect of the law at work; it serves to make sin known and to call sinners to repentance.

## Are All Sins Equal?

Whether we speak of "little white lies" or of "the ultimate sin," common, everyday speech betrays the widely held belief that individual sins can be weighed, measured, compared, and contrasted. Can sin really be quantified? Or are all sins the same?

Common sense and intuitive notions of justice recoil at the thought of equating deeds which differ drastically in their consequences. It seems incredibly obscene, for example, to weigh serial murder on the same scale with seemingly harmless fibs about the existence of Santa Claus. And in fact Scripture does recognize distinctions between various sins, their results, and the temporal penalties which they deserve (for example, see Exodus 21-22). The effects of all sins are not equal, nor are the human responses God judges appropriate.

But sin affects more than human society, nor is it judged solely by its effects on society.

*All Sins are Sins Against God*

Though there may be good reason to distinguish between various sins, such distinctions and classifications should not lead us to believe that sins differ fundamentally one from another. All sins are transgressions of the law of God; all, therefore, are sins against the Lord himself. To be sure, other people are affected by our sin, but we remain guilty primarily before God. An analogy from criminal law may prove helpful. Theft, assault, and murder are quite obviously crimes committed against individual persons. But they are defined as crimes because they break the objective laws of the state, not the personal rules or regulations of the victim. Law-breakers are therefore ultimately accountable to the state itself. Thus, when a criminal stands trial, his case is not introduced as The Victim v. John Doe, but as *The People* v. John Doe.

A very similar principle is evident in the biblical data regarding sin. Particularly telling in this regard is the well-known account of David and Bathsheba (2 Samuel 11). David's adulterous affair with Bathsheba was certainly a sin against Uriah, her lawful husband. (Significantly, according to 1 Corinthians 6:18, David was also sinning against himself.) Quite obviously, Uriah was also the victim of David's sin when he subsequently met his death by David's order. And yet, when David was confronted with his

By its very nature sin is a transgression of *divine* law; therefore it also affects one's relationship with the divine lawgiver. When viewed from this perspective, the effects of and response to all sins are indeed equal. The effect of breaking even one point of God's law is that one is judged guilty of breaking the whole of it (James 2:10). The divine response, no matter the sin, is condemnation (Galatians 3:10).

The question of whether all sins are equal can only be answered with both a "yes" and a "no." Within the context of this temporal life and our relationship with the rest of humanity, sins must be judged unequal and addressed individually. But within the context of eternal life and our relationship with the Creator and Redeemer, we dare not attempt to downplay the significance of even the most minor transgression. Instead, we repent in the sure knowledge that even as our smallest sins must separate us from the Lord, even the greatest are freely forgiven through the death of his Son.

awful treachery, his confession makes no mention of Uriah at all. Instead, he says, "I have sinned against the LORD" (2 Samuel 12:13). This is not to deny that he had in fact sinned also against Uriah. Rather, it indicates David's important recognition that he was guilty first and foremost before the God whose law he had so shamefully disregarded.

*Consequences of Actual Sin*

The fact that all sin is primarily against God himself is also the reason it carries with it such weighty consequences. The repercussions for actual sins are no less than those for the original sin which prompts them. With human guilt comes divine wrath (Galatians 6:8; Ephesians 2:3). The punishment for all sin, unless it is forgiven through faith in Christ, results ultimately in eternal death. Additionally, actual sins may have more immediate consequences. Some may be the direct result of divine punishment (for example, 2 Samuel 12:14). Others may be chastisements intended to prompt contrition leading to forgiveness, as when Paul demanded the excommunication of an unrepentant sinner (1 Corinthians 5:1-5). We must also realize that some sin carries with it results that flow naturally from the nature of the act itself. Lies lead unsurprisingly to distrust, theft often ends in imprisonment, promiscuity may result in disease, and adultery may lead to divorce. When we realize that God's law was given, in part, so that we might live peacefully and orderly in this world, we will not be surprised that an inevitable consequence of breaking this law is strife and disorder.

## 4. The Cause of Sin

As there are different kinds of sin and diverse consequences for sin, it will not surprise us to see that there are also various causes of sin. Three in particular—the devil, the world, and the flesh—are frequently mentioned throughout Scripture. A brief examination of the biblical evidence concerning sin's causes may help the Christian understand why he or she continues to stumble even while struggling to resist sin. But the topic is especially important as it serves to highlight a fact of central importance for the Christian faith: sin is not caused by God.

*Satan*

You have probably heard the old saying: "The devil made me do it." At best it is cliché; at worst a feeble excuse for wrongdoing. Nevertheless, it is not altogether incorrect in identifying the devil as a cause of human sin. As already noted, the first human sin was indeed suggested by the serpent who tempted Eve. St. John makes clear that this serpent was the devil himself. He names him "Satan, the deceiver of the whole world" (Revelation 12:9). John's use of the present tense here is also significant. Satan not only introduced sin at the fall; but he continues to do so even now. This important fact is further emphasized by Paul, who notes that the devil "is now at work in the sons of disobedience" (Ephesians 2:2; see also 1 John 3:8).

In addition to these biblical assertions that Satan is a cause of sin, Scripture also offers some illuminating examples in support of such claims. The Gospel of John mentions specifically that Judas Iscariot's betrayal of Christ was prompted by the devil (John 13:2). Satan's causal role in human sin also helps to explain Jesus' enigmatic but forceful statement to the apostle Peter: "Get behind me, Satan!" (Matthew 16:23).

### The World

As if the promptings of Satan were not enough with which to struggle, Scripture also informs us that the world can and does lead us into sin. And for those whose view of Satan is no more subtle than the popular smoke-belching, trident-wielding caricature, it is easy to imagine that the temptations of the world are far more enticing than those of the devil. It does not take manipulative advertising to make one aware that the world in which we live contains much that is sinfully desirable. Thus Jesus' strong pronouncement: "Woe to the world for temptations to sin!" (Matthew 18:7). Sinful cravings, lusts, boasting—all of these and more, St. John explains, come "not from the Father but. . . from the world" (1 John 2:16).

### The Flesh

External causes, such as Satan and the world, do not negate human responsibility for sin. Scripture also clearly emphasizes that a third, internal cause is also involved. The effects of the fall taint all humanity with original sin. Jesus himself thus points not only to the devil and the world as causes of sin; he also insists that sins of thought, word, and deed come "out of the heart" (Matthew 15:19). James is equally insistent that sin has an internal cause, that an individual falls into it "by his own desire" (James 1:14). This internal causation is what leads Paul to describe sinful acts quite bluntly as "works of the flesh" (Galatians 5:19).

That the causes of sin are not only external, but exist even within the sinner, has important practical and theological implications. Worth mentioning first is that this fact reinforces the Christian doctrine of original sin. Sin is not merely a deed one does that is distinct from who one is; it actually lives within a person and cannot be separated from his or her being. Furthermore, the recognition of our own flesh as a source of sin will discourage us from attempts to avoid responsibility for our actions. Though they too are causes of sin, we cannot simply lay the blame for our transgressions on either the world or the devil. When Adam ("the woman. . . gave me fruit") and Eve ("The serpent deceived me") attempted such blame-shifting, God was neither impressed nor convinced (see Genesis 3:12-24).

*God is Not the Cause of Sin*

Even less convincing are any efforts to implicate God himself as a cause of sin. This too Adam attempted when he sought to blame his own fall on "the woman *whom You gave* to be with me" (Genesis 3:12). This insinuated that the Lord was responsible for the first sin, since he created the one who committed it. This line of thought does not end with Adam; many today still raise the same point: How can God escape responsibility for sin if it was first introduced by his own creation?

The answer to this question may not be as tidy as we would like, but Scripture does make abundantly clear that God bears no responsibility for sin, either original or actual. The apostle John makes several comments relevant to this point in his first epistle. He first establishes that in God "is no darkness at all;" that is, he himself is without sin (1 John 1:5). Knowing this about God's nature, he therefore insists that sin is certainly "not from the Father" (1 John 2:16). To the contrary, he continues, "Whoever makes a practice of sinning is of the devil" (1 John 3:8). John concludes the same verse by emphasizing that God's relation to sin is not to be sought in its origins, but in its conquest: "The reason the Son of God appeared was to destroy the works of the devil." The Christian therefore looks to God not arrogantly to charge him with causing sin, but humbly to thank and praise him for conquering the sin for which we ourselves are responsible.

Sin in all of its manifestations—original and actual—drives a wedge between a loving God and those whom he seeks to love. Thankfully (and contrary to many cynical caricatures of Christianity), Christian doctrine does not climax or conclude with the topic of sin. Rather, we now move on to examine how a gracious God in his mercy has deigned to deal with the very real problem of human sin.

### Key Terms

| | |
|---|---|
| Actual sin | Guilt |
| Concupiscence | Hereditary sin |
| Depravity | Original sin |
| Fall, the | Shame |

## For Review and Discussion

1. Is all sin equal? In what way is this true? In what way is it false?

2. Why is it important to teach about both original sin and actual sin? What is lost if we ignore part of this reality?

3. Christians often limit their view of original sin to the issue of guilt. Why is it important that depravity or concupiscence be included? What does this doctrine help explain about our daily existence?

4. What is the cause of sin? How is it "caused" by Satan, the world, or our flesh? What is the role of God?

5. As Christians learn more about God's Word, they may discover that some things were sinful that they had previously done. What is the significance of such a discovery? How should they respond?

# 8

# Jesus the Christ

How do you introduce yourself to other people? You probably tell them your name, and briefly describe yourself. You may tell them about your background: your family, hometown, or the place you currently live. You might describe what you do: your job, interests or hobbies. As you get to know them better, they will learn more about you, but we usually start with these basics: who you are and what you do.

We follow that same basic pattern when we describe Jesus Christ. We talk about who he is and we describe what he does. In other words, we speak of his person and his work. When we look at these things, we see what God is really like. This chapter will examine Jesus and his gracious work as we study:

1. The Grace of God—*God's unexpected attitude*
2. Jesus Christ—*The promised Messiah*
3. The Humanity of Christ—*Fully human, just like us*
4. The Deity of Christ—*Jesus is truly God*
5. Heresies Regarding Christ's Two Natures—*Oversimplifying the person of Christ*
6. The Personal Union of Christ—*Christ is one person*
7. The Office of Christ—*Our Savior serves as the ultimate prophet, high priest and king*
8. The Atonement—*What does the death and resurrection of Christ do for us?*

## 1. The Grace of God

Perhaps you have found the last chapter of this book unsettling. Focusing on our sinful nature and actions crushes our pride and reveals God's righteous verdict. We are sinners, deserving death and everlasting condemnation in hell. Left to ourselves, this is what we would certainly receive. Praise be to God that he does not leave us to ourselves and does not give us what we truly deserve. Instead, he gives us grace.

We see evidence of God's gracious character in the way he responds to his fallen creation. All creation owes its existence and every good thing experienced to God. He made and he continues to care for us. In his goodness, our Father gives these gifts to all people—even those who reject him. Acts 14:17 summarizes this, saying "he did good by giving you rains from heaven and fruitful seasons; satisfying your hearts with food and gladness." Jesus notes that this goodness benefits "the evil and the good. . . the just and the unjust" (Matthew 5:45). The Father cares for his creation, allowing us to continue living when we deserve only death (Genesis 2:17). He provides us with all we need to support our earthly life and allows humanity to know many joys and pleasures. God gives his gifts freely and bountifully. When we recognize this truth, we are able to confess that "every good gift and every perfect gift is from above, coming down from the Father. . . ." (James 1:17). Even though our sin corrupts, misuses, and fails to appreciate these gifts, our loving Father continues to give them.

While we rejoice in God's goodness and enjoy the gifts that he gives to us and all people each day, the grace of God is seen most clearly in our redemption. Romans 3:23-24 describes this grace: "for all have sinned and fall short of the glory of God, and are justified by his grace as a gift, through the redemption that is in Christ Jesus." The **grace** of God is his undeserved love of people who deserve only punishment. This grace is not ours because of our merit but only because of Christ.

*Components of Grace*

*The Love of God*

If we want to understand God's grace towards human beings, we must realize that this is a one-sided relationship. Grace is God's undeserved love and mercy towards us. God does not merely act in a gracious manner; God *is* gracious. Grace is one of his attributes. "Gracious is the LORD, and righteous; our God is merciful" (Psalm 116:5 see also Psalm 103:8 and Exodus 34:6). God chooses to be gracious towards us because this is his nature and will. This grace is a disposition or attitude of God towards us. He is completely loving and gracious.

### *Apart from Human Merit*

This perfect, divine grace exists apart from any human merit. We do not deserve it in any way. Human merit and works are the antithesis of grace (Romans 11:6). Nothing in us causes God to be gracious. He does not give us what we deserve, for we deserve only death and punishment. Rather, he gives us what we could never deserve: forgiveness, life and salvation. There are no conditions to be met for this grace; God chooses to be gracious to us, apart from who we are and what we do.

But sinful pride may be offended by grace. Human beings want to feel like they are in control or that they contribute something to salvation. We want God to identify something in us that is lovable or worthy of his grace. But this is not the message of Scripture. God does not find us lovable; he redeems us when we are sinners and his enemies (Romans 5:8). Neither is God's grace a change that he works in us. God does not effect a moral transformation in us so that he can love us and be gracious to us. He loves and redeems us even while we are unworthy, sinful, and contemptible. Any insertion of human merit into grace misses the entire point. Grace is freely given to those who do not and cannot deserve it.

### *For Christ's Sake*

Grace is freely given to humanity, but it is not free to God. His grace has a terrible price. It is ours only in Christ Jesus (Galatians 1:6-7). The death and resurrection of Christ are both the price and the content of God's graciousness. Grace is not an abstract attribute or wish of God; it is always connected to the work of the Redeemer. God does not simply love us; he loves us in Jesus Christ.

## *Characteristics of God's Grace*

God is gracious through the work of Jesus Christ. This does not mean, however, that the grace of God was unknown before the incarnation. In Christ we see the fulfillment of God's gracious plan, but the grace of God is part of his eternal nature. In fact, many passages in the Old Testament specifically describe God's gracious nature (for example, Psalm 103:8, Exodus 34:6).

God's grace is also part of his will for all humanity. The grace of God is universal. Titus 2:11 says, "the grace of God has appeared, bringing salvation for all people." God has not limited his grace to a few people but offers it to all. God is free to offer his grace to anyone he chooses—and he chooses to offer it to all humanity.

Furthermore, the grace of God is active. He does not merely wish that humanity might be saved. No, when God wills to be gracious, he provides all that is necessary. With the will to save humanity comes his plan of salvation. Grace is carried out in action. What's more, this grace is **efficacious**. It has the power to accomplish an effect. This means that the grace which is available to all is also able to bring people to salvation. St. Paul summarizes this powerful grace, saying, "Now I commend you to God and to the word of his grace, which is able to build you up and give you the inheritance among all those who are sanctified" (Acts 20:32). The grace of God has the power to be effective in our lives.

But how does this grace of God reach us? How are we to know of God's gracious will for us in Christ? God does not leave us to search for his grace. He promises to offer us his grace in specific means. God promises to convey his grace to us as his Spirit works through the word and the sacraments. When God works through the **means of grace**, sinful human beings may either receive or resist his grace (see Jonah 2:8, Matthew 23:37), but human resistance does not alter the will and nature of God. He is gracious to us for the sake of Christ Jesus. Consequently, it is essential to know him and to be known by him.

## 2. Jesus Christ

The disciples had traveled with Jesus, heard him teach, and seen him perform amazing miracles. After all of these experiences, Jesus took the disciples aside and asked, "Who do people say that the Son of Man is?" They responded that some thought that Jesus was John the Baptist, while others likened him to Elijah, Jeremiah, or another prophet. Then Jesus redirected the question towards the disciples. "Who do you say that I am?" Peter answered Jesus, "You are the Christ, the Son of the living God" (Matthew 16:13-18). Hearing this answer, Jesus said that Peter was blessed because he knew the truth. Peter hadn't learned this truth from human beings but from God. Jesus is the Christ, the Son of the living God. Peter's answer seems to be simple, but in reality, it summarizes the doctrine of the person of Christ in only a few words. Scripture teaches that Jesus is the Christ: a human being but also the Son of God. This one person has two distinct natures: human and divine. But what do these words mean?

*Getting Our Vocabulary Straight*

For most of its history, Christian theology has described Jesus with these terms. He is one person with two natures. Theology precisely defines these words. "**Person**" describes someone who exists as a unique individual. Each person is distinct from other persons, is able to think, and is self-aware. A person is not part of another being, though he or she will usually be in relationships with other persons. Each one of us is a person.

Closely related to this concept is nature. "**Nature**" is a description of characteristics. It is the essential qualities that make something what it is. To have a human nature is to have those qualities and characteristics that are essential components of humanity. These characteristics include things like life, a body, or a sequence of DNA. It is the "humanness" of a person. Likewise a divine nature consists in everything that it means to be God. It is the "godness" of a person. (This divine nature is seen in only three persons: the Father, Son, and Holy Spirit).

In our ordinary use of these terms, a person has a nature. You are a human person with a human nature. In other words, you are a self-existing individual who exhibits the qualities and characteristics that we would expect to see, to some degree, in a human being. The need for a precise use of this vocabulary becomes more urgent when we describe the person of Christ. Scripture describes him with two natures: Christ is fully human and at the same time fully divine. Does this mean that there are two Christs? No, there is one Christ—one person—but this single person consists of two natures. The divine nature has existed from all eternity, even before the **incarnation**, but the human nature of Christ never existed independently or without the divine nature. He has a true human nature, but it is not a human person independent of the divine nature. Rather, the person of Christ consists of two natures. We use this specific vocabulary in order to uphold both of these biblical truths. This terminology can be confusing when we use it abstractly. It becomes clearer when we look at the specific biblical evidence.

## 3. The Humanity of Christ

One of the things that we need to know about our Savior is that he is truly a human being. Most people today, even non-believers, concede that there was a historical man from Nazareth named Jesus. Still, Scripture carefully notes Jesus' humanity. He is called human (1 Timothy 2:5), has a human ancestry (Romans 9:5) and had the characteristics of a normal (though unfallen) human nature. Like all other humans, his life began with his conception, gestation, and birth. He did not descend from heaven with a body, but obtained one in the ordinary way as he grew in the womb of his mother. He was truly human.

Every biblical description of human nature is applied to Jesus. He has a body that is subject to the same experiences of other humans. He experienced physical and mental growth (Luke 2:40, 52). He was psychologically and intellectually human, experiencing feelings such as love, compassion, sorrow, and joy. Like all humans he gets hungry when he fasts (Matthew 4:2), he experiences thirst (John 19:28), fatigue, (John 4:6) and the need for sleep (Luke 8:23). He feels pain and agony. When he is injured, he bleeds (John 19:34) and ultimately dies. At any point in the life of Christ, an observer would recognize a human being (Luke 23:47). All the evidence demonstrates that he is a genuine human being.

*Is His Humanity Like Ours?*

## The Virgin Conception and Birth

While Jesus has a full and complete human nature, there are several notable ways in which his human experience differs from that of other human beings. The first is probably the best known. While Jesus had an ordinary human gestation and birth, the nature of his conception was different than the ordinary human experience. Scripture clearly teaches that Christ was born of a virgin, deriving his human nature entirely from his mother. This miraculous conception is foreshadowed in the first messianic prophecy, Genesis 3:15, where the promised Messiah is called the seed of a woman. (In the ordinary way of speaking, only men have "seed.") Both by implication and by the specific reference to a woman, but not a man, the virgin conception is reflected. The prophecy is intensified in Isaiah 7:14, "behold the virgin shall conceive and bear a son, and shall call his name Immanuel."

Two Gospels directly testify to the miracle of the virgin conception and birth. Matthew 1:18-25 recounts Joseph's experience. Knowing that he had not impregnated Mary, he was going to end their betrothal. When an angel assured him of Mary's faithfulness and of God's miracle, Joseph believed. Even more compelling is Mary's perspective found in Luke 1:26-38. Mary knew that she had done nothing to become pregnant (Luke 1:34), but soon learned that God is able to do anything by his miraculous power.

Why does Scripture take such care to note the **virgin conception** and **birth** of Jesus? It is not implying a sexual relationship between Mary and God. Rather, it is a miraculous appearance of divine power that has several interesting implications for our understanding of the person of Christ.

The early Christian church saw the virgin birth as evidence of the true humanity of Christ. What was most significant to them was not the absence of a biological father but the presence of a biological mother. The virgin birth answers the question, "was Christ truly human?" with a solid "yes." Naturally, almighty God could bring about human life in any manner that pleased him, but it pleased him to do this through an ordinary human woman.

But the virgin birth also brings about some differences between Jesus and the rest of humanity. Jesus is fully human, but his unique conception implies a break with the ordinary. Jesus was not the first human to exist without a human father—indeed our first parents came into being without either human father or mother! They were directly created by God himself. In the virgin birth, we see Christ as the beginning of a new creation (see 1 Corinthians 15:47). As Adam had only God as his Father, so also Christ has no human father.

Many Christians stress the connection between the virgin birth and original sin. Our first parents were created without a sinful nature. Christ, who was conceived in a miraculous manner, did not inherit Adam's guilt. The virgin conception and birth marks a discontinuity in the transmission of both guilt and sinful desire.

These explanations are not mutually exclusive. In fact, they all express part of the fullness of God's miracle. Humanity is affirmed in the incarnation. In Christ real humanity is seen again. He is the second Adam, the unfallen human without the abnormalities that have plagued Adam's children. All of these are part of the biblical miracle of the virgin conception. Perhaps we might also marvel that Christ, who does many miracles for others, has a human life that begins with a miracle.[1]

### Sinlessness

The virgin birth shows both continuity and a difference between Christ and the rest of humanity. A further difference is seen when the question of sin is considered in more detail. Fallen human beings daily experience two realities: we are sinful by nature and we do sinful things. Original and actual sin permeate our existence. Yet this is not true of Christ.

Scripture teaches that Christ was sinless. In this, he is notably different from the rest of humanity. He lived the righteous human life that we

---

[1] The doctrine of the virgin conception and birth of Christ should not be confused with the "**immaculate conception.**" The later refers to the Roman Catholic teaching that Mary was conceived and born without original sin.

consistently fail to live. Had he been guilty of sin, Jesus would have needed a redeemer himself, but the word of God teaches that he committed no sin (1 Peter 2:22). He endured all the temptations which we face, but without yielding to temptation (Hebrews 4:15). Yet in the miracle of our redemption, God, "made him to be sin who knew no sin, so that in him we might become the righteousness of God" (2 Corinthians 5:21). Scripture clearly teaches that he was free from the guilt of his own sin. Christ Jesus was a holy, sinless human being.

### Consequences of Christ's Sinlessness

Christ did not sin (2 Corinthians 5:21). In this regard he is different from all other people. Because he did not sin, he is free from the effects of sin. Sin has alienated all other humans from God, but our sinless Savior does not have this separation. Human will is bound in sin; he alone has truly free will. The condemnation of death that comes from sin (Romans 6:23) does not apply to him. All other human beings are mortal because of sin, but Christ was potentially immortal. He did not need to die as a result of his own sin. It would have been possible for his human nature to live forever without dying. (And even after his voluntary death, he rose again and lives eternally with both his human and divine natures.) Of all humanity, only he was free from the curse of death. His death was not a necessary consequence of his own sin but a voluntary choice. He willingly chose to die in order to bring salvation to his fallen creation.

These differences in Christ's human nature are significant. Since other humans do not share in these characteristics of perfection, we might think him to be abnormal or not really human, but the truth is just the opposite. In Christ we see what humanity was meant to be. In Jesus we encounter a real human being free from the abnormalities that we know so well. He is fully and completely human.

### The Significance of Christ's Humanity

We have taken our time to demonstrate that Christ is a genuine human being. Perhaps you are wondering if this was really necessary. Why is it so important to discuss something as obvious as his humanity? The word of God reveals that the incarnation was necessary for our salvation. As human disobedience caused our problem, so human obedience, in Christ, effected our salvation (Romans 5:19). Hebrews shows the connection between the incarnation and our salvation when it says, "since therefore the children share in flesh and blood, he himself likewise partook of the same things, that through death he might destroy the one who has the power of death, that is, the devil" (Hebrews 2:14).

Our Savior needed to be one of us. Furthermore, the humanity of Christ gives us strength and support in our struggles and weaknesses. He understands what we experience. He knows by experience what it means to be human, to be tempted, to suffer, and to die. As the omniscient God he had always known this, but in the incarnation, we are made confident and sure that this is true. Again, Hebrews says, "we do not have a high priest who is unable to sympathize with our weaknesses, but one who in every respect has been tempted as we are, yet without sin. Let us then with confidence draw near to the throne of grace, that we may receive mercy and find grace to help in time of need" (Hebrews 4:15-16).

We should also recognize that the incarnation of our Savior is an affirmation of the goodness of creation and of human flesh. The material world is not inherently evil. The spiritual and the physical are not opposed to each other. In Christ God enters his creation, taking on human flesh, and makes it his own. We see the goodness of his creation as he uses it to come close to us. Our Savior is Immanuel, God with us, God in the flesh.

## 4. The Deity of Christ

Today, most people acknowledge that Jesus was a genuine human being. Unbelievers may doubt his virgin birth, sinlessness or immortality, but most would agree that he was truly human. Today people are more likely to stumble on Christ's divine nature, but this also is an essential Christian teaching. Because this is fundamental to our understanding of the Christ and to our salvation, Scripture provides us with evidence of his divine nature.

*Evidence of a True Divine Nature*

*Scripture Calls Christ God*

The Bible testifies to the deity of Christ. He is the one true God, the second person of the Trinity. 1 John 5:20 calls him "true God and eternal life." St. John begins his Gospel, "In the beginning was the Word, and the Word was with God, and the Word was God" (John 1:1). He is not *a* god, but *the* God. Nor is he partially divine, rather, "in him the whole fullness of deity dwells bodily" (Colossians 2:9). We should not be surprised to find these affirmations of Christ's deity in the New Testament, for it was prophesied that the Messiah would be divine (Isaiah 7:14; Isaiah 9:6).

## *Christ Identifies Himself as God*

This claim is not simply a conclusion of his followers. Christ himself claimed to be God. At Jesus' trial, the high priest demanded that he tell them whether he was the Son of God. Jesus did not deny this charge, even though denial would have saved his life. Instead, he admitted his divine identity (Matthew 26:63-64a).

When Peter called Jesus, "the Christ, the Son of the living God" (Matthew 16:16), he was not rebuked for blasphemy. Instead, Jesus called Peter "blessed" for knowing this truth. Jesus taught Philip that anyone who had seen him had seen the Father (John 14:9). One of the best known passages in which Jesus claims to be God is John 10:30 "I and the Father are one." Following this astonishing claim, John records the following:

> The Jews picked up stones again to stone him. [32]Jesus answered them, "I have shown you many good works from the Father; for which of them are you going to stone me?" [33]The Jews answered him, "It is not for a good work that we are going to stone you but for blasphemy, because you, being a man, make yourself God." (John 10:31-33)

His enemies did not believe what Jesus said about himself, but they did not misunderstand him. Jesus was obviously claiming to be the true God.

## *Christ has Divine Characteristics*

Further evidence for the deity of Christ is seen in the way that the Bible describes him. Jesus is described with attributes and characteristics that belong to God, but not to any mere man. Because Jesus is fully God, all of the divine attributes belong to him, but as a demonstration of his deity, a few notable examples will suffice.

Our Savior is described as eternal, existing before his conception and even before creation. He was with the Father, in glory, before the world began (John 17:5). He exists before all things and is the creator of all things (Colossians 1:16-17). Because he is true God, he exists before all of creation. Unbelieving Jews wanted to stone Jesus for blasphemy when he said, "before Abraham was, I am!" (John 8:58). Only God can make such statements truthfully. Jesus is the eternal God.

We also see the Christ claim to have and use divine authority and power. Those who heard his teaching were amazed that he didn't teach like one of the teachers of the Law, but as one who had God's authority (Matthew 7:28-29). Jesus claims that his Father had given him "authority over all flesh" (John 17:2). Before ascending into heaven, he tells his disciples "All author-

John's Gospel records seven different statements of Jesus in which he gives a vivid depiction of his identify, introduced with the opening statement "I Am." Since God's personal name, Yahweh means "I am," pious Jews considered it blasphemous for any human being to use these precise words. Thus these statements not only describe Jesus, they affirm his deity. The I AM statements are:

> I am the Bread of Life—John 6:35
> I am the Light of the World—John 8:12
> I am the Door of the Sheep—John 10:7
> I am the Good Shepherd—John 10:11
> I am the Resurrection and the Life—John 11:25
> I am the Way, the Truth, and the Life—John 14:6
> I am the True Vine—John 15:1

ity in heaven and on earth has been given to me" (Matthew 28:18). Only God has complete authority and Jesus claims that it is his own.

Furthermore, Christ is described with the divine attribute of omnipresence. No ordinary human being could sensibly make such a claim, yet Jesus says "I am with you always, to the end of the age" (Matthew 28:20). He promises that, "where two or three are gathered in my name, there am I among them" (Matthew 18:20). If we trust his promises, we recognize that he is claiming to be present with us in a way that a mere human cannot. Ephesians describes this presence saying that he fills all things completely (Ephesians 1:23). This can only be true of God.

The Bible also shows us that Christ has knowledge that surpasses human limitations. Jesus surprised Nathanael (John 1:47-51) and the Samaritan woman (John 4:4-26) by his inexplicable knowledge of their lives and conduct. His disciples clearly testify, "Now we know that you know all things" (John 16:30). Christ demonstrated divine knowledge.

### Christ Does Divine Works

By these and other attributes, the Christ is depicted as God. Further evidence of his divine identity is seen when we consider the works that are attributed to Jesus. He is described as one who does things that only God can do. A significant example is the work of creation. Almighty God is the creator of the universe, yet Scripture clearly testifies that Christ is involved in creation. John says that all things were made by Christ (John 1:3; see also

Hebrews 1:1-3, and 1 Corinthians 8:6). Colossians shows that he was directly involved in the entire work of creation when it says, "by him all things were created, in heaven and on earth, visible and invisible, whether thrones or dominions or rulers or authorities—all things were created through him and for him. And he is before all things, and in him all things hold together" (Colossians 1:16-17). The world is not only created through Christ, it is upheld and sustained through him. This same passage shows that he is involved in the preservation of creation. Hebrews 1:3 adds that Jesus "upholds the universe by the word of his power." This is the work of God himself, and it is done by Christ.

Christ reveals the word, will, and person of God to humanity. Divine revelation can only be given by God himself. "No one has ever seen God; the only God, who is at the Father's side, he has made him known" (John 1:18). Moreover, this revealer claims authority over God's prior revelation. This is seen as he clarifies the obligations of the Sabbath (Mark 2:28), something that is incredibly presumptuous for anyone but God.

Jesus freely forgives sins with God's authority (Matthew 9:2-8). He performs miracles—even the astounding miracle of resurrection and the bestowal of life (John 5:21). He invites others to believe in him, making himself the object of faith (John 14:1). He tells his listeners that he will ascend into heaven and ultimately return to judge the nations of the earth. (Matthew 25:31-46). All of these things are divine works that are performed by Jesus.

## Other Persons Recognize Christ as God

Hearing his testimony and seeing all this evidence, many individuals in Scripture, and in many generations since, have confessed the biblical truth that Jesus Christ is true God. Skeptical Thomas calls the resurrected Jesus "My Lord and My God" (John 20:28). The magi worship the infant Jesus (Matthew 2:2); his disciples (Matthew 28:17) and even the angels worship him (Hebrews 1:6). Ultimately, Scripture teaches that, "at the name of Jesus every knee should bow, in heaven and on earth and under the earth, and every tongue confess that Jesus Christ is Lord to the glory of God the Father" (Philippians 2:10-11). This worship is the rightful response of his creation to Christ Jesus, the true God.

## The Significance of Christ's Deity

The direct claims of Jesus, the testimony of his followers and of Scripture, the evidence of his attributes and works all teach the same truth: Jesus Christ is the true God. Because this is who he is, he is our Redeemer. It is no mere human who sacrifices himself for us, but the precious Son of God. God comes to us to be our Savior.

Moreover, through Jesus Christ we have God's supreme revelation (Hebrews 1:1-3, John 1:18). We know God because he has personally come to reveal himself to us. There is no higher authority, no other source of knowledge or hope than this perfect revelation in Christ Jesus. Many prophets and messengers were sent from God to his people, but the greatest revelation was in his only begotten Son.

## 5. Heresies Regarding Christ's Two Natures

Exploring the doctrine of Christ's two natures, it soon becomes apparent that this biblical teaching challenges our understanding. Human minds struggle to comprehend the person of our Savior. He alone is the incarnate God who unites these two natures in one person. But our logical minds stumble on the paradox of these two natures. Could we adjust our teaching to make it more understandable? Certainly we should try to communicate the biblical text more clearly, but if we discard parts of its teaching to fit our understanding, we distort its message. This is how many heresies begin. People reject or change portions of Scripture to make them more appealing or simpler. When this relates to the two natures of Christ, two main heresies emerge.

### *Arianism: Christ is Not Fully God*

In the fourth century, a bishop named Arius wanted to uphold the absolute uniqueness of God who cannot divide himself, change, or share his being with another. Arius identified this God not with the Trinity or divine essence, but with the Father alone. Thus he thought that only the Father is uncreated and eternal. Arius would not say the same thing about the Second Person of the Trinity. He thought that the Son was less than, or subordinate to the Father. (For this reason, **Arianism** is frequently called **Subordinationism**.) Arius believed that the Father made or created the Son. The Son then created the rest of the world. Because of this, the Son is higher than everything else except the Father, but he is a lesser god than the Father. The persons of the Trinity are not equal. Arius stressed the differences between the Father and the Son. Later Arians modified this teaching by emphasizing the similarities of the two persons. They said the Son is of a similar substance with the Father, but not of the same substance. He is close, but not fully God.

Orthodox Christianity recognized that Arianism denied essential biblical doctrines and condemned this heresy at the Council of Nicea in AD 325. To this day, Christians confess the words of that council. Christ is

> . . .the only-begotten Son of God,
> begotten of his Father before all worlds,
> God of God, Light of Light,
> Very God of very God,
> Begotten, not made,
> Being of one substance with the Father. . .

The words of the Nicene Creed strongly confess that Christ is not part of creation, but its Creator. Whatever you can say of the Father (for example, that he is God, the Light, or very God), you can say of the Son. Against the Arians and other subordinationists, the Christian church confesses the full and complete deity of Christ. We see Arianism alive today in groups like the Jehovah's Witnesses that teach that Jesus is *a* god but not *the* God. Any teaching that makes Jesus a lesser God or a super-human reflects Arian tendencies. Any reduction in his deity takes away from our Savior.

## Docetism: the Denial of Christ's Humanity

Unlike the Arianism, **Docetism** is willing to accept the deity of Christ, but makes the opposite error of denying his humanity. Recognizing the work and power of Christ, the Docetists found it easy to believe that he was God, but they were uncomfortable with the material world. Influenced by another philosophy known as **Gnosticism**, they thought that spiritual things were good and physical things were evil. God, who is spirit, would not want to enter into the evil of a physical body. Still, God wanted to save humanity. He carried out this salvation by sending Jesus who appeared to be human, but did not actually become flesh and blood. (Their name comes from the Greek word *dokeo* which means "to appear" or "to seem.") Jesus appeared to be a human being, but they said he was really only a spirit or phantom. Because of this, Jesus did not truly suffer and die on the cross, but only seemed to do so. The Docetists thought that this was an improvement on the orthodox teaching of the atonement. But in taking away the humanity and the genuine suffering and death of Jesus, they deleted the sacrifice of Christ, leaving us without a real Savior. While Docetism is not as common today as some other heresies, we see reflections of it in religions like "Christian Science" which maintain that physical existence is an illusion. They deny the physical world and so deny the incarnation of Christ as well.

## 6. The Personal Union of Christ

It is not surprising that heresies arose to explain the person of Christ. This is a complicated topic. But when we find scriptural teachings that are in tension or paradox, we are not called to modify God's word. Rather we are to hear and believe. Since this may be difficult, St. Paul reminds us, "great indeed, we confess, is the mystery of godliness: he was manifested in the flesh. . ." (1 Timothy 3:16). It is ultimately a mystery to us how these two natures are united. We will not be able to figure this out completely, since Christ is unique and not subject to our manipulation. We are not called to solve the mystery of godliness but to believe in our Savior. As we do this, we simultaneously uphold two biblical truths.

*Two Distinct Natures*

The first teaching is what we have been discussing. Christ Jesus has two natures. He is fully human and fully divine. Each nature is complete with all the attributes, characteristics, and functions that are expected of that nature. When we see paradoxical attributes that belong to each nature we simply confess that these are the attributes of Christ. For example, since Christ is God, he is the creator. Since he is human, he is part of creation. Both of these statements are true because Christ has two natures. We maintain both of these natures because this is what Scripture does. Christ is fully human and fully divine.

*One Person*

But we also confess with the Athanasian Creed that "there are not two Christs but one Christ." We deal with the individual natures only in the abstract. With Christ, we never encounter one nature apart from the other; he is the God-man. These two natures are joined together in one person. The Athanasian Creed compares the personal union of God and man in Christ to the union of body and soul in a human being. A human is one person. The incarnate Christ is one person. The two natures are inseparably and eternally united.

In addition to being biblically accurate, this is an immensely practical doctrine. We don't need to debate about which nature of Christ deserves our attention, our faith, or our worship. Rather, as the Nicene Creed says, "I believe in one Lord Jesus Christ." The Incarnate God is one person.

*Maintaining the Paradox*

In AD 451, the council of Chalcedon summarized the orthodox Christian teaching on the person of Christ. These two natures are joined together in one person but without division, without separation, without change, and without confusion. In other words, we want to make sure that we maintain the completeness and integrity of both natures while at the same time maintaining the unity of the person of Christ. The mystery of godliness is great, but Christians need not be troubled by the complexity of his person. Indeed, we rarely understand what it means for us to be persons. But this is the Christ who reveals himself to us. Hearing his word, we confess our faith in this one Christ who has two natures.

*The Two Natures and Our Redemption*

The biblical teaching of two natures in one person describes the Savior that we needed. Our Savior needed to be human so that he could be a substitute for us. Since humans caused the problem, a human would be the solution (Hebrews 2:14). As a human, he would fulfill the Law that we are unable to keep (Galatians 4:4, 5). Moreover, our Savior needed to give his life for humanity. The Christ needed to be human so that he could die.

At the same time, we needed a Savior who was divine. Only God has the perfection necessary to win our salvation. All other humans had succumbed to temptation, but God would not. Only his death could be valuable enough to pay for the sin of the entire world. Only God has the power to conquer sin, death, and the devil on our behalf. We needed a human Savior. We needed a divine Savior. All of our needs are perfectly met in Jesus Christ the God-man.

*Heresies Regarding the Personal Union*

Because the doctrine of the personal union challenges our limited reason, it quickly was distorted by people who thought they could make it more logical. While the major christological heresies already addressed focused their attention on one nature or the other, these last two affect the teaching of the personal union.

### Nestorianism: a Split Personality

Nestorius was the patriarch (the eastern title for bishop) of Constantinople early in the fifth century. He was involved in a number of debates regarding the two natures of Christ. One of the more famous ones involved the question of whether Mary could be called the "mother of God." Because of his role in these debates, his name has become attached to a distortion of the personal union. **Nestorianism** emphasizes the distinctness of Christ's two natures to an extreme degree. Christ was fully human, and Christ was fully divine, but these two natures have little to do with each other. There is no communication of attributes between the two natures. A consistent Nestorian will ascribe any individual act of Christ to one nature only, not to the entire person. A human being was born, not God. Only God was (and is) worshipped. It was only the human who died, not the God-man. Every act of Christ is attributed to one nature or the other. The Nestorian understanding of the person of Christ is often illustrated by two boards that are glued together. They are related by proximity, but really share nothing but space. They are isolated and separated. Nestorianism effectively denies the personal union and seems to offer two distinct Christs.

## Eutychianism: Confused Natures

**Eutychianism** is the opposite error of Nestorianism and is named for another fifth century church leader named Eutyches. Trying to avoid the Nestorian separation of the two natures, Eutychianism eliminates any distinction between the two natures. Humanity and deity are completely mixed and confused. There is no uniqueness to either nature in Christ Jesus. Sometimes this is described as the divine nature absorbing the human nature into itself. Humanity is still present, but diluted and imperceptible. At other times it is described as the formation of a new nature (Christ has only one nature in this description). In either case, the distinctness of both natures is lost. Since we need both for our salvation, Eutychianism destroys the work of Christ.

The council of Chalcedon rejected both of these extremes. The Christ is true God and true man, but against Eutychianism, "without confusion or change" and against Nestorianism, "without division or separation." We see the same vigilance in the Athanasian Creed which repudiates Eutychianism by calling Christ "perfect God and perfect man. . . one not by confusion of substance but by unity of person." Nestorianism is also rejected since "although he is God and man, yet he is not two but one Christ."

## Christ's Humiliation and Exaltation

Jesus Christ has both human and divine attributes, but how does this function in his life and ministry? How can an immortal divine nature be united with a mortal human nature and communicate its attributes to this person, yet this Christ is able to die? How can he be omniscient as God yet, as a human, be ignorant of things like the timing of his return (Mark 13: 32)? The answer to these questions is found in the twin doctrines of Christ's humiliation and exaltation. Here we see not only how the person of Christ functions but even more, we see the grace of God in action.

### *Christ's Humiliation*

In ordinary speech, humiliation entails the lowering of a person from one level to another, or it may describe an embarrassing situation. However, humiliation can also describe a voluntarily change in status or power in order to serve another. When we speak of Christ's **humiliation**, we are referring to the latter meaning. Even though he had, by nature, all the divine attributes, rights, and abilities, during the time of his earthly ministry he did not always or fully use these things. He voluntarily refrained from using these divine powers in his human nature. While there were times within his state of humiliation when he did use his divine power (for example, when he performed miracles), he did not constantly use this power, nor was he using it to its full extent.

Notice that in this definition, we are not saying simply that Christ was a humble person. He was indeed humble, but the humiliation was far more significant. Neither is the humiliation a synonym for the incarnation. Christ continues to have his human nature even after the state of humiliation is complete. Nor are we saying that Christ gave up his divine attributes or left them behind when he became human. He continued to have these abilities, but voluntarily chose not to use them.

There are many portions of God's word that reveal Christ's humiliation. One of the most significant is found in Philippians 2:

> Have this mind among yourselves, which is yours in Christ Jesus, ⁶who, though he was in the form of God, did not count equality with God a thing to be grasped, ⁷but made himself nothing, taking the form of a servant, being born in the likeness of men. And being found in human form, ⁸he humbled himself by becoming obedient to the point of death, even death on a cross. (Philippians 2:5-8)

Christ Jesus became a human being and became our servant in order to bring about our salvation. He humbled himself and died so that we would be his own. The humiliation was necessary for our salvation. If he had fully used his divine power, he would not have been able to die. If his glory had always been manifest as it was at his transfiguration, the people would not have condemned him. If he had done miracles at every opportunity, they would have saved his life—if only to exploit that power. Instead, he became a servant, not using his divine attributes constantly or fully. Because of this, we are redeemed.

The humiliation of Christ is evident when his life and ministry is examined. From his conception and birth to his death and burial, Jesus was in his state of humiliation. He had all the divine powers and attributes available to him, but he did not always or fully use these abilities. Since the humiliation is not about the possession of these divine abilities but about their use, it is inappropriate to classify events in Christ's humiliation in a way that implies that certain things involve a greater humiliation than others. There are no greater or lesser degrees of humiliation. The crucifixion is part of Christ's humiliation, but it is not more a part of the humiliation than his birth, childhood, or ministry. During all of these things, Christ is in his state of humiliation for us.

### Christ's Exaltation

In Christ's **exaltation**, he resumes the full and unrestricted use of his divine privileges, power, and glory that he had voluntarily restricted in his humiliation. This state of exaltation begins with his return to life and continues forever. Even today, Christ is in his state of exaltation where he uses all of his attributes in any way that pleases him. Amazingly, he chooses to use these on our behalf.

Philippians 2, which spoke of Christ's humiliation, also describes his exaltation.

> Therefore God has highly exalted him and bestowed on him the name that is above every name, [10]so that at the name of Jesus every knee should bow, in heaven and on earth and under the earth, [11]and every tongue confess that Jesus Christ is Lord, to the glory of God the Father. (Philippians 2:9-11)

Just as the humiliation is not synonymous with the incarnation, so the exaltation does not mean that Christ abandons his humanity. The Savior remains fully human, but also resumes full use and exhibition of his divine attributes and glory. Now that his saving work is complete there is no reason for him to continue in the humiliation. He accomplished the work he came to do and so returns to the full use of his glory and majesty.

### The Significance of the Humiliation and Exaltation

Our Lord did not have to do any of this. He was not compelled to be our Savior. He did not have to give up the full and complete use of his divine attributes in the humiliation. Yet this was the only way that we would be

saved. All of this he has done out of his great love for us. This is who he is:
Jesus is the God-Man. Fully human and fully divine, he has given himself
to be our Savior.

## 7. The Office of Christ

The work of Christ—the central or "official" things he comes to do— is
called his **office**. In the 33 years that Jesus lived on this earth he did many
things, but why did he come? He came to be the Savior of the world: our one
Redeemer who would reconcile us to the Father (Matthew 1:21). Only Jesus
Christ can and does offer us the gift of eternal life.

In order to describe his work, many Christians have found it useful to
divide his work into several smaller aspects that may be examined more
closely. While the Scriptures describe his work and ministry with many different images, many Christians find it helpful to focus on three particular
images: prophet, priest, and king. These roles help us understand his work
and communicate it to others.

### The Christ of God

These three aspects of his work may have been initially used to describe
his work because each was an important office in the life of ancient Israel.
God sent prophets, priests, and kings to his people. Each served Israel in
unique ways. Some have suggested that one thing that all three offices have
in common is that their occupants were anointed. Anointing was a sign that
someone was set apart or consecrated for a specific service. Oil was poured
on their heads as a visible sign that they were authorized and empowered
to carry out the responsibilities of their office. This was common for priests
(Exodus 40:13) and kings (2 Kings 9:3). Some prophets were also anointed
(1 Kings 19:16). Anointing showed their legitimacy and authority.

When we call the Savior "Christ" we are not using his name. "**Christ**"
is the Greek word for "anointed one." In Hebrew, this word is "**Messiah**."
He is the anointed one, the Messiah, the one set apart and consecrated by
God for a specific task. He is anointed to be our Savior. In fact, the New
Testament specifically notes that Jesus was anointed with the Holy Spirit
(Acts 10:38). Many Christians who have gone before us have connected the
title Christ with the offices of prophet, priest, and king. He was anointed to
do this work.

Saying that Christ holds all three of these positions, however, recognizes something unique about him. There are specific requirements for each
of these offices. Two of them, priest and king, require a specific ancestry.

Kings were descended from David in the tribe of Judah, but priests had to be Levites. One person would ordinarily not be able to serve in both of those positions. Moses came close. He was a prophet, led his nation, and established the regulations for the priesthood (Leviticus 8-10), but he was not really a king or a priest. David was a king. Like a prophet, he wrote portions of the Bible, but he wasn't a priest. But Jesus is truly a prophet, priest, and king. Only he is able to unite these offices.

*The Prophetic Office—Christ the Prophet of God*

People often equate the work of a prophet with predictions of the future. While Jesus does predict future events (for example, in Matthew 26:34), this is not the sole work of a prophet. A **prophet** brings the word of God to human beings as God's representative.

Some Christians are reluctant to call Jesus a prophet. Perhaps this is a reaction against those who would describe Jesus merely as a prophet while rejecting his deity. Even in his ministry, Jesus was, at times, misunderstood as being only a prophet (John 9:17; Luke 24:19). Yet no one who takes his prophetic message seriously can mistake what he says. Jesus calls himself God. He is not merely a prophet, but this truth does not take away the fact that Jesus is also a prophet. We uphold this scriptural truth because it is an important part of his work. Jesus brings the word of God to us (John 17:6-8). He is the supreme prophet, greater than all others. The book of Hebrews notes that he fulfills this office, but it also shows his superiority. While other prophets spoke God's word to the people, Jesus is God. He speaks his own divine word directly (Hebrews 1:1). Where the other prophets declare, "God says. . ." Jesus boldly proclaims, "I tell you. . . ." Other prophets speak the word of God through sinful lips (Isaiah 6:5). Christ is the supreme messenger of God because he is God. St. John reminds us, "No one has ever seen God; the only God who is at the Father's side, he has made him known" (John 1:18). The **prophetic office** of Christ continues today as he speaks to us through his word. As ministers are sent with his word and in his name, it is Christ's voice that is proclaimed and heard.

*The Priestly Office—Christ the Great High Priest*

The second aspect of Christ's work is his **priestly office**. A prophet represents God to humanity; a priest represents people to God. Priests intercede with God, offering gifts, sacrifices and prayers to God on behalf of others (Hebrews 5:1). They have God's invitation and command to do this priestly work for his people. We see this office when Scripture calls him a **priest**. We also see it when he does priestly work or is called as a sacrifice. Words like intercessor (Hebrews 7:25), sacrifice (Romans 3:25), offering (Romans 8:3), and even Lamb of God (John 1:29) all reflect the priestly office of Jesus.

### The Necessity of the Priestly Office

If we are to receive the forgiveness of sins and salvation, we need the services of a priest. God has decreed the conditions of our forgiveness. The Old Testament teaches the need for sacrifice. The New Testament summarizes this, "under the law almost everything is purified with blood, and without the shedding of blood there is no forgiveness of sins" (Hebrews 9:22).

This requirement of the Law did not disappear with the coming of Christ. We still needed a proper sacrifice of blood for our sins. Jesus comes as our sacrifice. He is "the Lamb of God, who takes away the sin of the world" (John 1:29) and "the propitiation for. . . the sins of the whole world" (1 John 2:2). He was sacrificed on the cross so that we might have life and forgiveness. What's more, his sacrifice was perfect and so effective that no further sacrifices are ever needed again (Hebrews 10:10).

Jesus is our sacrifice, but this raises a theological question. A sacrifice must be offered by someone. It is not sufficient to simply buy or even kill an animal. A legitimate priest must offer the sacrifice in the proper way if it is to be valid. Without the priest a creature might be killed, but it would not be a sacrifice.

So if Jesus was the sacrifice, who was the priest? Not the priests in Jerusalem. They had rejected him and helped arrange his death, but they did not think they were offering a sacrifice. Certainly it was not the faithless soldiers who carried out the crucifixion. The New Testament offers a different explanation. Jesus was both the priest and the sacrifice. But can this be true? God declared through Moses that priests must come from the tribe of Levi. At the same time, the Messiah was a descendent of David in the tribe of Judah (Hebrews 7:14). How could one man be the Messiah who is sacrificed and also the priest? Are not these roles mutually exclusive?

Hebrews considers the question in detail and proves that it is possible. It notes that Scripture describes a great priest who lived before the Levites. Melchizedek was a priest who served Abraham (Genesis 14:18-20). Though he was not a Levite, Melchizedek was a legitimate priest, because he lived before that regulation had been given. Jesus was a priest in the same way. As God, he existed from all eternity and so is exempt from the Levitical requirement. (He is, in essence, "grandfathered in.") Jesus is a priest forever, "after the order of Melchizedek" (Psalm 110:4, Hebrews 5:4-10). Jesus is the great high priest, anointed by God to offer the final sacrifice of himself for the sin of the entire world.

Not only is Christ a legitimate priest, he is the supreme high priest. All priests who preceded him served only for a short time and then died. Jesus lives forever and so is our high priest forever (Hebrews 7:23-25). Other priests offered sacrifices for sins, but before they did this, they had to offer a sacrifice for their own sin. Jesus did not have to do this. He had no sin, and so was able to serve us completely (Hebrews 7:27-28). Other priests served God in the tabernacle and temple, but these were temporary structures. Jesus serves in the true, heavenly temple for all eternity (Hebrews 9:11). Other priests offered animals as God commanded, but Jesus offered a priceless offering—himself (Hebrews 9:12-15, Ephesians 5:2). Other priests needed to offer many offerings day after day. Whenever sins were committed more sacrifices had to be offered. Jesus offered one great and final offering that was sufficient to atone for all sins: past, present, and future (Hebrews 10:10, 14). Once he offered that sacrifice, everything necessary had been completed. No further sacrifice would be needed (Hebrews 8:1; 10:12; John 19:30). In fact, no other sacrifices have been offered since AD 70 when the temple in Jerusalem was destroyed. There is no longer any place to offer those sacrifices and no further need for them. Jesus has fulfilled and completed them all when he sacrificed himself.

### The Intercession of Christ Our High Priest

Priests represent people to God when they offer sacrifices. They also represent people through intercessory prayer. A priest brings the petitions and prayers to God on behalf of others. This too is part of the priestly office of Christ.

In his ministry on earth, Jesus prayed for his disciples. John 17:1ff records one of his prayers (usually called the High Priestly Prayer) for his followers. His intercession was not only for the disciples that day, but also for "those who will believe in me through their word" (John 17:20). We are included in that prayer. He prayed for all believers and his intercession continues today. St. Paul assures us, "who is to condemn? Christ Jesus is the one who died—more than that, who was raised—who is at the right hand of God, who indeed is interceding for us" (Romans 8:34). Jesus our high priest is our advocate to the Father (1 John 2:1). He served us as high priest by sacrificing himself, and he serves us still by interceding for us.

*The Royal Office—Christ the King*

The third office of Christ is his kingly or **royal office**. Christians often call Jesus their king. Unfortunately, as with the title prophet, there are some who use this description in a misleading way. Some call Jesus a king, thinking that he only sought to rule one of earth's kingdoms. Some think that he will return to this earthly reign in the future. The kingship of Jesus can also be described in a way that eclipses his priestly office. All of these are misunderstandings of the scriptural teaching of Jesus' kingship.

Biblical prophesy foretold that the Messiah would be a king, from David's royal line, who would reign forever (2 Samuel 7:12-13, Isaiah 9: 6-7). When Jesus was born, the magi recognized him as a king (Matthew 2: 2). When, later in his ministry, people called him the "Son of David" (for example, in Matthew 21:9), they acclaimed him as the Messiah.

Sadly, the people did not really understand what it meant for the Messiah to be a king. They sought an earthly leader but not a divine Savior. After Jesus fed more than 5000 people with his miraculous power, they wanted to make him king by force (John 6:15). Jesus refused, knowing that this would keep him from the work of salvation. His own disciples at times acted as though he came to be simply an earthly king (Acts 1:6). The leaders of this world, interested only in power, were jealous that Jesus was called a king and sought to keep him from taking that power (Matthew 2:13-18). No one seemed to understand or believe Jesus when he said, "My kingdom is not of this world" (John 18:36).

These misunderstandings of Jesus' kingship cannot negate his authentic royalty. At Jesus' trial, Pontius Pilate asked Jesus if he was a king. Jesus agreed that this was true (Luke 23:3). The cross carried the inscription, "Jesus of Nazareth, the King of the Jews" (John 19:19). Although they were meant in mockery, the words were true. Scripture hails Jesus as the King of kings (Revelation 17:14) and speaks of his eternal kingdom (2 Peter 1:11). Misunderstandings do not change the fact that Jesus truly is a king. So how do we maintain the biblical teaching of Christ's kingship without falling into these errors? We can do this by recognizing that there are several related, yet distinct aspects to his reign. These are ordinarily called the kingdom of power, kingdom of grace, and kingdom of glory.

### *Christ's Kingdom of Power*

The **kingdom of power** is Christ's rule over all creation. This kingdom is his by divine right since he is true God and the creator of the universe. All things were made by him and are subject to his rule and command. So Jesus says that all power in heaven and earth is his (Matthew 28:18). All things are under him, and he is the "head over all things" (Ephesians 1:22).

In this aspect of rule, Christ reigns by his Law and power, not by his Gospel. Here the Law is functioning in its first use: to restrain and limit the effects of sin and wickedness. All of his creation is part of his kingdom of power. Indeed it is a great blessing that this is so.

Christ's providential care is part of the kingdom of power. He works through the natural order that he created to cause the rain to fall on the righteous and the unrighteous alike (Matthew 5:45). He upholds the universe and causes it to function properly not only for those who believe in him, but for all (Hebrews 1:3). These gifts of creation and providence are all part of his kingly bounty. He rules and guides through society, government, and human authority. All governments are established by God (Romans 13:1) and are accountable and subject to Christ their maker.

Christians, like all other people, are citizens in the kingdom of power. We are not exempt from natural laws or from obedience to the government. We still live in societies and know the effect of the Law. We also are constantly receiving the benefits of our master's providence and care.

### Christ's Kingdom of Grace

While the kingdom of power extends over all people, the kingdom of grace is more limited. This kingdom includes those who have heard and believed the Gospel—in other words, the church. Jesus describes this kingdom as "the kingdom of heaven" or "the kingdom of God" (Matthew 13:44-45; Mark 10:15).

In this kingdom he rules not by the power and force of the Law, but by his Gospel. This is why it is the **kingdom of grace**: he creates and gathers this kingdom together solely by his gracious work and will. There is no coercion or force in this kingdom, only his gracious and free invitation. Where the kingdom of power works through natural laws and institutions that wield the power of the Law, the kingdom of grace is spread gently through the proclamation of the Gospel and service of the sacraments.

As the children of God, we are now citizens in his kingdom (Ephesians 2:19). This does not, however, remove us from the kingdom of power. Christians simultaneously live in both kingdoms.

### Christ's Kingdom of Glory

When people speak of Christ's kingship, some overlook the first two kingdoms and refer only to the kingdom of glory. While this is part of Christ's royal office, we should not neglect the first two kingdoms. The third kingdom, called the **kingdom of glory**, refers to the majestic, eternal reign of our Savior in heaven. He has a heavenly kingdom and he will take us there (2 Timothy 4:18). This kingdom will be manifest on earth when he returns to judge the nations (Matthew 25:31). This does not mean, however, that this kingly reign of Christ is only a future reality. While we continue to await the return of our Savior, he is already reigning in the kingdom of glory. The saints who have gone before us, along with the rest of the heavenly host, all know the glorious reign of our Savior. Even though we have not yet been brought into this kingdom, the kingdom is already a reality and our King is reigning.

### *The Relationship of the Three Kingdoms*

These three kingdoms reflect different ways in which Christ Jesus exercises his kingly office. They are distinct from each other, but they are also related. There are three kingdoms, but one king. Christ rules over all things, though in different ways. He rules in the kingdom of power by his Law and power. Among those who receive his Gospel on this earth, he works tenderly through the Gospel in the means of grace. In the kingdom of glory the redeemed, having been freed from sin and all its effects, see him face to face and know his presence. Paul describes part of the relationship of these kingdoms:

> [The Father] worked [his great might] in Christ when he raised him from the dead and seated him at his right hand in the heavenly places, [21]far above all rule and authority and power and dominion, and above every name that is named, not only in this age but also in the one to come. [22]And he put all things under his feet and gave him as head over all things to the church, [23]which is his body, the fullness of him who fills all in all. (Ephesians 1:20-23)

In his kingdom of glory, Christ is above all things, and possesses every title and honor that is due him. He is also over all things (kingdom of power) but uses that power for the church (kingdom of grace). He works in the kingdom of power for the sake and benefit of his church. His work in the kingdom of grace creates and prepares citizens for the kingdom of glory. In his kingdom of power he protects us, in his kingdom of grace he nurtures and nourishes us until we reach his eternal, heavenly kingdom. The kingdoms are related because all are ruled by the same king.

## Some Cautions

Imagery of Christ as king is often exciting to Christians, and rightly so. We belong to a great and glorious king who has made us his own. In excitement, however, it is easy to slip into errors regarding the kingly office. One is the danger of treating Christ's kingly office as only a future reality. Sometimes Christians describe Christ's return as the time in which he will finally become king. This is not an adequate depiction of the biblical teaching. While the return of our Savior will mark a change for those who live on earth, he is not waiting to become king. Jesus Christ already is king. Today he rules over all creation. He reigns in the hearts of his people and in the life of his church. Even now he reigns in heaven. Christ is king already! The fact that we do not always recognize his reign or live as his citizens marks a problem in us, not in him. Do not delay the kingship of Christ. Our Savior reigns.

A second danger is also significant. It is easy to get caught up in the majesty and power of the kingship of Christ and allow it to eclipse other parts of his work. In particular, it is easy to allow the kingly reign of Christ to become more important in our minds than his priestly office. Yet Christ reigns in his kingdoms of grace and glory precisely because of his priestly work. He has redeemed us with his blood and made us his own. The reign of Christ was not interrupted by his crucifixion and death. They are the heart of his work.

Our Savior is the Christ, the anointed one, the Messiah. He serves us as prophet, revealing God's will to us. He serves us as our great high priest who offers himself as the greatest and final sacrifice for the sins of the whole world. He continues to intercede for us as our high priest. He serves us as king as he reigns over the world, his church, and heaven itself. This is the office of Christ, the work that he was sent to do. He has accomplished this for us. All three of these offices are expressed in this work of salvation. If we change our focus from this work, we lose our proper perspective and misunderstand our Savior. He did not come only to proclaim the word as a prophet. He did not come for a coronation. He came to be our redeemer.

## 8. The Atonement

As we focus on the core work of Christ for our salvation, we arrive at another question. Jesus Christ is the incarnate Son of God who saves us by his death and resurrection. This is the very heart of Christianity. Many Christians are content to simply know and believe this truth. Some, however, seek to go a little deeper. I believe that this is true, but how does it work?

What exactly does Christ's incarnation, death and resurrection accomplish? How does Scripture describe this work and its effects? Why did our salvation take place in this way? Was this the only way possible or could God have done it another way? Perhaps the most significant question is, "how should I describe and explain his work to other people?"

Christians have asked these questions since the very beginning. They are not expressions of doubt or unbelief, but rather show a desire to dig deeply into the riches of God's word. They seek a biblical description of the **atonement**. Those who search the Scriptures will find several descriptions of the work of Christ. His service to us is described in several images and patterns so that we might better understand it.

One of the most important biblical descriptions of Jesus' work centers on the need for perfect obedience to God and his law. God demands holiness and perfection, and since we have failed, we need to pay the appropriate penalty. The penalty for sin is death (Romans 6:23): a cost that is too great for us to pay. Even if we paid the just penalty, we would be dead and still would have not kept the Law perfectly. We would be punished but will not have attained salvation.

God was not satisfied with this situation. He is perfectly righteous and so cannot overlook the sin that has been committed. If he were to do so, he would not be just and holy; rather, he would be arbitrary and capricious. This is inconsistent with his changeless nature (Malachi 3:6). At the same time, God is merciful and wants to forgive his creatures. How is God able to be just and merciful? He can be true to both of these attributes in Christ Jesus. The Son of God comes to stand in our place as a substitute.

Christ Jesus earns our salvation by his obedience to the Father. He fulfills both of our needs before God. Since humans failed to keep God's Law perfectly and without sin, the Savior does this for us. This is called his **active obedience**. He is born under the Law's demands (Galatians 4:4), lives a sinless life and fulfills all the commands of our righteous God. This obedience was expected of all humanity, but only Christ was able to do this. He lived the life that we were meant to live: a life of holiness and perfection. He does this as our substitute so that his obedience is credited to us.

But our second need still remained: we owed a debt to God for sinning against him. Again, Christ is our substitute by taking the punishment that we deserved: the punishment of death. This is his **passive obedience** where he voluntarily took our fate upon himself. Isaiah prophesied this of the Messiah:

> But He was wounded for our transgressions; He was crushed for our iniquities; upon him was the chastisement that brought us peace, and with his

stripes we are healed. [6]All we like sheep have gone astray; we have turned every one to his own way; and the Lord has laid on him the iniquity of us all. (Isaiah 53:5-6)

He did not deserve this suffering or death, but chose to pay the price of our sin. His life was of such great value that he has paid the penalty for all humanity. Notice that in this substitution the sin is not forgotten. God does not ignore or arbitrarily forget sin. The penalty is truly paid. God's justice has been satisfied. Moreover, it has been paid in God's way. Blood has been shed (Hebrews 9:22) and God's wrath has been covered (Romans 3:24; 1 John 2:2). He exchanged our sinfulness for his righteousness and we are reconciled with the Father.

This is one significant biblical description of Christ's work, but it is not the only one. Another biblical theme depicts his work in terms of victory over sin, death and the devil. Elsewhere the Bible shows us that Christ's love powerfully demonstrates God's love to us. The Scriptures describe the work of Christ in many ways. Indeed, these portrayals do not encompass everything that the word says about our Savior. It presents his work in many ways so that we will hear it, understand it better, and rejoice in what he has done for us. Some of these biblical motifs will seem more meaningful to one person than another. Different Christians may have their own favorite passages. As we explain the work of Christ to other people, we will likely emphasize specific verses and explanations that we found helpful. This is appropriate, since it is normal for us to focus on a few key themes. We should not, however, think that this focus represents the entire content of Scripture. The richness of God's word allows us to present the work of our Savior in several complementary ways. Recognizing this, the response of the Christian is not to choose one, but to trust the Savior that they reveal. Indeed, knowing the work of Christ, his people can know him more deeply through other biblical descriptions. Our Savior is also our Shepherd (John 10:11), our Light (John 1:9), our Mediator (1 Timothy 2:5), our Advocate (1 John 2:1), and many other things.

Our Savior has blessed us beyond our comprehension. He serves us as our prophet, priest, and king. He dies and rises again to reconcile us with the Father, destroy our enemies, and bring us into his kingdom. He does not come with demands and conditions, but freely offers his grace and mercy. This is what he has done for us and, when we see that, we know him.

### Key Terms

| | |
|---|---|
| Active obedience | Kingdom of Power |
| Arianism | Means of grace |
| Atonement | Messiah |
| Christ | Nature |
| Docetism | Nestorianism |
| Efficacious | Office |
| Eutychianism | Passive obedience |
| Exaltation | Person |
| Gnosticism | Priest |
| Grace | Priestly Office |
| Humiliation | Prophet |
| Immaculate concep- | Prophetic Office |
| tion | Royal Office |
| Incarnation | Subordinationism |
| Kingdom of Glory | Virgin conception |
| Kingdom of Grace | and birth |

## For Review and Discussion

1.  Christianity is unique among all the world's religions in that it is the only religion that is based not on works but on grace. Yet many Christians seem to ignore grace and turn Christianity into another religion of works. Why do you think they do this? How can we keep our faith focused on God's grace in Christ?

2.  God proclaims his gracious will to humanity throughout the Bible. What examples of his grace can you find in both the Old and the New Testaments? How does recognizing his grace strengthen your faith?

3.  When faced with trials, people may make statements suggesting that God does not really understand the human situation. How does the incarnation of Christ demonstrate God's full understanding and awareness of our existence?

4.  Many heresies have developed regarding the person and work of Jesus Christ. Why do you think these doctrines attract so many errors? What does this suggest about the importance of

these doctrines? What does this reveal about human sinfulness?

5.  In Philippians 2, St. Paul says that the humiliation of Christ
    demonstrates the type of attitude that we should have. (Even
    while it also shows us many other things.) How is Christ's
    humiliation a model for our lives? Is there a danger in overem-
    phasizing this function of the humiliation? How can we keep it
    in proper perspective?

## For Further Reading

Athanasius. *On the Incarnation: The Treatise De Incarnatione Verbi
Dei.* Crestwood, New York: St. Vladimir's Seminary Press, 1977.

Aulén, Gustaf. *Christus Victor: An Historical Study of the Three Main
Types of the Idea of Atonement.* New York: MacMillan, 1986.

Baille, D. M. *God was in Christ: An Essay on Incarnation and Atonement.* New York: Scribner's, 1948.

Bray, Gerald. *Creeds, Councils, and Christ.* Downer's Grove, Illinois:
Intervarsity Press, 1984.

Hengstenberg, Ernst Wilhelm. *The Christology of the Old Testament
and a Commentary on the Messianic Predictions.* Grand Rapids:
Kregel, 1970.

Lewis, C. S. *Mere Christianity.* New York: Macmillan, 1952.

Morris, Leon. *The Apostolic Preaching of the Cross.* Grand Rapids:
Eerdmans, 1955.

Sasse, Hermann. *We Confess Jesus Christ.* Translated by Norman Na-
gel. St. Louis: Concordia Publishing House, 1984.

Scaer, David. *Christology.* Confessional Lutheran Dogmatics, vol IX.
St. Louis: The Luther Academy, 1989.

_____. *What Do You Think of Jesus?* St. Louis: Concordia, 1973.

Strobel, Lee. *The Case for Christ: A Journalist's Personal Investigation
of the Evidence for Jesus.* Grand Rapids: Zondervan, 1998.

# 9

# Justification

Imagine that you are sitting in an airport terminal, waiting for a flight. A stranger sits down near you and notices that you are reading this book. "So you're a Christian? I'm not really religious myself, but I've always wondered what your religion is all about. Can you tell me what the difference is between Christianity and other religions?" It is an amazing opportunity to share your faith, but there is a catch: her flight boards in five minutes. What will you say? Hopefully, you will introduce her to Jesus. You will describe what God has done for her in the death and resurrection of his Son. You will describe God's free gift of salvation which he gives to us—a gift we cannot earn or deserve. You likely will not use deep theological vocabulary, but you will be presenting the doctrine of justification. This is the very essence of the Christian faith—the core doctrine on which all other teaching rests. Looking at this teaching, we will consider:

1. The Context of Justification—*God's response to our sinful state*
2. The Definition of Justification—*God declares us righteous for Christ's sake*
3. Essential Components of Justification—*Details of this central doctrine*
4. Challenges to Justification—*Human distortions of God's gracious plan*
5. The Comfort of Justification—*God's truth brings us peace and joy*

## 1. The Context of Justification

If justification is the central doctrine of Christianity, why have we wait-ed so long to discuss it? We have held our examination of justification to this point so that we could place it in context. The doctrines that we have already studied show humanity's need for justification and the means by which God brings it about. A brief review will help contextualize justification.

Almighty God, our creator, is holy and righteous and he demands righ-teousness from his creatures. Our first parents failed to keep his commands and by their fall into sin broke the relationship that God had established with them. Their rebellion justly earned his condemnation and wrath. Moreover, the effect of their sin was not limited to them alone. As the first human be-ings, they have passed on to all of their descendents both the guilt of sin and the desire to sin. We have followed in their image by sinning in actions, inactions, words, thoughts, and intentions. All humanity is now sinful by nature and behavior. Because of this, we rightly come under God's wrath. His sentence of death and hell are appropriate, just, and fair. We are guilty and deserve this fate.

At some level, humanity is aware of our separation from God, but we are unable to do anything about it. Even though it is impossible, people still make vain attempts to save themselves, earn God's favor, or appease his anger. Most of the world's religions suggest ways to do this, but the true God shows us how pointless this is. We do not do our best to please him, and even if we did, it is not enough. God does not demand our best efforts; he demands perfection and holiness (Leviticus 19:2), a standard that we cannot meet. As Isaiah said, even our *righteous* acts are like filthy rags (Isaiah 64:6). The very best we offer is still not enough. We cannot save ourselves.

The living God expects perfection, but he does not ask us to save our-selves. He knows that if we are to be saved, it cannot be up to us. He must intervene. It is all up to God and, in Christ Jesus, he accomplishes the work that we are unable to do. He brings about our forgiveness and salvation. It is entirely his work.

## 2. The Definition of Justification

As we saw in the last chapter, Scripture describes the work of Christ with a variety of images, but how are we connected to that work? How are the benefits of his actions applied to humanity and to us as individuals? This is the topic of justification.

The word justification is not used much outside of Christianity. Many people are most familiar with this term in the context of word-processing.

Our documents are right justified, left justified, or full justified. This means that they are arranged on the right margin, left margin, or on both margins. The margin that is justified has all the words lined up in a straight line. While that definition seems to be a long way from theology, it does reflect the sense of justification.

Justification is concerned with being or becoming just, right, righteous, or fair. In a document, the words are lined up in the proper way and so are justified. They are exactly where they are supposed to be. If a person is to be justified, they need to be exactly where and exactly what they are supposed to be. If we could justify ourselves, we would need to be perfectly righteous and holy—exactly what God wants us to be.

Because we cannot meet this demand, God has revealed something else to us. He does not ask us to justify ourselves, he justifies us. In its theological sense, **justification** refers to God's declaration that, because of the merit of Christ and without any merit of our own, we are righteous in his sight. Our sins are forgiven and we are credited with the righteousness of Christ. Closer examination of this biblical teaching reveals two complementary senses in which the Scriptures use this term. They are known as objective justification and subjective justification.

*Objective Justification*

**Objective justification** describes the extent of Christ's saving work. By his holy life, death and resurrection, Christ Jesus has atoned for the sin of the whole world. His work is sufficient payment for every single human being and all of our sins. No one is excluded from his gracious work. There is no one for whom he has not died.

The Bible frequently makes this point. Jesus is the Lamb of God who takes away the sins of the world (John 1:29). He is called "the propitiation for our sins, and not for ours only but also for the sins of the whole world" (1 John 2:2). Second Corinthians 5:19 says, "in Christ God was reconciling the world to himself, not counting their trespasses against them." John 3:16 reminds us that God's motive for sending Jesus was love for the world, not just for some people in the world.

Objective justification acknowledges this divine work. Christ has reconciled the world to the Father. This is an objective fact whether we believe it, reject it, or are ignorant of it. Christ's work is sufficient to pay for the entire world, and the Father has accepted the sacrifice of Christ. His wrath has been appeased and the payment for sin has been made.

Unfortunately, not all Christians agree with this summary of scriptural truth. Some would limit the work of Christ to the elect or to Christians only. Many who hold such a view (called **limited atonement** or particular atonement) believe that they are stressing the effectiveness of the work of Christ. In their view, everyone for whom Christ died will receive the gift of salvation. They fear that objective justification will lead to **universalism** (the teaching that everyone will eventually be saved, regardless of their faith). They need not have this fear. A proper understanding of subjective justification will keep universalism at bay. This biblical teaching must not be removed or neglected in order to protect another biblical teaching. They all fit together.

Because Christ objectively justified the world, we do not question whether he died for any individual. I know he died and rose, but did he do it for me? Yes. For me; for everyone. The whole world was reconciled by the death of Jesus.

## Subjective Justification

Objective justification is the truth that Christ died for the sins of the whole world and has reconciled the world to the Father. But how does this connect to the individual? We know from Scripture that not all will be saved. How can some be damned when Christ has justified the world? The solution is found in subjective justification. **Subjective justification** is the work of Christ applied to and received by an individual in faith. Christ Jesus has paid for the sins of the whole world, but this truth becomes my own, and a benefit for me, when I believe the Gospel and have faith in Christ my Savior. Objective justification applies to all people, but those who reject the Gospel do not receive the benefits or blessings of that justification. They have chosen to exempt themselves from the gifts that God has given them in Christ.

## God's Forensic Declaration

The doctrine of justification rightly places all the effort on God's side. Justification is not a human work; it is the work of God. So how does God justify us? It is important for us to recognize that we are justified because God declares us to be just for Christ's sake. God doesn't pronounce us righteous because we have done enough good works. God doesn't make us perfectly holy in this life before calling us just. Instead, God justifies us while we are still sinners (Romans 5:8).

Justification is God's declaration that, because of the merit of Christ, and without any merit of our own, we are righteous in his sight. This is a verdict of almighty God. Despite the overwhelming and indisputable evidence of our guilt, he has *proclaimed* us innocent. As a judge's verdict proclaims a defendant guilty or not guilty, so God's verdict proclaims our status in his sight. We are declared righteous. This is known as **forensic justification**. ("Forensic" is a description of legal issues, or things related to a court.) God has forensically declared that we are innocent. This verdict should perplex us. How can he say I am righteous? I know my sinfulness. I am completely guilty and unrighteous. How can a just God act in a way which seems so unjust? I am happy that God considers me to be innocent, but is this fair?

God does not violate his own Law when he declares us innocent. There is a legitimate penalty for sin and that penalty is not ignored. A defendant is still convicted of sin and sentenced to pay its penalty. The legal, forensic verdict of guilt falls upon Jesus. The sentence of death is carried out. The Law is upheld, but God allows our substitute to exchange places with us.

## Imputation of Righteousness

Forensic justification is a direct application of the work of Christ. In this declaration, God permits Christ to stand in our place to bear our punishment and credits us with the righteousness of Christ. He exchanges our guilt for his holiness. Theologians generally refer to this as imputation. **Imputation** is another legal or accounting term that refers to the charging or crediting of something to a person. In the Bible, we see this idea reflected in terms like "credit," "reckon," or "account" (as in Galatians 3:6 "Abraham believed God, and it was *counted* to him as righteousness").

Justification involves a two-fold imputation. The first deals with our sins. God does not impute our sins to us. In other words, he does not hold us accountable for those sins. But sin is not overlooked; God imputes our sin to Christ. Our guilt is charged against him and Jesus bore the sentence of death for that sin. He did nothing to deserve death; it is our fault. 2 Corinthians 5: 19 shows how this occurs when it says, "in Christ God was reconciling the world to himself, not counting their trespasses against them." He did not count (or impute) our sins against us. Rather, he charges them to his Son as "he made him to be sin who knew no sin, so that in him we might become the righteousness of God" (2 Corinthians 5:21). This imputation is complete. All human sins and sinfulness are imputed to the Redeemer (1 John 1:7).

In the second imputation, God imputes Christ's righteousness to us. We have not lived holy and perfect lives, but God credits us with the holiness that was actually seen in the life of Christ. He regards us as his obedient, holy children. When he sees us, he sees the righteousness of Christ. This righteousness is truly credited to us, but it is not based on anything we have done. Martin Luther referred to this as **"alien righteousness."** It comes from outside of us, from Christ. We have done nothing to deserve the imputation of his righteousness; he has done it all for us.

Jeremiah prophesied that the Messiah would be known as "the LORD is our righteousness" (Jeremiah 23:6). St. Paul calls him "our wisdom and our righteousness and sanctification and redemption" (1 Corinthians 1:30). The only way that sinners can be called righteous is if that righteousness is given to them. We see this in Philippians 3:9 where Paul says that he does not have ". . .a righteousness of my own that comes from the law, but that which comes through faith in Christ, the righteousness from God that depends on faith."

This righteousness is not our own; we do not contribute anything but our sin. God imputes the righteousness of Christ to us. It is his forensic decree. This righteousness is "from faith for faith" (Romans 1:17). It is all up to God. He has done everything for us. We are declared righteous because of Christ Jesus.

## *Not an Infusion of Righteousness*

Some Christians consider this biblical teaching to be dangerous. Relying on alien righteousness may lead people to ignore their own morality and behavior. While this concern is addressed in the Scriptures (for example, see Romans 6:15), it is still frequently raised within the church. Hoping to safeguard pious behavior, some Christians have sought to make justification not an imputation of righteousness but an infusion of righteousness. **Infused righteousness** is another way of saying that God makes us actually righteous. He works within us to make us holy people. While that might sound good, it is not the biblical doctrine of justification. At best, it is a confusion of justification and sanctification. At worst, it can deny the work of Christ.

Infused righteousness would mean that God changes us in order to save us. He gives us the strength and power so that we actually become holy and righteous people. On the basis of those actually holy lives, he then pronounces us righteous. Put another way, God changes us so that we are able to save ourselves, with his help. Notice that this ignores the many passages of Scripture which speak of our inability to contribute to our salvation. Note also that infused righteousness robs us of the comfort of justification. How do you know you are saved? One must look at the evidence of a holy life. The sins that we commit daily call that holy life into question. At best, I can only try my hardest and hope that is good enough.

In contrast, **imputed righteousness** gives comfort and assurance. God has not changed our nature, he changes our status. We continue to struggle with sin each day, but God has already imputed those sins to Christ. We are declared righteous and just because of Christ. How do you know you are saved? Not because of anything you have done, but only because of Jesus.

### Not a Process, a Verdict

With this forensic understanding of imputation, justification is not a gradual process but a complete and certain verdict. There is nothing lacking. Either we are fully justified by his grace or we have rejected it. Either we are the children of God through Christ or we are not. The Christian need not doubt the forgiveness and salvation that is ours in Christ. The forensic verdict has already been made. For Christ's sake, we are fully justified.

## 3. Essential Components of Justification

The doctrine of justification permeates the Scriptures. As we consider the details of this teaching, four essential components of the doctrine are evident. We see them all reflected in a familiar verse from Ephesians.

> For by grace you have been saved through faith. And this is not your own doing; it is the gift of God, [9]not a result of works, so that no one may boast. [10]For we are his workmanship, created in Christ Jesus for good works, which God prepared beforehand, that we should walk in them. (Ephesians 2:8-10)

The four essential components are that we are justified (1) by grace, (2) through faith, (3) for the sake of Christ, (4) apart from works.

### By Grace

"For by grace you have been saved. . ." (Ephesians 2:8). This first component of justification is a clear reminder that we do not deserve salvation, nor can we do anything to earn it or prepare for it. In fact, we deserve damnation and the wrath of God. Grace is God's undeserved mercy and love which is seen in the voluntary death of Jesus for humans and our salvation. Because sinful people are so prone to give themselves credit for salvation, Scripture reminds us again and again that this is a free gift of God's grace (Romans 3: 21-24, Titus 3:7; Acts 15:11; 2 Timothy 1:9). We are saved by God's grace, not by our merit or works. "But if it is by grace, it is no longer on the basis of works; otherwise grace would no longer be grace" (Romans 11:6).

*Through Faith*

Still, some people ask, "how do we receive this grace? Surely we must do *something* to deserve it." Human pride wants to think that we make some contribution to our salvation, but the biblical answer is that we do not. All that is asked of us is faith. "For by grace you have been saved through faith. . ." (Ephesians 2:8). Hebrews teaches us that "without faith it is impossible to please him" (Hebrews 11:6). So is this what we have to do? Is faith the work that earns salvation?

Faith is not a human work. Ephesians continues to say that this faith "is not your own doing; it is the gift of God" (Ephesians 2:8). Even faith is his gift to us. American Christianity, heavily influenced by revivalistic pleas to "accept Jesus," has often tended to describe faith as a human action or a decision that we make. This is not an accurate description of faith. Ephesians reminds us that faith is not from ourselves. By ourselves we resist God. Faith is the means by which we receive the blessings of God and even this faith comes from him.

Scripture clearly teaches that we receive God's grace through faith. Romans 3:22 says that righteousness from God comes "through faith in Christ Jesus for all who believe." Romans 1:17 tells us that the righteousness "is from faith for faith." No one receives salvation in any other way. We receive God's grace through faith or we do not receive it. Even Abraham was not saved by his works. Rather he was justified by faith (Genesis 15:6; Romans 4:3).

*For Christ's Sake*

The third essential element of justification is not explicitly listed in Ephesians 2, but it is certainly implied in these verses and in the rest of Ephesians (and throughout Scripture). Faith must have an object. We do not simply have faith in the abstract; we have faith in Christ. It is not the believing that saves us but the one in whom we believe. So St. Paul teaches, "a person is not justified by works of the law but through faith *in Jesus Christ*" (Galatians 2:16).

This biblical qualification prevents us from transforming faith into a human work. Every human being has some sort of faith. We may trust our God, other people, science technology, or any number of other things, but not all of these things are worthy of our trust. If the object of faith is not appropriate or trustworthy, we are lost. Justifying faith trusts Christ and his merits. It does not try to substitute our pitiful efforts for his holy work. Faith clings to Jesus Christ alone.

## The Reformation Solas

Students of the Reformation often summarize its teachings with three Latin phrases:

*Sola Scriptura* — "Scripture alone" is the source of true Christian doctrine and the norm by which we evaluate teachings and practices.

*Sola Gratia* — "Grace Alone." Salvation is a gift from God. We do not deserve it or merit it in any way.

*Sola Fide* — "Faith Alone" receives this gift of God. Faith is not a human work but is a gift of God. Saying that we are justified by faith alone is another affirmation that our works do not contribute to our salvation.

All of these are summaries of the greatest statement of all:

*Solus Christus* — Christ alone. His word that is the source of doctrine, his work is the essence and heart of grace, and faith clings to him alone.

### Apart from Works

"For by grace you have been saved through faith. And this is not your own doing; it is the gift of God, not a result of works, so that no one may boast" (Ephesians 2:8-9). The final component of justification is the exclusion of works. We are "justified by faith apart from works of the law" (Romans 3:28). There is nothing for us to contribute to salvation. All that we give God is our sinfulness which he imputes to Christ. All the good things are given by him to us.

You have probably noticed the redundancy in this list. Justification is by grace, which is the opposite of works. It is through faith, not works. It is through Christ and his merits, not our own. It is apart from works. Why are we (and Scripture) making this point so emphatically? It is stressed so strongly because sinful humans continually try to give themselves a role in their own salvation. But this is not accurate. We have nothing to offer to God but our sin, yet we continually try to usurp his place. St. Paul shows us the logical conclusion of making our works part of salvation: ". . .if justification were through the law, then Christ died for no purpose" (Galatians 2:21).

Do good works have a place in the Christian life? Of course. But they are not part of our justification. After stressing these truths, Ephesians shows us that works are a response of faith (Ephesians 2:10). Sanctification is part of the lives to which God has called us, but we can not improve sanctification by altering justification. Our justification is by grace through faith in Christ, apart from works.

### 4. Challenges to Justification

Justification is the central Christian doctrine. Without it there is nothing to distinguish genuine Christianity from any worldly philosophy. Consequently, there are many attacks on this teaching. Certainly there are unbelievers who will attack basic Christian teachings, including justification, but the greater threat to this teaching comes from Christians themselves. Any time we attempt to earn our salvation or suggest that our own efforts might have a role in justification, we challenge this biblical teaching. This may be done by focusing on human works, morals, or actions instead of Jesus. We do the same thing when we try to be more subtle and suggest that we cooperate with God's grace. Either way, we insert our sinful will into salvation. This detracts from our Savior and leads us away from his merit.

A further danger may be seen in efforts to justify ourselves not through works but through knowledge. This is a subtle temptation that may trouble those who see that salvation is apart from works. While we are to believe, teach, and confess the truth, it is not our knowledge that saves us. Christ Jesus saves us, not our intellectual understanding. Faith certainly may contain elements of knowledge, and the maturing Christian will continually seek to grow in knowledge, but we must not make this knowledge into a work. God doesn't love us because of our intelligence. He doesn't love us because of our works. He loves us because of Christ.

### 5. The Comfort of Justification

The doctrine of justification is the central doctrine of the Christian faith. Believing, teaching and confessing this doctrine not only gives testimony to the very essence of Christianity, it also proves to be a very comforting doctrine. If we take the witness of Scripture seriously, we know that we cannot save ourselves. When we try, we fail—and we seldom even try. But our salvation is not dependent on our own efforts. Our salvation is in God's hands. He has already done all that needs to be done, and he gives us the benefits of that work.

Because of Christ Jesus, God has declared us righteous. Even though we continue to sin, the righteousness of Christ is imputed to us. This is not a fictional construction or a pious wish; it is God's own truth. We can trust his word. Knowing this truth, we rejoice with St. Paul, "since we have been justified by faith, we have peace with God through our Lord Jesus Christ" (Romans 5:1). The wrath of God has been covered. Justice has been fulfilled. We need not be afraid of God when we are clothed in the righteousness of his Son. We live in peace.

We live in peace because we know that our salvation is certain. He has proclaimed us righteous by faith. Since we are in Christ Jesus, there is no doubt about our salvation. We need not worry if we have done enough. We haven't, but Jesus has. We are justified. Our salvation is certain.

---

### Key Terms

| | |
|---|---|
| Alien righteousness | Justification |
| Forensic justifica-tion | Limited atonement |
| Imputation | Objective justifica-tion |
| Imputed righteous-ness | Subjective justifi-cation |
| Infused righteous-ness | Universalism |

---

**For Review and Discussion**

1.  Despite the clear biblical teaching, human beings often try to insert some works into the plan of salvation. Why do you think this is such a common problem? Why is it so important that we keep our own works out of justification?

2.  The book of Romans discusses the doctrine of justification in great detail. Read through this Epistle noting how many times Paul stresses that we are justified by grace through faith in Christ alone.

3.  Many Christians describe justification as a moral transfor-mation or an infused righteousness. Can you think of any examples of times when this is done? How does this teaching overshadow the biblical truth of forensic justification?

4. How does the biblical teaching of objective justification provide an extra degree of confidence and certainty to the Christian? How does a right view of subjective justification keep this from being distorted into universalism?

## For Further Reading

Chemnitz, Martin. *Justification: The Chief Article of Christian Doctrine as Expounded in Loci Theologici*. Translated by J. A. O. Preus, edited by Delpha Holleque Preus. St. Louis: Concordia Publishing House, 1985.

Dantine, Wilhelm. *Justification of the Ungodly*. St. Louis: Concordia Publishing House, 1968.

Forde, Gerhard. *Justification by Faith: A Matter of Death and Life*. Philadelphia: Fortress Press, 1982.

Luther, Martin. *Lectures on Galatians*. Luther's Works, American Edition, vols. 26, 27. St. Louis: Concordia Publishing House, 1964, 1973.

Preus, Jacob A. O. III. *Just Words: Understanding the Fullness of the Gospel*. St. Louis: Concordia Publishing House, 2000.

Senkbeil, Harold. *Dying to Live: the Power of Forgiveness*. St. Louis: Concordia Publishing House, 1994.

*Theses on Justification*. A report of the Commission on Theology and Church Relations of the Lutheran Church – Missouri Synod. St. Louis, Missouri: The Lutheran Church – Missouri Synod, 1983.

# 10

# Conversion and Faith

You can invite Jesus Christ into your life right now by praying to God something like the following.

Dear Lord, I know that I am a sinner and that I need Your forgiveness. I believe that Christ died in my place to pay the penalty for my sin and that He rose from the dead. I now invite Jesus Christ to come into my life as my Savior. Thank you for making me Your child. Help me learn to please You in every part of my life.

My Decision: On _____ [Date] I, _____
[Your Name], received Jesus Christ as my Savior.

This quote comes directly from a tract written by the famous twentieth-century American evangelist, Billy Graham. Similar prayers and appeals to choose to believe in Jesus are common among various groups of Christians. How do you react to this familiar way of describing conversion? It presents the essential truths of the Gospel, but it frames these truths with an additional emphasis. Stress is placed on a person inviting Jesus into their life or on their own decision. How do these ideas relate to the biblical teaching of conversion? What abilities do humans have regarding their salvation? What is the role of the Holy Spirit? These vital issues confront us in this chapter as we consider:

1. The Holy Spirit—*The Third Person of the Trinity*
2. The Work of the Holy Spirit—*God's continual involvement with his people*
3. Conversion—*Our connection to Christ's work of redemption*
4. Faith—*What is it and how it works*
5. Human Choice—*A free will or a bound will?*

## 1. The Holy Spirit

The doctrine of the Holy Spirit is a vital Christian teaching that is interconnected with every other doctrine. As one person in the Trinity, the Holy Spirit is the God we rightly worship. Yet many Christians find it difficult to conceptualize the Holy Spirit. This may be due, in part, to a lack of analogies. When we describe Jesus, we rightly think of a human being. If we focus on his divine nature, we generally call him the Son. The first person of the Trinity is the Father. While we know that the Father and the Son are different than us, we do have a point of comparison. We understand what it means to be a parent or a child. We have analogies to begin to understand them. The third person of the Trinity, however, provides a different challenge. Scripture commonly refers to him as the Holy Spirit (or in earlier English, the Holy Ghost). But what is a spirit?

"Spirit" is a common word in the Bible. We should be careful to note that not every use of the word "spirit" refers to the Holy Spirit (just as not every father is God). Both the Hebrew word for spirit (*ruach*) and the Greek (*pneuma*) can refer to a variety of things. They can be translated as breath or wind. They can mean life or the soul, as distinguished from the body. Spirit can also refer to living beings that do not have a material body. Calling something "spirit" does not make a moral judgment about it, since spirits can be holy or fallen (1 John 4:1-3). The highest example of spirit is God himself, who, apart from Christ's incarnation, is spirit (John 4:24).

Along with these meanings, Spirit is also the name of the Third Person of the Trinity. He is *the* Spirit or the Holy Spirit. When we encounter this word in the Scriptures, it is important to recognize how it is being used in that particular context. For example, Psalm 51 uses "spirit" in different senses:

> Create in me a clean heart, O God, and renew a right spirit within me. [11]cast me not away from your presence, and take not your Holy Spirit from me. [12]Restore to me the joy of your salvation, and uphold me with a willing spirit. (Psalm 51:10-12)

The psalmist asks for a right (verse 10) and willing spirit (verse 12). These characteristics, which he seeks for himself, are gifts of God that can be his because he has the Holy Spirit (verse 11). God, the Holy Spirit, can give him these other blessings.

## The Person of the Holy Spirit

The context of Scripture indicates whether it is referring to God or to some other spirit. Many religions refer to spirits. It is common today to talk about "spirituality" or spiritual things. When the Bible speaks of the Holy Spirit, it is not depicting any of these things, but instead refers exclusively to God. This Spirit is not a vague or generic force, power, energy, or emotion. The Holy Spirit is not a thing or an object; he is a divine person. The Holy Spirit has an identity, he is knowable, and he reveals himself to us in Scripture.

### Names and Titles of the Holy Spirit

We have been calling the Third Person of the Trinity "the Holy Spirit." This is the most common biblical title (for example, Matthew 28:19). Scripture also names him with other titles and descriptions. He is the Spirit of God (2 Corinthians 3:3), the Spirit of the Lord (Acts 8:39), the Spirit of the Father (Matthew 10:20) and the Spirit of Christ (Galatians 4:6, Philippians 1:19). These descriptions remind us that the Holy Trinity is one God, not three gods. Other descriptions of the Holy Spirit reveal his character. He is the Spirit of truth (John 14:17), the Spirit of life (Romans 8:2), and the Spirit of wisdom and revelation (Ephesians 1:17). Jesus called the Holy Spirit the helper (also translated as counselor, comforter, or **paraclete**) (John 14:16) who will guide and bless the church.

### The Deity of the Holy Spirit

The Holy Spirit is called all of these things and can do these wondrous works because he is God. Directly and indirectly, the Bible asserts the deity of the Holy Spirit. The Spirit is identified as the Lord (2 Corinthians 3:17-18, 1 Corinthians 12:4-6), a title that properly belongs only to God. St. Peter taught that when a person lies to the Holy Spirit, he is lying to God (Acts 5:3-4). The church is called the temple of God because the Holy Spirit, who is God, lives within us (1 Corinthians 3:16).

Furthermore, the Holy Spirit is described with attributes and characteristics that belong to God alone. The Spirit is **omnipresent**; there is nowhere the psalmist can go to escape the presence of God's Spirit (Psalm 139:7-10).

Likewise the Spirit is **omniscient**, having full knowledge of all things (1 Corinthians 2:10-11). The Spirit has and uses the limitless power that belongs to God alone (Luke 1:35, Romans 15:19). As God, the Spirit is eternal, unlimited by time (Hebrews 9:14), and because he is God, he can be sinned against (Matthew 12:31).

We previously considered the deity of the Holy Spirit while considering the doctrine of the triune God (chapter 4). He is present in the manifestations of the Trinity (for example, at Jesus' baptism, Matthew 3:16-17). He is invoked in the trinitarian benedictions and formulas (see 2 Corinthians 13:14, 1 Peter 1:2, Ephesians 4:3-6, Matthew 28:19). From the beginning of Genesis (1:2) to the end of Revelation (22:17), Scripture reveals the person and work of God the Holy Spirit.

## 2. The Work of the Holy Spirit

We also see the identity of the Spirit and know him in his work. The Holy Spirit works in many ways. Our knowledge and understanding of his work does not restrict him or confine him to certain activities. The Spirit does what he pleases (John 3:8), but our knowledge of his work is limited to the things that he has revealed. He has promised us that he will act in certain ways and describes that work to us. We are quickly led away from the Holy Spirit if we do not focus on the work that he reveals. In fact, the Spirit has shown us so much of his work that we have enough to contemplate for a lifetime.

### The Revealing Spirit

A significant part of the work of the Holy Spirit is the work of revelation. Throughout this book, we have been reminded that God must reveal himself to us if we are to have accurate and helpful knowledge of him. God does not ask us to guess about his nature or his will; he chooses to reveal himself to humans. This revelation is the work of the Spirit. The Israelite prophets declared that the Spirit spoke God's word through them (see, for example, 2 Samuel 23:2). The New Testament continued in this affirmation of the Spirit's work. Before his passion, Jesus promised his disciples that they would not be left alone. After his saving work was complete, he would send them another comforter, the Holy Spirit. When he comes, that Spirit ". . .will teach you all things and bring to your remembrance all that I have said to you" (John 14:26).

Jesus said that the Spirit gives him glory by revealing God's truth to us (John 16:14-15). The disciples would face opposition from other people and would be given the opportunity to testify before many people. They did not need to worry about what they would say, because the Holy Spirit would speak through them and give them the words to say (Matthew 10: 19-20). The revelatory work of the Spirit is manifest in the Scriptures that he inspired (2 Peter 1:21). On account of this truth, the Christian church confesses in the Nicene Creed that the Spirit "spoke by the prophets." This revelation is vital, for no mere human being has seen all of the things addressed in the Scriptures. St. Paul summarizes this truth,

> . . .as it is written, "no eye has seen, nor ear heard, nor the heart of man imagined, what God has prepared for those who love him"— [10]these things God has revealed to us through the Spirit. For the Spirit searches everything, even the depths of God. [11]For who knows a person's thoughts except the spirit of that person, which is in him? So also no one comprehends the thoughts of God except the Spirit of God. [12]Now we have received not the spirit of the world, but the Spirit who is from God, that we might understand the things freely given us by God. [13]And we impart this in words not taught by human wisdom but taught by the Spirit, interpreting spiritual truths to those who are spiritual. (1 Corinthians 2:9-13)

The Spirit reveals God and his will to us in the Scriptures. He gives us that word, "the sword of the Spirit" (Ephesians 6:17) and conveys his grace to us through that word.

*The Life-Giving Spirit*

As important as the work of revelation is, it is only a portion of the Spirit's work. In the Nicene Creed, Christians confess that the Spirit is "the Lord and giver of life." The Holy Spirit gives life in two ways: spiritually and physically. While many people think that physical life is the most important thing, the gift of new spiritual life is even greater. This new life of faith is the principle work of the Holy Spirit. Salvation is a free gift of God through the work of Jesus Christ. We receive that gift through faith, but the Scriptures show that faith is not our work, it is a gift of God. "No one can say 'Jesus is Lord,' except in the Holy Spirit" (1 Corinthians 12:3). The Spirit awakens faith in us through the means of grace. The Spirit reveals Christ to us. We are given "the washing of regeneration and renewal of the Holy Spirit" (Titus 3: 5). We are Christians because the Holy Spirit has worked faith in us.

The Holy Spirit's life-giving work continues in the life of the Christian in his work of **sanctification**. He equips us and guides us as we live as God's children in this world (Galatians 5:25, Ephesians 5:8-9, Galatians 5: 16). Even sanctification is the work of the Spirit as he works in and through us to accomplish his purposes. Knowing that we are weak, God freely gives us his Spirit to strengthen us in our weakness, bless us, and intercede for us (Romans 8:26-27).

### Creation

The Holy Spirit works faith in our hearts and gives us life and salvation as he connects us with the benefits of Christ's saving work. For this reason, we call him the giver of life, but he also is the giver of physical life. The Holy Spirit participates in all the works of the Trinity, including the work of creation. As God created the heavens and the earth, Genesis says, "the Spirit of God was hovering over the face of the waters" (Genesis 1:2). After forming man from the dust of the earth, God "breathed into his nostrils the breath of life, and the man became a living creature" (Genesis 2:7). Job reflects on God's creation, saying, "the Spirit of God has made me, and the breath of the Almighty gives me life" (Job 33:4). Clearly the Holy Spirit was directly involved in the work of creation. We would also do well to note his role in providing the human nature of Christ. Our Savior was born of a virgin, who miraculously conceived by the power of the Holy Spirit (Luke 1:35).

### *The Gifts and Fruits of the Holy Spirit*

The Spirit continues in active relationship to human beings and to the Christian church today. He continues to give physical and spiritual life. He reveals divine truth and offers his comfort and guidance. He equips Christians with his gifts and gathers us together in the church. He blesses us as individuals so that we may be a blessing to his church and to the world. These blessings are often divided into two categories: gifts of the Spirit and fruits of the Spirit.

**Spiritual gifts** include special abilities, roles, offices, functions, or a number of other things that God has promised to give. Whatever the gift is, it is a gift from God for use in his church. Spiritual gifts call Christians to serve one another and to confess Christ before the world. Some of the gifts described in the Bible are obviously supernatural (for example, performing miracles). Others seem more "ordinary," like helping, teaching, or administration. The important thing is that spiritual gifts are given by the Holy Spirit for use in his church. Peter reminds us, "as each has received a gift, use it to serve one another, as good stewards of God's varied grace" (1 Peter 4:10). Furthermore, the Spirit gives different gifts to different Christians, placing us in his church in such a way that we need one another and are able to serve each other and the world (1 Corinthians 12:12-31).

A second type of blessing from the Holy Spirit is generally known as the **"fruits of the Spirit."** Paul describes these fruits:

> But the fruit of the Spirit is love, joy, peace, patience, kindness, goodness, faithfulness, [23]gentleness, self-control; against such things there is no law. [24]And those who belong to Christ Jesus have crucified the flesh with its passions and desires. [25]If we live by the Spirit, let us also walk by the Spirit (Galatians 5:22-25).

Unlike spiritual gifts which are given to different Christians, the fruits of the Spirit are available to all believers. Paul shows these fruits in contrast to the "works of the flesh" (Galatians 5:19-21). Here he describes the life of the justified child of God. When our sins have been forgiven, the work of God in our lives is evident. The Spirit equips us with these virtues as a fruit of faith. As sinners, we may not always manifest these characteristics but the Spirit will graciously guide us in these things. By properly recognizing these fruits as the work of the Holy Spirit we can thankfully receive these blessings he desires us to have.

### 3. Conversion

Before these gifts and fruits can be ours, however, we need to belong to God. By his life, suffering, death, and resurrection, Jesus has graciously redeemed the world. All humanity has been objectively justified by Jesus. But, as we have already seen, an individual person may reject Christ and his work. Lacking faith in Christ, the individual will not receive the benefits that Christ has already won for all. As sinful human beings, we need some kind of a connection with Christ's great act of salvation. Unless that event is connected with our personal lives, it does not benefit us (1 Corinthians 15:14).

Because of Christ's saving work, God's attitude toward us is changed. In conversion and faith, our attitudes about God change. One of the works of the Holy Spirit is the creation of a new attitude in us, who believe. This attitude change is called conversion. The New Testament Greek word for **conversion** is *metanoia.* It literally means to "change one's mind" or heart. Such a change of heart or mind occurs when the gift of faith is given to an individual (Psalm 51:10).

This gift of faith is something that only God can provide (Galatians 5: 5). He alone can do this because of the sinful nature that clings to our humanity. After the fall, Adam and Eve were still rational human beings, yet their descendents were unable to grasp the spiritual reality of God's truths (1 Corinthians 1:23). So St. Paul reminds us that "The natural person does not accept the things of the Spirit of God, for they are folly to him, and he is not able to understand them because they are spiritually discerned" (1 Corinthians 2:14). Since the fall, our human minds are inclined away from God and his will. The reality of our human condition is that we continue to rebel and go our own ways in opposition to God. (Genesis 8:21; Romans 8:5). We are unable to save ourselves, unable to convert ourselves, and because of our sin, uninterested in the things of God.

*Our "B.C." condition*

St. Paul profoundly shows this human condition in Romans 5: 6, 8, 10:

> For while we were still weak, at the right time Christ died for the ungodly. . . . God shows his love for us in that while we were still sinners, Christ died for us. . . While we were enemies we were reconciled to God by the death of his Son. . . .

Notice the four characteristics of our "B.C." (before Christ and before conversion) human condition: we are ungodly, weak, sinners, and enemies. In his letter to the Ephesians, Paul describes this condition as being "dead" (Ephesians 2:1-2). Our human condition is a state of unbelief or "un-faith." If we are to live, God and God alone must move into our hearts and change our attitudes toward him (John 6:44). Once he creates that faith in us, we are converted.

| Our B.C. Condition | | A Believing Christian |
|---|---|---|
| Un-faith | by God's grace | Faith |
| Ungodly | | Godly |
| Weak | | Empowered |
| Enemy of God | →→→ | God's Child |
| Sinner | | Saint |
| Dead | | Alive |

## 4. Faith

Faith is the connecting link between what Jesus has done for the entire world and a person's individual salvation. Faith in Christ is the bridge that overcomes the separation between sinful humanity and a holy God. Faith is the gift that the Holy Spirit provides which enables an individual to appropriate the saving grace that God offers in Christ.

*What Faith Isn't*

Sometimes it is easier to talk about something by stating what it is not. This is particularly true of faith. Faith is not a general belief in the existence of God. Non-Christians may have such knowledge, but that is not saving faith, as Paul says:

> For what can be known about God is plain to them [the people of the world], because God has shown it to them. [20]For his invisible attributes, namely, his eternal power and divine nature, have been clearly perceived, ever since the creation of the world, in the things that have been made. So they are without excuse (Romans 1:19-20).

Likewise, faith is not mere knowledge about Jesus and the historical facts of the Gospel. James 2:19 speaks of that kind of "faith," which the demons have, but which causes them to tremble in fear. Demons could identify Jesus as God's Son, yet they were not saved by that knowledge (Luke 4:34). Just knowing the facts about Jesus isn't saving faith.

Neither is faith something that we can do or a decision that we can make (John 1:13). In spite of what many Protestants teach about "deciding to follow Jesus," we do not have the ability, power, or desire to make this choice. Because of sin, our natural human inclination is hostile to God and we would never choose to be in his presence (Romans 5: 6, 8, 10).

*What Faith Is*

**Faith** is not a human work, but a gift that is experienced and expressed as trust and reliance (Psalm 3:5). We trust God's words of promise and rely upon Christ's work of salvation in our place (Romans 4:13, 16). The gift of faith enables us to say "yes" to God's offer of forgiveness, life, and salvation and to thank him for that gift. While faith is not equivalent with knowledge, faith does involve knowledge of God's saving act in Christ (Romans 10:13-14). Because no one can believe in someone they do not know, the relationship of faith always includes some kind of knowledge about the person we believe in. It also includes some kind of assent to that knowledge as being something reliable, true, and certain (John 6:69). Finally, there is a sense of trust and assurance that results in an absolute reliance on God's revealed grace in Christ (2 Corinthians 1:20-21).

Perhaps the analogy of a relationship with a girl or boyfriend might be helpful. You first need to be acquainted with the person you intend to date. It may take some phone calls or brief encounters. Even a "blind date" relies on some kind of basic information about the person. Once you have met the person, you may want to get to know him or her better. You agree to the invitation to go on a date with that person. The relationship begins to grow. As trust develops, you may consider the person reliable and agree to continue dating. Finally, over time, you may find that you want to spend your life with that person—you are ready to commit yourself to the person and trust him or her for the rest of your life. So it is in a relationship with Jesus. We cannot believe in him unless we first know him (Romans 10:14). A relationship develops which includes intellectual knowledge and recognition of certain facts (Hebrews 11:1), but most importantly these facts are personally meaningful and trustworthy; there is a confidence of the heart (John 17:3). This is faith, the full commitment of body, mind, and spirit (see Matthew 15:21-28; Luke 7:1-10; John 4:47-53).

This example of an adult relationship helps us consider various aspects of faith. It is important to remember, however, that persons of all ages are involved in relationships. Even infants can be in loving, trusting relationships with parents and other individuals. These relationships grow and may deepen over time, but they remain relationships of love. The relationship of faith is not a matter of age or of intellectual ability. It is a gift that is given and sustained by God himself and so is available to all human beings.

Faith, then, is a matter of God's working in us to establish and maintain a relationship with him. We trust the Father's word because of what he has done for us in the world, and especially in Christ. He has established a growing relationship between Jesus and us through the working of the Holy Spirit. As we get to know his Son by the power of his Spirit, we find that we learn to know the Father better, too. Thus, a Spirit-created faith changes, grows, and matures for each individual believer (Ephesians 4:15-16).

Another way of speaking about faith would be to say that faith is the tool, instrument, or power that enables the believing heart to take hold of the forgiveness of sins that Christ won for all people. A person with a prosthetic arm and hand initially needs help to put on that arm. Faith is like a prosthetic arm that God gives to us which then enables us to cling to Jesus. Without that arm, we are powerless, but with that arm of faith we are restored to a full relationship with our creator and redeemer. Notice that faith does not achieve forgiveness, earn it, make us worthy of it, or even move God to give it. Rather faith merely receives what God has worked for us, it is the instrument for grasping hold of God's promises.

*The Object of Our Faith*

The object of our faith is a key in this whole issue of faith. Faith is always *in* something, or better yet, *in someone*. We can't cling to an empty phantom or to a dream. Nor can we really trust in material things which will erode over time (Matthew 6:19). Such false objects of faith will inevitably prove untrustworthy. Faith holds on to Jesus, the founder and perfecter of our faith (Hebrews 12:2). He is the substance of all Scripture (John 5:39; Luke 24:27). Faith clings to God's promises which are based on the certainty of the effectiveness of Christ's death and resurrection (Romans 4: 24-25). God's word of promise and our human faith are directly connected (John 3:36). A promise without someone believing it is ineffective; believing in something without substance is dangerous superstition or misleading imagination (Hebrews 11:1-3).

We sometimes differentiate between faith and believing. In Greek this is the same concept, but in English they seem to be different things. Perhaps it would be helpful to say that faith is the gift and believing is the act. With such a distinction, it would be correct to say that faith is our "believe-ability." Thus, faith is an act, but it is a work that God has done in us and not something that we do ourselves. Another comparison would be to eating: we eat, but our act of eating does not give us strength, rather it is the food we eat that nourishes us.

*Faith is not Fideism*

"I have faith. That's why I'm saved." Such a remark is heard occasionally when someone is asked whether they are confident that they are going to heaven. While they likely mean the right thing, there is something wrong with that statement. As this phrasing puts it, the object of their reliance is not Christ, but something they have identified as "faith." This is sometimes called **fideism**, or "faith-ism." It's the reliance upon an empty faith or faith in "faith," rather than faith in Jesus as one's Lord and Savior.

Faith must never be looked at as something we do to earn God's favor. A person is not saved "on account of faith" but always "through faith" (Ephesians 2:8-9). Faith is the instrument that takes hold of the forgiveness God offers in the life, death, and resurrection of his Son for the sins of all people. It saves because it is in Jesus (the object to which it is related), not because of any act on its own part.

*Conversion in the Bible*

But let's get back to our main topic, conversion. We first come to faith in conversion, and conversion means change. Some Christians describe conversion as a change of lifestyle. When confronted by their sins some people may stop swearing or excessive drinking, recognizing that such behavior is harmful or offensive; but that does not mean they are converted. To amend one's life is not the biblical understanding of conversion any more than to change the oil in one's car makes it a new vehicle. They may only be complying with what someone else has asked them to do while their heart is unchanged (Matthew 15:8).

"I'm sorry" is a natural response when confronted by one's sins. Some people are very remorseful when they are caught in a crime or a sin. Think about how you respond to the flashing lights of a police car—many people immediately slow down and look at their speedometer. If they are stopped, they may even say to the officer, "I'm sorry." But that sorrow is usually not a sorrow over sin, rather it is the sorrow at being caught. People's behavior may even change for a while—they may drive more cautiously or obediently—but their heart or attitude has not changed. Actually, making that heart-felt inner spiritual change would be impossible for a person to do on his or her own, since we are naturally sinful.

Many evangelical Protestant Christians define their conversion as "accepting Jesus" or "inviting Jesus into my heart." Interestingly, in John's gospel, this idea is dismissed rather clearly as John says that we are **born again**, "not by human decision" (John 1:13 NIV) or "the will of the flesh" (ESV). Later in the Gospel, Jesus says, "You did not choose me, but I chose you" (John 15:16). From a human point of view, we may see a point at which we seem to make a decision, but this is really a response to a conversion that has already occurred. Moreover, this conversion is always the work of the Holy Spirit. Once a person is converted, they may recognize their need for expressing that change with their lips (Romans 10:10). This is a response of faith, a response to the conversion that God has already worked in their hearts. This is why Paul stresses that "no one can say 'Jesus is Lord' except in the Holy Spirit" (1 Corinthians 12:3). Any apparent "decision," confession, or testimony is a response to the faith that God the Holy Spirit has already created.

### The Means of Grace in Conversion

How does God do this? God always uses "means" or channels to communicate with us. God says that he will give the gift of faith, and he does this through his word. Paul clearly says this in Romans 10:17, "Faith comes from hearing, and hearing through the word of Christ." When we hear the word of God, two specific messages are given—the Law and the Gospel. The Law convicts us of our sins, points to our need for a Savior, and creates in us a sense of sorrow over our sins. The technical term for this sorrow is **contrition**. Contrition is not being sorry one is caught or just knowing that one should feel sorry, it is true sorrow for offending God with our sins (2 Corinthians 7:10). The Gospel then tells us what God has done—how he has sent his Son as our Savior and how his Spirit has drawn us to himself—so that we have the divine promise of salvation for Christ's sake. As a result of the working of God's Law and Gospel, repentance occurs, faith accepts the forgiveness of sins (Luke 13:5) and a new changed life begins. Various other biblical images also refer to this change or conveyance of faith.

We may speak of **regeneration** (Titus 3:5) or being "born again" (1 Peter 1:23). In John's Gospel (John 3:5-7), Jesus uses this image to convey baptismal rebirth "by water and the Spirit." This new spiritual life is implanted by the power of the Spirit and is also called the "second birth" or being "reborn." John records Jesus' clever play on words in this passage. Jesus' comment to Nicodemus conveyed the idea of being born "from above," not "again." Later in this same chapter of John, we see the same Greek word (*anothen*) translated as "from above" (John 3:31). Conversion is the giving of life and the establishing of a spiritual relationship (John 3:6-8), which brings eternal life. Nicodemus misunderstood it at first, so Jesus had to explain that this regeneration is "by water and the Spirit" (John 3:5).

Another biblical image for conversion is being "awakened" from death. We enjoy sleeping, but being dead is beyond our experience. We saw how Paul described our human condition of being "dead in trespasses and sins" (Ephesians 2:1), yet "even when we were dead in our trespasses, [God] made us alive together with Christ" (Ephesians 2:5). This making alive is the result of God's action alone—no dead person can revive or resuscitate herself (Revelation 20:5). We, who were spiritually dead, are made alive with Christ through baptism (Colossians 2:11-13).

Perhaps you have experienced situations where you found it difficult or impossible to see. Scripture uses blindness and sight as a metaphor for conversion. We are living in a world of darkness (John 12:46), blinded by sin, and the Light comes to give us vision (2 Corinthians 4:6). Actually, Paul says that we "*were* once darkness, but now you *are* light in the Lord" (Ephesians 5:8). We were not merely "in darkness," but that we had taken on the characteristics of darkness. Only God's light—the Light of the World (John 8:12)—changed our condition (1 Peter 2:9 and John 12:36). This perspective on conversion is sometimes called illumination or being enlightened (Ephesians 1:18).

Losing a friend can be a devastating experience. However, regaining a friend or making new friends is often exhilarating. The Bible, as we saw above, speaks of our human condition as being "enemies of God" (Romans 5:10). That condition is changed, however, by Christ. Jesus became the reconciler between us and God, creating in us a new relationship with the

Father. Thus conversion is God's **reconciliation** with us (2 Corinthians 5:18-19). Christ has called us God's friends (John 15:14-15) and so we are.

A final biblical image for conversion is that of an invitation. Paul reminded the Corinthian Christians that "God is faithful, by whom you were called into the fellowship of his Son, Jesus Christ our Lord" (1 Corinthians 1:9; compare this with Romans 1:6). The very act of being called is God's action and is not something we can do ourselves. This calling is an invitation to follow Jesus through and in our callings or vocations. This invitation or calling is done through the Gospel (2 Thessalonians 2:14) as we hear the good news of God's love and forgiveness.

---

*A closer look at God's invitation*

Let's stop a moment and look a little closer at this concept of invitation and see how it works. When we think of the Gospel as an invitation to get to know Jesus we can think of five distinct elements.

First, there is the Inviter, God himself, who is the authorizing agent or the "host." For example, a host may personally invite us to a party. Or the host may use a mediating agent such as another person, an email message, a phone call, or a printed invitation.

Second, there is the invited guest. It could be an individual person or many people may be invited at the same time.

Third, there is the medium of communication, something that is common to both the inviter and invitee, whether gestures or words (spoken or written).

Fourth, there is the end or goal of the invitation. What are you being invited to? It could be a party or a lecture or eternal life.

Finally, the invitation is based upon an assumption that there is a separation between the inviter and the invitee which is bridged by the invitation. For example, if I invite you to my home, you are an outsider until you receive my invitation. You cannot come into my home unless you are invited (if you enter uninvited, you are a trespasser

*An Instantaneous Event*

The change we call "conversion" is not a slow process in the sense that we gradually become converted or facilitate our conversion in any way. Rather conversion is instantaneous. As an analogy, just as a woman is or is not pregnant, so a person is or is not converted. When a human egg is fertilized, a pregnancy begins. A mother-to-be is not "a little pregnant." Her pregnancy may be more visible to the rest of the world as time passes, but she is no more pregnant. Either she is or she is not expecting a child. When God's Spirit plants the seed of faith in a person, Christian life begins—we are no longer ungodly, powerless, blind, sinners, and enemies of God, but we are God's empowered saints who live in his full and free forgiveness as

and may be subject to legal action). Similarly, you cannot properly be invited to sit in your own seat in your room, since it is already yours.

The crux of the invitation is that in one sense it informs the invitee of being in a "separated state." You didn't belong until you were invited and even the invitation makes you aware of that separation. The invitation serves as a bridge to overcome the separation.

Your response to the invitation is critical. You may have no reason to doubt the legitimacy of the invitation and so accept the invitation. The efficacy of the invitation is sufficient for you acting on it. Once you are clear that the invitation is real and addresses you, your actions follow naturally. Your "decision" to at-tend the affair is the result of the inviter and is not a result of your own initiative.

On the other hand, you may doubt the legitimacy of the invitation as a skeptic. It may be that other people with authority or credibility need to prove to you the legitimacy of the invitation. They need to show you that the invitation is sincere and it is meant for you. The invitation is able to bridge the gap and render the inaccessible (my home) accessible to you. So it is with God's word of invitation.

This understanding of conversion as an invitation is centered is the Inviter's invitation and not on the recipient. Whether the recipient responds or not, the invitation is real and is worthwhile. So also is God's Gospel invitation for the whole world.

his friends who have seen the light. There is no partial conversion or half-conversion. Either you are or you are not!

But all this may sound mechanical and one-sided. Isn't there something that humans have to do? This may seem logical, but Scripture teaches that God alone is the cause of our conversion. This is sometimes called "divine **monergism**," meaning that God alone is the one who works conversion. The sinner is absolutely passive, as St. Paul notes: "So then it depends not on human will or exertion, but on God, who has mercy" (Romans 9:16). This perspective is confirmed by scriptural example: Jesus says that believing is God's work (John 6:29). Such believing is the result of God's drawing us to come to Christ (John 6:44). God is the one who rescues us (Colossians 1: 12-13). Christians are born again by the will of God, not by human desires (John 1:12-13).

Perhaps a comparison might help illustrate the passiveness of faith. The Bible tells us that "faith comes from hearing" (Romans 10:17). Hearing is a passive activity—that is why alarm clocks are supposed to be effective. We can, however, actively ignore or reject the sounds—perhaps by putting a pillow over our heads. Faith is like our ears; we passively receive the blessed relationship that the Holy Spirit establishes between Jesus and us. Yet, people can reject that relationship and go their own way. As we will note below, the grace of conversion is resistible.

Some Christians teach that humans have the ability to do something in conversion. They maintain that, at a minimum, individuals need to cooperate with God or assent. Yet we have seen that Scripture says humans have no power to believe or even know the Gospel (Romans 8 and 1 Corinthians 2: 14). We cannot and would not cooperate, because our hearts are not changed. Once God changes us, we are already converted. Any activity which seems to be cooperation or a participatory action by humans is actually a consequence of conversion and thus is more accurately understood and explained as part of our sanctification.

### 5. Human Choice

Sometimes people object that this biblical teaching cannot be sustained. They argue that humans have free will and can choose to be converted or not. We have already seen that our "B.C. condition" places us in opposition to God and his will. But do human beings have free will? No Christian theologian would deny that human beings have some freedom. To be human means that we have some choices. This ability to choose is sometimes called **formal freedom**. We can decide on what clothes to wear, what university to attend, whether we will go to all our classes or not, whether and who to marry, etc. Outwardly and formally there is a genuine freedom of choice in many (but not all) circumstances.

The human will, however, does not act of its own accord but is always moved or influenced by something outside itself—events, circumstances, or ideas. Humans therefore do not have **material freedom**, real or complete freedom that allows them all options and choices. This is particularly true when it comes to spiritual things. What actually occurs in our human experience of spiritual things is not a free will to do whatever we desire, but rather what Martin Luther described as "the **bondage of the will**." The choices we make are bound and affected by sin, the world, and Satan (Romans 8:5, 7; Ephesians 2:2-3; 4:22); as a result, they are always choices against God, opposed to his will, and destructive of a relationship with him. There are only two efficient causes for our conversion—God the Holy Spirit and his life-imparting word. We cannot convert ourselves.

*Resistibility of Grace*

One of the mysteries of the Christian faith is that the grace of God is resistible. While we have asserted and affirmed that God does the converting, a person can resist the grace of God as he comes to them through the various means of grace (Matthew 23:37). This should never be interpreted to imply that those who are converted resisted less than the unconverted. On the other hand, some people do believe for a while and then lose their faith. Jesus' parable of the soil depicts such a concept (Matthew 13:3-9). Paul mentions this, too, in 1 Timothy 1:19: "By rejecting this, some have made shipwreck of their faith." Particularly when persons continue to commit mortal sins (sins that separate them from God), they may lose their faith (Galatians 5:4). We cannot understand why this is the case, except that this is what God has revealed through his word.

The individual person is converted and thus believes, yet it is the Spirit who makes the unwilling person willing and so believe. Paul says this clearly in Philippians 2:13 when he notes that it is God who is at work both to will and to do his good pleasure. Similarly, Jesus says (John 6:44) that "No one can come to me unless the Father who sent me draws him."

*False Teachings Associated with Free Will and Conversion*

*Pelagianism*

Around the turn of the fifth century, a monk from Britain came to Rome with a teaching that caught the attention of many. His name was Pelagius, and his message was simple. There is a spark of goodness in everyone which needed to be fully recognized and realized in the Christian life. That spark of goodness, which God would see and bless, was sufficient for one's salvation. Conversion was the result of this innate goodness (or at least moral indifference) which only needed to be tapped. This distorted teaching is now known as **Pelagianism**.

Augustine, recently converted to Christianity, soon recognized a flaw in that message of Pelagius. Augustine emphasized the truth that God's grace alone saved and that if one looked within, there was certainly only corruption and sin. In addition, if people looked at themselves, they took their eyes off Jesus. Pelagius wasn't presenting the biblical view. As a result, the church, meeting in several councils at Carthage (411 and 416), condemned the unbiblical position of Pelagius and affirmed Augustine's view (which was particularly based on Paul's writings) of salvation by grace alone.

### Semipelagianism

However, some successors of Augustine were not as supportive or certain of Augustine's biblical position and saw some merit in the teachings of Pelagius, particularly as they reflected on the need for sacramental activity in the life of the church. This teaching became known as **Semipelagianism**, since its adherents held a position similar to Pelagius. They believed that the Christian could start his own conversion, but then needed the aid of the seven sacraments to continue to do the good works that saved. So the individual believer is said to have the ability to begin his own conversion while needing God's assistance to complete it. While more nuanced than pure Pelagianism, this teaching again gives human beings more abilities than Scripture does. Semipelagianism was officially condemned in A.D. 529, though its influence is still felt today.

### Arminianism

Although the positions of the Pelagians and Semipelagians were condemned long before and again during the time of the Reformation, the human desire to "do something" persisted. A Protestant pastor named Jakob Arminius (1560-1609) proposed that humans had to do something for their salvation—at a minimum, they had to "decide" or "accept" Jesus into their hearts. Neglecting the concept of original sin, Arminius' argument went something like this: free will is only partially impaired by sin; it needs only divine assistance to complete the process of conversion. Therefore, humans could cooperate with God in bringing about their conversions. Although never becoming a specific denomination, **Arminianism** influenced several Protestant groups since then, including Wesleyan Methodists, some Dutch

Reformed groups, many evangelical Christians, and revivalistic strains of Christianity. Noteworthy is Billy Graham and his crusade-messages which enjoined people to make a decision for Jesus. Because of its emphasis on the alleged human ability to choose or reject God, Arminianism is sometimes called "decision theology." It is a popular position, but lacks biblical support.

## Synergism

Although the position of Pelagius was condemned, and the Semipelagian position questioned, other theologians offered the view that there still needed to be some cooperation with God in one's conversion. This became known as **synergism**, from the Greek word for "working together" with someone. This view is similar to the Semipelagian and Arminian view, but gives more weight to God's actions as initiating conversion and then placing more responsibility on the individual to follow through with appropriate responses. (It is important to remember that these teachings are related to conversion. After conversion, in the realm of sanctification, there are proper ways to speak of Christians working with God. This is a different concept than conversion.) Synergism in the area of conversion emphasizes the cooperative responsibility of the individual in responding to God's invitation. Unfortunately, such a subtle emphasis still takes a person's eyes off Jesus.

## Can We Accept Jesus?

If we look at the spiritual pre-conversion (the B.C.) condition of humanity, we see why self-generated conversion is impossible. Look again at Ephesians 2:1-2. "You were dead in your trespasses and sins. . . ." Can a dead person open a door? Can a spiritually dead person open up their heart? Conversion has already occurred for the person who says, "I accepted Jesus," or "I decided to let Jesus into my life." Before they did anything, God in his grace and mercy changed them—that was their conversion (instant, miraculous, and gracious). The story of Lazarus' resurrection (John 11:43-44) is a graphic illustration of the sequence of events. Lazarus didn't raise himself, Jesus had to speak the word first: "Lazarus come forth." Only then, in response to that word of command, was Lazarus revived and able to obey the command to come out. So also a person is converted as a result of the Spirit's reviving work through the means of grace.

## Some False Assumptions Answered

Most of these erroneous views are based upon some false assumptions, as alluded to in the previous paragraphs. For the sake of clarity, let's look at the assumptions more specifically. First, some people say that the biblical call to "repent" (Mark 1:15; Acts 2:38) implies that we have the power to repent. If people can hinder their conversion (Matthew 23:37 and Luke 7:30), then, these theologians argue, cooperation must be possible. If one can resist, then one must also be able to stop resisting and, thereby, do a good work to save oneself. But the Bible is clear that no one can turn to God on their own power (Romans 8:7); this is God's work alone (Jeremiah 31:18).

Others think that to say that a person is entirely passive makes conversion mechanical. If a person cannot do anything, then a person will become careless or fatalistic. Quite the contrary is true. Giving credit to human abilities clearly takes some credit away from God. That is why Paul's words in Ephesians 2:8-9 are so important: "For by grace you have been saved through faith. And this is not your own doing; it is the gift of God, not a result of works, so that no one may boast."

Still others argue that God makes conversion "possible," but the individual makes it "real." This distinction is certainly unbiblical and is unfounded. Such a questionable semantic assumption appeals only to someone who does not fully recognize the joy of God's love in Christ (Galatians 3:1-3). In the end, it takes away God's grace.

In contrast to all these other explanations, the biblical view of conversion is that God alone is the cause of conversion and sinners are completely passive (John 6:29 shows conversion is God's work; John 6:44 illustrates how the Father draws people to Jesus; Colossians 1:12-13 uses the imagery of God rescuing us; Ephesians 2:8-9 certainly shows that our salvation is not something humans can do; finally, John 1:12-13 asserts that Christians are born again only by the will of God.) Therefore, conversion is entirely an act of God's grace. In this monergism, the convert doesn't cooperate, since he has no power to know or believe the Gospel (1 Corinthians 2:14 and Romans 8:7).

### 6. How Justifying Faith Works

An illustration might help explain the relationship between faith, the believer, and the object of faith—Jesus Christ and the good news of God's love through him. Let's begin with the premise and promise that the next few paragraphs will help you understand what faith is. You may believe this claim immediately. That is fine. On the other hand, you may doubt it. There are at least three possible reasons you might doubt this promise. First, you may be unsure of my competence to accomplish what I promised you. After all, you may not have had me as a instructor and you are only reading this chapter that I have written. Or, you may question whether I really meant what I said. This may only be a rhetorical exercise that I've created and I'm not really sincere about my intentions. Therefore, your doubt may be founded on a question of my sincerity. A third reason that you may question this exercise is that you don't see the value in even trying to understand what faith is.

If you doubt, I need to work to help you. Perhaps I need to help you recognize my competence. It might be in showing you my academic training (although that may be a rather dry and boring approach). You might be more impressed with the successes I have had as a teacher over the past years.

On the other hand, you may question the sincerity of my claim. In this case, I would need to show the validity in my sincerity. My students know that I joke with them, yet when it comes to teaching theological truths, I am sincere. If you question my sincerity, interviewing former students or faculty members who know me would be helpful in confirming the sincerity of my claim. At that point, however, it isn't your soliciting of information that would confirm my claim since my claim stands on its own. The information would only support my original statement and promise.

Finally, you may question the benefits of this exercise. Why bother trying to understand this doctrine? With such an attitude I would have to show you any advantage in following this process. Every task has its benefits and this exercise does, too. You will be able to see how faith works as well as understand the grace of God better. You may be able to articulate the faith more convincingly to others, also.

In all of this, notice that the burden lies in the "message" (in the case of justification, the Gospel), not on the recipient. Whatever is done by you, the burden of proof and the strength of the promise is always on the side of the speaker and the message, not on the skeptic. If you do believe, you have not done anything except to "receive the promise" given. The passiveness of conversion and God's gracious and one-sided activity remains.

Finally, you, the recipient may still reject my offer. That is the difficult dimension of God's Gospel promises. He does not force us to take it. But the offer is always good, as my (and his) promise always stands.

## How Does God Work This Conversion?

God chooses to use means or vehicles to express his loving relationship with us. Rather than allowing human beings to wonder whether or not they are converted or have done the right thing, God accommodates himself to our human condition and uses tangible means to work our conversion. The faith that is worked in the hearts of believers is the result of the Holy Spirit's activity. Scripture tells us that the Holy Spirit uses the word, specifically "the word of Christ" (Romans 10:17) to create faith. James confirms this when he says that we are begotten by the word of truth (James 1:18). Paul in several of his letters adds his support to this understanding that God uses the word to create faith. 1 Thessalonians 2:13 affirms that it is the word that works in those who believe. In Romans 1:16, Paul even calls the Gospel the power of God, referring to its power to create and sustain faith.

The Law prepares the sinner for conversion. When the Law is preached and heard, the Holy Spirit convicts people of their sinful condition and of the fact that they are under God's wrath (Psalm 51:17; Acts 2:37-41). Through the Law comes the knowledge of one's sin (Romans 3:19-20). The result of this preaching of the Law is what is sometimes called the "terrors of conscience" as exemplified by the jailor at Philippi (Acts 16:29-30). When individuals know their sin and feel the burden of a guilty conscience, they are ready for the sweet message of the Gospel.

The Gospel converts the sinner. When the sinner hears the promise of forgiveness that comes from Christ, faith is created (Romans 10:17). This is a miraculous and mysterious work which cannot be sufficiently explained, although Scripture does tell us that this is how God works (Romans 1:16; 1 Thessalonians 2:13; 2 Thessalonians 2:13-14). As the good news about God's forgiving love in Christ is heard, the promises of God no longer seem foolish, but become his wisdom (1 Corinthians 1:23-24). The voice of the Good Shepherd is recognized as a good voice and no longer that of a righteous Judge (John 10:14-16; 1 Peter 2:25).

In addition to the spoken, written, and proclaimed word, the sacraments are also used by the Holy Spirit as a means of grace. Matthew 26:26-28 supports this idea. Titus 3:5 shows how the Spirit creates faith through baptism. Paul shows that the Lord's Supper also is a vehicle for sustaining faith (1 Corinthians 11:26).

Finally, how this actually "works" is a mystery. Just as psychologists cannot actually tell us how thoughts create emotions, so theologians cannot explain how the Spirit of God changes knowledge about God into faith. Jesus' comparison to the growth of a seed (Mark 4:27) illustrates that we don't have to understand how something works in order to appreciate it.

### 7. Preservation in Faith

Having worked to give us faith, the Holy Spirit also works to keep us in the faith. While we do not cooperate in our conversion, once we are Christians, we do work with the Spirit in maintaining our faith. We keep in touch with God through Bible reading, worship, and participation in the Lord's Supper. These are the vehicles the Spirit promises to use to strengthen us so that we can continue to grow in our faith. In the face of trials and difficulties, it is important that Christians remember that the Spirit not only calls us to faith; he continually works to keep us in that Christian faith. God does not leave us to our own resources alone, he constantly strengthens and defends us. This work of the Holy Spirit to keep Christians in the faith is known as **preservation**. The gift of faith comes from him and it is preserved by him.

One of the realities of faith is that we will experience fluctuations in the strength of our faith. This is not due to the Spirit's perfect gift, but to the influence of our own sinful nature. Sometimes our faith is strong (Matthew 15:28), sometimes it is weaker (Matthew 14:31). The same thing can be said about any relationship. The more we stay in touch with the one we love, the stronger that relationship will be. If we lose contact with a person, our relationship may grow stale, yet it remains. It is the same way with our relationship with God. Faith may fluctuate in its strength; the stronger our faith the more able we are to resist temptations and enjoy the fruit of faith in our lives. We may grow weaker through spiritual starvation, avoiding Bible reading and the means of grace. But, even when we are strong, we need to be vigilant so that we do not fall from faith (1 Corinthians 10:12).

*The Gift of Faith*

Our gracious God has done everything necessary. He has created us. He has redeemed us in Jesus Christ. He calls us to faith through the means of grace. The Holy Spirit works in us to create faith and then continues to work to preserve us in the faith until life's end. God continually fills us with grace, forgiving our sin and restoring us to righteousness again and again. He does all the work, and gives it to us as a gift. Sinful human beings try to take credit for the gift through their supposed works, worthiness, cooperation, or by their decision, but this is futile. We contributed nothing but our sin. God has done it all. He has chosen us.

## Key Terms

| | |
|---|---|
| Arminianism | Omnipresent |
| Bondage of the Will | Omniscient |
| Born again | Paraclete |
| Contrition | Pelagianism |
| Conversion | Preservation |
| Faith | Reconciliation |
| Fideism | Regeneration |
| Formal Freedom | Sanctification |
| Fruits of the Spirit | Semipelagianism |
| Material Freedom | Spiritual gifts |
| Monergism | Synergism |

## For Review and Discussion

1. Many Christians limit their understanding of the Holy Spirit to events that follow the day of Pentecost. Why is this a critical mistake? What evidence of the Holy Spirit's presence and work can you see before Pentecost?

2. God works a dramatic change in us through his work of conversion. Contrast the "B.C." (before Christ and before conversion) condition of a person to their condition after conversion. How does this demonstrate our need for the Holy Spirit in conversion?

3. In what sense does a person have "free will" before conversion? In what way do they not have free will? Is anything changed after conversion? Why is this such an important topic?

4. Most people have faith in something, but not everyone has saving faith. Why is it vital that the person have faith in the right person (Jesus Christ)? How can we guard against the dangers of fideism?

5. Many Christians continue to believe that they contributed something to their conversion or that they "chose" or "accepted Jesus." Outline a discussion you might have with someone who believes this. How can you gently guide their faith back

to a biblically accurate description without crushing the enthusiasm of their faith?

## For Further Reading

Dallmann, William. *The Holy Ghost.* St. Louis: Concordia Publishing House, 1930.

_____. *I Believe in the Holy Spirit.* Minneapolis: Augsburg Publishing House, 1949.

Gritsch, Eric W. *Born Againism: Perspectives on a Movement.* Philadelphia: Fortress Press, 1982.

Kauffeld, Eugene P., ed. *God the Holy Spirit.* Milwaukee: Northwestern, 1972.

Lockwood, Gregory J. "Spiritual Gifts in 1 Corinthians." In *1 Corinthians*, 426-440. St Louis: Concordia Publishing House, 2000.

Senkbeil, Harold L. *Dying to Live: the Power of Forgiveness.* St. Louis: Concordia Publishing House, 1994.

*Spiritual Gifts.* A report of the Commission on Theology and Church Relations of the Lutheran Church—Missouri Synod. St. Louis, Missouri: The Lutheran Church—Missouri Synod, 1994.

Wunderlich, Lorenz. *The Half Known God.* St. Louis: Concordia Publishing House, 1963.

# 11

# Sanctification

Have you ever watched a butterfly emerge from a cocoon? It is hard to believe that something so beautiful is coming out of the cocoon when you remember that a rather ugly "worm" made it. The new insect is the same animal genetically as it was before the change, yet it looks so very different that we wonder if it is really a new creature. In a small and inadequate sense, that is what sanctification is about. Because of Jesus, God works a wonderful, miraculous transformation in us. In this chapter, we will look at this transformative activity of the Holy Spirit as we consider:

1. Sanctification Defined—*Wide and narrow senses*
2. Biblical Images of Sanctification—*Different descriptions of the Spirit's work*
3. Helpful Resources—*Where Christians can find assistance in life*
4. Good Works—*What Christians do naturally*
5. Is Perfect Sanctification Possible?—*The completion of sanctification*

## 1. Sanctification Defined

When we examined the Holy Spirit, we saw that his life-giving work continues throughout the years of a Christian's existence. **Sanctification** is this lifelong work of the Spirit. The word "sanctification" comes from two Latin words meaning "to make holy." But what does this mean? This one word can be used to describe two biblical concepts. In a wide or general sense, sanctification refers to the working of the Holy Spirit in the lives of people. This broader work includes his participation in creation and redemption as well as everything he does to bring us to faith in Jesus and nurture our relationship with him (2 Thessalonians 2:13; Hebrews 13:12). While this is one biblical description, sanctification is more often used in a narrower, more precise sense. This narrower sense refers to an inward spiritual transformation of a believer through the miraculous working of the Holy Spirit. When we speak of sanctification in this chapter, we are referring to this narrow sense.

Sanctification in this more precise scriptural sense is the Holy Spirit's creation of a new spiritual life in a person (1 Thessalonians 4:3). Through the means of grace (John 17:17; Galatians 5:25) the image of God which was lost after the fall (Colossians 3:10) begins to be restored and we grow in our relationship with our God. However, as we explore the biblical data on sanctification, we will discover that this does not mean that we attain spiritual perfection or that we are free from our sinful nature. The biblical picture is much more complex and true to life, since it accounts for both our fallen nature and our new life as children of God.

## *The Relationship of Sanctification to Justification*

Sanctification begins immediately at our justification. As soon as God declares us acceptable and his children because of Christ (justification), the gradual process of becoming what-God-has-declared-us-to-be (sanctification) begins. God has declared us holy; he has declared us to be saints; he has declared that we are his children. Immediately the Holy Spirit works a change in us through the same means that created our faith: the Gospel. As a result of this subjective justification, good works flow from the Christian's life (John 15:5).

The faith that justifies us has another dimension. God produces a renewed desire and a holy life in the believer (Galatians 2:20). Prior to our conversion, we were God's enemies, hostile to anything that had to do with God (Romans 5:6, 8, 10). But the Spirit gave us the gift of faith in Christ, and we were justified. A false or pretended faith that does not justify cannot sanctify either. But as we will see, a saving faith naturally and inevitably produces good works (Ephesians 2:8-10). Sanctification is God's will for his redeemed people (1 Thessalonians 4:3) and involves the whole of a person's life (1 Thessalonians 5:23).

## *Divine and Human Roles in Sanctification*

Because of human sinfulness, we cannot do anything for our justification. We cannot save ourselves, convert ourselves, contribute anything, or do anything to make God love us. We don't have to, since Jesus did it all for us. As we discussed conversion, we noted that the concept of "synergism" is biblically incorrect and theologically erroneous. However, once a person is converted and the Holy Spirit gives the gift of faith, a new relationship with God begins.

One of the biblical descriptions of conversion is "reconciliation." God has made us his friends because of Jesus' death and resurrection. As a result of being God's friends, we want to please him, grow closer to him, and learn more about him. In that sense, we can speak of a working with the Holy Spirit—not in justification, but in sanctification (2 Corinthians 6:1). Because of the gift of faith, we want to work with the Holy Spirit. Yet, even this cooperation is a product of God's activities (Philippians 2:13) and not something we can do by our own innate human power.

*The Means of Grace in Sanctification*

The Holy Spirit awakens faith in us through the Gospel and sacraments (together known as the means of grace), but the means of grace are not limited to conversion. The Spirit uses the same means to create the transformation of sanctification in our hearts and lives. Jesus clearly states that his word makes us holy (John 17:17). Paul says God works in a Christian "according to the Spirit" (Romans 8:4). That same Spirit creates a new attitude along with new actions (Philippians 2:13). God's word of Law not only convicts us of sin, but also now serves as a glorious guide (Romans 12: 1-2). God's word of Gospel serves as our motivation and inspires us to keep up the good works (1 Peter 2:2). The sacraments, particularly the Lord's Supper, nurture and strengthen our faith as we receive Jesus into ourselves weekly (Acts 2:42, 46; 1 Corinthians 10:16). Through these means, the Spirit produces the fruit of faith in each believer's heart and life. The means of grace demonstrate, once again, that it is God who works in and through us in sanctification; our response is not merely a matter of our own efforts.

## 2. Biblical Images of Sanctification

The Bible presents a number of different depictions of sanctification. In a sense, each of these images communicates an outward demonstration of the inward transformation. Because sanctification begins with the renewal of one's heart through faith, sanctification is not always visible (Ephesians 3:16). Yet, there are always manifestations of that inward change which are evident in a believer's life.

The transformation of sanctification begins with a transformation of the heart and mind (Romans 12:2). Because conversion refers to a change in mind or attitude, a Christian will no longer be as concerned with worldly things, but will begin to have a heavenly perspective (Philippians 3:7-8; Colossians 3:2). The believer will think of spiritual things more frequently and focus on eternal issues (Romans 8:5; Philippians 3:17-21). This transformation is not simply a mental focus or concentration; it is a gift of God.

A complementary image of sanctification is **vivification**. St. Paul used this image to describe justification (Christ gives us his life), and then continues to apply it to sanctification. Christians are now "dead" to themselves but alive to God (Romans 6:11). As a result, the believer will live life to God's glory (Romans 14:8; 1 Corinthians 10:31; Galatians 2:19-20). This vivifying is the work of the Spirit as "Lord and giver of life."

Growth is another picture of sanctification. Second Peter 3:18 says that we are to grow in grace. Paul uses this idea, too, when he speaks of the love of the Philippians abounding more and more (Philippians 1:9). He also spoke of the fruit of the Spirit, indicating that the sanctified life produces actions that are God-pleasing (Galatians 5:22-23). Particularly pleasing to God are works of love toward others (2 Thessalonians 1:3). This growth is always in relationship to Christ and his perfect gift of eternal life to us through the Holy Spirit.

Sanctification is sometimes described as an inner, spiritual struggle. St. Paul describes his own life after being converted (Romans 7:14-24): "For I do not do the good I want, but the evil I do not want is what I keep on doing" (Romans 7:19). What he portrays in this section of his Letter to the Romans is readily understood by Christians who struggle daily with their sins, knowing the good and the right but not always doing it. Luther was not only particularly sensitive to this struggle, but he was able to label this struggle with helpful Latin phrase. He said he was ***simul iustus et peccator*** (simultaneously justified and a sinner; often rendered, "saint and sinner"). This condition of struggle remains until we are glorified in heaven. All Christians experience fluctuations in faith and struggle with their sinful nature. Fluctuations in faith vary within a person over time as well as between believers depending upon their life circumstances. Yet, through it all, the Spirit works to strengthen our relationship with Jesus.

St. Paul used another image when he spoke of the Christian life as having old soiled clothes removed and putting on new ones that are clean and fresh. We have our old sinful selves (Paul sometimes calls this our "Adam" or "old man" or "flesh"). These old selves are removed, like the sloughed off skin of a snake or the shell of a crab, and our new selves emerge. But this is not a once-in-a-lifetime event. When Paul speaks of this, he says that it is a continuing work of God (Ephesians 4:22-24; Colossians 3:8-10; Romans 13: 14 and Galatians 3:27). As a snake continually sheds its old skin throughout its life, so a Christian regularly needs to have the old self removed. In fact, this is a constant need! In the Small Catechism, Luther says that we "daily drown" the old self and that "daily a new person is to come forth and rise up to live before God in righteousness and purity forever." This is done most evidently through the means of grace. Of course, we also need to remember that it is not enough to remove the sin. We need to be dressed again, and the "clothing" that we put on is not one of ourselves, but the very righteousness of Christ (Romans 13:14).

## 3. Helpful Resources

The sanctified life is not something that a Christian undertakes alone. Rather, the Holy Spirit provides assistance on the journey: resources that Christians can easily use for help in their struggles and experiences in their Christian walk.

We have already seen that God uses his word to create and sustain faith. These are the resources that the Spirit uses to stimulate and strengthen that faith. The Gospel energizes our faith, producing the power to live and the Law directs us toward those things that God wants us to do (Romans 12:1-2). Through regular Bible reading and worship, a Christian will have these resources focused on day-to-day issues. We live in the grace of our baptism, hear God's certain word of absolution, and receive the body and blood of Christ in the Lord's Supper. In addition, the Christian community, the church, is a resource which provides support and encouragement. God gives us each other so that we can be sources of strength, help, and blessing.

### The Gifts of the Spirit

In chapter 10, we considered the gifts and fruits of the Holy Spirit. While some Christians have over-emphasized these gifts, or presented them in a way that obscures the biblical data, we still remember that God gives gracious gifts to all Christians. Every Christian has been given the gift of faith and certain other gifts for service (Romans 12 and 1 Corinthians 12). These gifts, or God-given abilities for use in the kingdom, are part of the sanctified life. Through his gifts, the Spirit equips us to be the people that God intends us to be.

The idea of being gifted by God does not help in our sanctification if our attention is directed at ourselves. That's why God continues to provide us with the real help we need for living our transforming lives. Scripture's message of Law and Gospel is part of the daily life of a Christian. The Spirit uses the Law to show us our sinful condition so that we daily recognize our need for Jesus in our lives. We see the sin that we commit and the sin that we are. We recognize things that inhibit our spiritual growth. The Spirit then comes into us and renews us through word and sacraments with the forgiveness we daily need to sustain our relationship with Jesus. He builds us up and strengthens us in faith each day. This is the sanctified, gifted life of the child of God. We do not have this experience only once. God does not give us an initial spiritual experience before leaving us to our own devices. Instead, this pattern continues throughout our lives as we live in relationship with Jesus by the power of his Spirit.

### 4. Good Works

The transformation that occurs in the life of a believer is evident by the fruit of faith (Psalm 1:3; Matthew 7:16-20) or, as St. Paul terms it, faith working through love (Galatians 5:6). Because, as Luther said, faith is a living, active, mighty thing, it will be eager to do good works (Titus 2:14). A faith without works is not a saving faith (James 2:17-18), but only a mental idea or emotional feeling that lacks substance and reality.

A definition of **good works** is necessary in the area of sanctification, because there are two different perspectives on works—human and divine. Our concern is chiefly with God's viewpoint, although we need to recognize the human perspective, too. The world recognizes some things as "good works" that God rejects and some things the world does not consider "good works" conform precisely to God's understanding and will. In theology, this distinction is referred to as **"civil righteousness"** versus Christian righteousness. Three things are necessary for a work to be considered "good" in God's eyes: it must conform to his will (Matthew 12:50), it must be done from faith (Romans 14:23), and it must proceed from a love for God (Romans 13:10; 1 John 5:3).

### *Two Different Perspectives*

A work could be considered good from the world's perspective (1 Samuel 16:7) and would then fall under the category of "civil righteousness." Consider a wealthy non-Christian who donates money for many philanthropic projects, supports charities and building programs, and is well-respected in a community. Since this person is not a Christian, these works were obviously not done from faith or for love of God. In fact, when asked why she was so generous, she responds that she wanted the community to remember her family. Her actions were certainly generous and good in the world's eyes. But God does not see them in the same way. (John 15:5; Romans 14:23; Hebrews 11:6). God looks at the heart, not the act. Apart from Christ and his forgiveness, even our righteous acts are like filthy rags (Isaiah 64:6). Similarly, if a non-Christian is a morally upright or an honest person, these are good acts which conform to God's will, but they are not done as a result of faith in Jesus or out of selfless love for God (2 Corinthians 5:14).

It is possible, and even probable, that two people can do exactly the same things—one is a good work and the other is not in God's eyes, because one does it out of obligation, fear of punishment, or the desire for reward and the other does it out of love for God and gratitude for Christ Jesus. For example, a student may study hard in order to receive special honors or respect, or an individual may work industriously for high wages, but these are not good works. Another student may study hard or work hard because it is God's will to use the gifts he has given and to express appreciation for what God has provided. Because of this, he has done a good work. The same acts are the result of different motives.

Perhaps a visual illustration may communicate the distinction. Which of the following numbers is larger?

000,000,000,000        OR        1,000

Obviously, the number with the "1" in front of the zeros is larger, since zero is an empty set. The works that a person does are like the zeros. No matter how many they are, without number one (Jesus) they are valueless.

*What God's Word Says*

While faith in Christ is an essential component of good works, we should be careful to note that not everything a Christian does is a good work. It is not up to us to decide what is a good work and what is not. God's word alone is the standard or norm for valuing good works. God says we are to bear fruit (Matthew 3:8) and not grow weary in doing good (Galatians 6:9). Human opinions or churchly regulations are good things to follow when they conform to Scripture. But these things are not the standard to judge whether something is a good work. Indeed, sometimes the most mundane activity is a good work in God's eyes. Luther often scolded the church leaders of his day for exalting monastic devotional piety, which was often a show to the world, while ignoring more humble works such as a loving parent who humbly and quietly took care of a child's dirty diaper. By living in their vocation or calling as a Christian, they were doing God's will. Such things may truly be good works.

Some actions are neither specifically commanded nor categorically condemned in Scripture. Theologians describe these with the Greek term **adiaphora**. These activities cannot be commanded or condemned by other Christians, since God does not speak of them. Therefore, the final standard for evaluating good works is that God is pleased by whatever one does, in faith, which conforms to his will (1 Corinthians 10:31).

These actions are described by Paul as "the fruit of the Spirit" (Galatians 5:22-23). The Spirit motivates our activities and provides avenues for us to serve God. For example, he wants us to be cheerful givers (2 Corinthians 9:7), not giving our monetary offerings out of selfish compulsion or a sense of obligation (2 Corinthians 8:12). When a faithful Christian sees a need in the world that can be met, and they respond in faith by assisting that need, they have done a good work. Thus it is that the Spirit gives both the incentive and the power to perform that which is pleasing in God's sight.

*Bearing the Cross*

While a sanctified life is God's plan for us, and while it is a blessed thing, it is not always easy. Luther described the Christian life as a "life under the cross." That meant that there will be suffering, as Jesus predicted and promised (Matthew 16:24). God does not promise us a perfectly happy and trouble-free life on this earth, but he does promise us his presence in times of trouble. This is one of the great paradoxes of the Christian life.

Not all sufferings, however, are crosses. Some suffering is the consequences of our own or others' sin. "The **cross**," as Christians understand it, is suffering experienced for the sake of the Gospel. It may be evident in snide remarks that people make about you at work because you are a Christian. More conspicuous are the persecutions that Christians suffer at the hands of a secular or pagan culture. Within the past century, more Christians died martyrs' deaths than occurred throughout the first centuries of Christian history. These Christian martyrs were "faithful to the point of death" (Revelation 2:10).

## 5. Is Perfect Sanctification Possible?

In this life, the Christian will continue to struggle with these challenges. We face opposition from without, and from our own sinful nature. So it should be obvious to us that the Christian or sanctified life is never complete or perfected in this life (Philippians 3:12). There will always be obstacles and detours on the way to life in heaven. As long as we live on this side of heaven, we will continue to fall short of God's perfect pattern of life.

## *Perfectionism*

Despite the clear evidence of Scripture, some Christians believe that the child of God can be perfectly sanctified and holy in this life. This misguided teaching is called **perfectionism**, though some Christians try to make it more appealing by labeling it the "victorious life." In its extreme form, these "Christians" claim to be free from sin (1 John 3:9 is taken out of its context of 1 John 1.) The argument is something like this: 1) Jesus can keep those who trust in him from sinning; 2) If a Christian "truly" trusts in Jesus, he will preserve the believer from any and all deliberate sins; 3) Unintentional wrongs will be regarded as "errors" rather than as sins. There are several obvious flaws in this argument. Primarily, we can see a rejection of the biblical concept of sin and an attempt to deny the sinful nature that permeates all human life this side of the grave. This causes us to overlook many sins, or to be hypocritical in how we consider our own failings.

Perfectionism fails to take the depth of human sinfulness seriously. The Scriptures are filled with accounts of struggle and warning. Paul describes his own struggle with temptation and sin in Romans 7. Peter warns us to "Be self-controlled and alert. Your enemy the devil prowls around like a roaring lion, looking for someone to devour" (1 Peter 5:8). But most importantly, God's word specifically reminds Christians of our sinfulness. We continue to need God's grace and forgiveness, because we continue to sin. St. John definitively shows us that we will not achieve perfection in this life when he tells us, "If we say we have no sin, we deceive ourselves, and the truth is not in us" (1 John 1:8). Our holiness comes not from our efforts but from Christ's sacrificial death and resurrection. Scripture is clear: only in heaven will we be truly perfect (Revelation 20).

## *A Continuing Struggle*

In the sanctified life, Christians will find that they experience a continuing struggle with sin. As mentioned earlier, Luther recognized this condition and said that Christians are simultaneously saints and sinners. The struggle with (or better, against) sin will continue throughout the life of Christians because Satan is always on the prowl seeking to get us back into his territory and possession (1 Peter 5:8). That is why God provides concrete sources for strengthening the Christian.

The Spirit strengthens us for this spiritual struggle through the Scriptures. Through that word comes the conviction of sin, but more importantly the comfort of forgiveness. When a Christian struggles with a particular sin, God's Spirit provides a word of strength, comfort and hope (Romans 16:25-

27). The word may come from personal Bible study or from the mouth of a fellow Christian or pastor. That word may come from a devotional reading or the words of a hymn. In all of these avenues, God's Spirit brings strength for the struggle (1 Peter 5:10).

In addition, the Christian finds strength for daily living through absolution and Holy Communion. The words of absolution bring us back to our baptism and recall the fact that we live in baptismal grace. Luther loved to recall this by saying, "I am baptized," rather than "I *was* baptized" (Large Catechism). For him, baptism was a "daily drowning and dying" so that "daily a new man come forth to live in righteousness and holiness" (Small Catechism). In absolution, we hear the words of God himself, through the voice of the pastor, speaking his forgiveness. In addition, the Lord's Supper assures us of God's real strength for daily living. Jesus comes to us in and with the bread and wine. With Jesus comes all the assurance and power for living our Christian lives. As Paul reminds us, it is "Christ. . . in me" (Galatians 2:20) that is really living the sanctified life.

We have not yet reached that state of perfect holiness and bliss. But because of Christ's work, and not our own, we will. In the meantime, Christians will strive for the good things of God (2 Corinthians 7:1), not because we must, but because we are grateful to the God who loves us. So in love, we strive to not grow weary in doing good (Galatians 6:9).

## Key Terms

| | |
|---|---|
| Adiaphora | Sanctification |
| Civil righteousness | *Simul iustus et* |
| Cross | *peccator* |
| Good work | Vivification |
| Perfectionism | |

## For Review and Discussion

1. Why are fluctuations of faith something to be concerned with, yet something not to worry about?

2. Read Paul's remarks in Romans 7:14-24 and describe his dilemma in terms of sanctification.

3. How does the idea of being "simultaneously saint and sinner" help explain the incompleteness of one's sanctified life?

4.  When is the experience of a difficult time in one's spiritual life not necessarily "bearing the cross"?


**For Further Reading**

Hordern, William. *Living by Grace*. Eugene, Oregon: Wipf and Stock. 1975.

Lange, Lyle W. *Sanctification: Alive in Christ.* Milwaukee: Northwestern Publishing House, 1999.

Middendorf, Michael. *The "I" in the Storm: a Study of Romans Seven.* St. Louis: Concordia Academic Press, 1997.

Saarnivaara, Uuras. *Salvation and Sanctification According to Luther*. Plymouth, MN: Inter-Lutheran Theological Seminary, 1988.

Senkbeil, Harold L. *Sanctification: Christ in Action: Evangelical Challenge and Lutheran Response*. Milwaukee: Northwestern Publishing House, 1989.

# 12

# The Means of Grace

Imagine receiving a phone call telling you that you have won first place in a drawing. Even though you did nothing to earn it, a wonderful prize is yours. There are no strings attached or conditions to be met. You won. You thank the caller, and are about to hang up and begin celebrating when they stop you. Wait! Don't you want to know how to get it? Feeling a little foolish, you stop to listen to the delivery details. After all, it will only be useful to you when it is delivered.

Any gift must be given in a tangible way. There is a time and place where it is given. A person gives the gift, and someone receives it. If the gift is not delivered and received, it cannot be used or enjoyed. Even though it may have been valuable and freely given, a gift will not benefit the recipient until it is received.

God has given humanity an amazing gift in the person and work of Jesus Christ. His gift is genuine, sincere, and of priceless worth. Yet many do not know this or benefit from the gift. Our Father wants us to receive the benefits of Christ's work, so he is very clear about how he makes those benefits available to his children. We will explore how God bestows the gifts that Jesus won for us on the cross as we examine:

1. The Nature of the Means of Grace—*Understanding God's gifts*
2. The Gospel and the Sacraments—*God's promised blessings*
3. Baptism—*Sacrament of rebirth*
4. Absolution—*Living in forgiveness*
5. The Lord's Supper—*The taste of forgiveness*

## 1. The Nature of the Means of Grace

In many ways, this entire book has been about grace. The center of Christian theology is the wonderful truth that, for Christ's sake, God is gracious to sinful people. We are justified by grace, through faith in Jesus Christ (Ephesians 2:8-10). That grace is delivered to and received by individuals in certain ways which are known as "the **means of grace**."

*Defining the Means of Grace*

To understand the means of grace, it is important to remember that our entire relationship with God is one-sided. He always takes the initiative, coming to us, and blessing us. Only after he does this can we respond. Knowing our need, and desiring to be gracious towards us, God gives us precisely what we need. He did not first consult humanity and ask if we wanted to be saved. Nor did he survey his creation to determine the means of our salvation. Instead, he determined to save humanity, sending his Son into our flesh to be our Savior (Hebrews 2:14). He gave us exactly what we needed. In the same way, God did not ask us how he should give us the gifts that Christ won for us; he simply established the means by which he would deliver those gifts to us. The means of grace are the instruments which the Holy Spirit uses to give us the forgiveness of sins and to create and strengthen faith. God has promised to act through these things. Specifically, the means of grace are the **Gospel**, and those applications of the Gospel known as the sacraments. Through the life-giving word of the Gospel, baptism, absolution, and the Lord's Supper, the Spirit conveys the grace of God to people.

*The Means of Grace and Justification*

Despite God's institution and promise, some Christians are skeptical about the means of grace. This skepticism may arise from a fear that an emphasis on these means may lead to an attitude that we are doing something to earn our salvation. A distorted teaching on baptism, for example, might lead one to think that it is something that the individual is doing for God. Yet this is not the biblical teaching of the means of grace. These things are not human institutions or works of the Law. If this were so, they would not be means of *grace*. Rather, the means of grace are simply the application of Christ's work. Jesus won the gifts of forgiveness, life, and salvation for us. He delivers them to us in the means of grace. Consequently, these means are not something different than justification. They are the ways in which God applies the benefits of justification to us. The means of grace are justification—applied to the lives of individual Christians.

*The Promises and Freedom of God*

It should amaze and astonish us that God gives his grace to us at all, let alone in so many ways. Yet he has chosen to do this and is always faithful to his promises. Faithful believers strive to know his will and seek him where he promises to be (Isaiah 55:6). But if we reject the ways in which God has promised to act, we have no way remaining where we can be sure that we will receive his grace. God promises to bless us in these means, but this does not mean that he is limited to these means. God can work in any way he desires, but what we need to remember is that he promises to work in these means. So a Christian seeking God should rightly look where he has promised to be. Furthermore, if a Christian believes that God is revealing himself in other ways, it is important to follow God's command to "test the spirits" (1 John 4:1) to be certain that it is God who is acting, and not something or someone else.

## 2. The Gospel and the Sacraments

So what are these means of grace? The first, and most vital means of grace, is the Gospel. It is important to recognize that the Gospel, and not just the Bible, is a means of grace. Though both Law and Gospel are the inspired word of God (2 Timothy 3:15-17), the Law is not a means of grace. Indeed, "through the law comes knowledge of sin" (Romans 3:20).

The Gospel is a way in which God's grace is given to us. It is not simply stories about Jesus, but the "power of God for salvation" (Romans 1:16). Any statement of the Gospel conveys God's grace. When we hear it, God pronounces absolution. People may hear it proclaimed or read it; either way, they are presented with the power of God in his Gospel.

In a way, it may properly be said that there is only one means of grace: the Gospel of the grace of God in Christ Jesus. The Gospel is made known by preaching and teaching. But that Gospel also comes to us in other ways. God has located his promise of forgiveness with certain external acts or elements. These physical applications of the Gospel are generally classified as "sacraments." Unfortunately, this common term is sometimes contentious and the source of division in the church. The primary reason for this is that the word "sacrament" is an extra-biblical term that is used to summarize biblical teaching. As we have repeatedly seen in this book, this is a common and legitimate practice. (The term "trinity" is a good example.) However, unlike many other theological terms, "sacrament" has not found a consensus of definition. Some Christians define it differently, and some reject the word altogether.

A common definition, used by Lutherans and some other Christians, describes a **sacrament** as a (1) sacred act that is (2) instituted by God, (3) has the promise of granting God's grace or forgiveness, and (4) is connected with a visible means or external element. We should recognize that while this is a common definition, it is not the only definition. Yet it is a serviceable description. As sacred acts, sacraments are distinguished from ordinary washing, eating and drinking. God is the one who deals with us in his sacraments; he institutes them and they belong to him. They are not ours to do with as we please but they are to be used as God has instructed. Changing things in a sacrament may alter God's institution and cause doubt as to whether God is working through these means.

Those who adopt a definition of "sacrament" generally use their definition to assess various acts to determine if they are or are not sacraments. Because the definitions vary, the resulting numbers of sacraments will also vary. It is not particularly helpful to debate the number of the sacraments or the term sacrament, since this is often based on the presupposed definition. It is far more profitable to focus on the meaning and use of particular things than to argue about numbers of sacraments. For example, what does the Bible teach about the Lord's Supper, and how are we to use it? This is much more fruitful than the question of categories.

### 3. Baptism

There is no question that **baptism**, the application of water with the word of God, is an important part of Christianity. Jesus Christ told his church to baptize. Most Christians have been baptized, and their churches practice baptism. Scripture is filled with stories of baptisms and references to it. The Nicene Creed confesses belief in "one baptism for the forgiveness of sins." Yet baptism is often a contentious topic in Christianity. Christians and denominations debate about who should be baptized, how it should be done, whether it should be repeated, and what it means. In light of these challenges, it is important to return to the roots of baptism.

Christianity is not unique in having a religious rite involving water. Many of the world's religions feature purification rites in which a person is ceremonially washed. Hindus may bathe in the Ganges River. Moslems wash themselves before prayer. Some Jewish women engage in ritual washings. These and many other religious practices all employ ritual washing. They represent or bring to mind the need for spiritual cleansing. Some may see Christian baptism as just another example of these washings. Others view baptism as an important rite of passage. It gives families a religious opportunity to celebrate the birth of a child, or offers an individual the chance to announce a transformed life to the world. Baptism certainly invokes images of cleansing and it may function as a rite of passage, but Christians do not baptize for these reasons.

Similarly, the fact that influential historical figures practiced baptism is not the foundation of Christian baptism. The Gospels all tell the story of John the Baptist. He preached a baptism "of repentance for the forgiveness of sins" (Mark 1:4; Luke 3:3). John's baptism pointed to Jesus, and when Jesus arrived, both John and his baptism moved aside (John 1:29-34). This baptism was important and by it, Jesus "fulfilled all righteousness" (Matthew 3:15), but Christians do not baptize because John the Baptist did. Similarly, while the apostles, church fathers and other Christians practiced baptism, they are not the source of baptism.

*Baptism was Instituted by Jesus Christ*

Christians baptize for one simple reason: Jesus told us to do this. It is a divine institution, given by God to his church so that, through it, we might receive his gifts. At the end of Matthew's Gospel, he says, "Go therefore and make disciples of all nations, baptizing them in the name of the Father and of the Son and of the Holy Spirit, teaching them to observe everything I have commanded you" (Matthew 28:19-20a). He tells us to baptize all nations. His word teaches us the meaning of baptism and shows its benefits. He blesses his people as we receive baptism.

It is important to note that the commission to baptize is not a legalistic command. Baptism is not a work of the Law; it is a proclamation and application of the Gospel. Through this sacrament, he gives us forgiveness, life and salvation. Baptism is God's work, not our own.

Christ's followers received his institution of baptism and immediately began using it, just as he had told them to do. On the day of Pentecost, the apostles baptized approximately 3000 individuals who had come to faith (Acts 2:41). After Pentecost they continued to baptize those who believed the Gospel (see Acts 8:38, Acts 16:15). Second Century Christian writings, including *The Teaching of the Twelve Apostles* (also known as the *Didache*) and the writings of Justin show that baptism in the name of the Father and of the Son and of the Holy Spirit was a common practice that was known by all Christians. Throughout the centuries, the Christian Church has continued to follow Christ's institution of baptism.

*The Blessings of Baptism*

The institution of Christ is, in itself, sufficient reason for the church to continue to baptize today. He gave this to us to do; it is not left to our discretion as to whether we want to baptize or not. Even if we had no further instruction on baptism or were told of no other blessings that accompany it, we would follow this divine institution. God has called us to baptize, so we do. But baptism is not simply a command; he has also attached many blessings to this sacrament—blessings that move us to receive his gifts with joy and thanksgiving.

## Forgiveness of Sins

In baptism, the Lord has promised to forgive sins. The forgiveness that was won for us on the cross is delivered to us in the waters of holy baptism. Peter makes this clear as he proclaims, "Repent and be baptized every one of you in the name of Jesus Christ for the forgiveness of your sins, and you will receive the gift of the Holy Spirit" (Acts 2:38). St. Paul likewise connects baptism with the forgiveness of sins, saying "rise and be baptized and wash away your sins" (Acts 22:16). Baptism forgives sins because in it, God applies the righteousness of Christ to us. "For as many of you as were baptized into Christ have put on Christ" (Galatians 3:27). God forgives in baptism, just as he promised he would do.

## Life and Salvation

Since baptism brings forgiveness of sins, it also frees us from the eternal consequences of our sins. Clothed in Christ and his righteousness, we share in his life and resurrection. Since the wages of sin is death (Romans 6:23) forgiveness means that the penalty of death has been paid for us. We died when we were baptized into the death of Christ (Romans 6:4, Colossians 2:12). We may yet face physical death, but because of Christ, death has now lost its sting (1 Corinthians 15:55-56). Death, for the Christian, is now the portal to eternal life. As our bodies were washed with the water of baptism, so our bodies will share in the resurrection of Christ at the last day (Romans 6:4-8) and we will live with him forever.

As wonderful as the blessings of eternal life and salvation are, this gift is not limited to heaven. God's gift of new life is a blessing to us here as well. Our new life is hidden in him (Colossians 3:3). It is no longer we who live, but Christ who lives in us (Galatians 2:20). We have been born again to a new life that begins now and continues, in Christ, for all eternity (John 3:16; John 10:10).

Just as birth from the womb was a gift from God so also our new birth through baptism is a gift. We did not cause our natural birth, and we do not cause our rebirth. Since we were dead in our trespasses and sin, our consent or cooperation was not possible. Salvation by grace through faith in Christ is pure gift (Ephesians 2:8-9).

## The Holy Spirit

Yet another blessing is implied through the gifts already mentioned, and is specifically promised in the Bible. In baptism, God promises to give his Holy Spirit. When Peter tells the Pentecost crowds about baptism, he not only tells them that their sins will be forgiven, but also that they "will receive the gift of the Holy Spirit" (Acts 2:38). Indeed, one could not have forgiveness, life, and salvation without the Spirit, since these are works of the Holy Spirit. There is no question or condition placed upon this gift. The Spirit is given in baptism.

## Essential Components of Baptism

Baptism, along with the other means of grace, conveys these blessings of God's grace. But what constitutes baptism? It is not just the application of water to a person, but water connected to the word of God and the Holy Spirit working through that word. These two things are essential components of baptism: the word of God and water.

## The Word of God

When Jesus instituted baptism, he instructed his disciples in what to do and say. They were to baptize, "in the name of the Father and of the Son and of the Holy Spirit." Those words are an essential part of baptism. Although it is performed by human hands, baptism is God's own act. Here God promises to be our Father and adopts us as his children.

While the words of baptism are brief and simple, we are not free to omit them. Without the word of God, we perform only a human washing but not a divine baptism. Similarly, we are not free to substitute other words for the holy word of God. At a minimum, changes to the baptismal formula may raise doubt in the minds of Christians about whether they are truly baptized. This is the opposite of the confidence that God would provide to us in baptism. Worse, substituting our own words for the word of God may make it only a human ritual and not the sacrament that Christ instituted. For example, the church should not substitute functions such as "Creator, Redeemer, and Sanctifier" for the divinely revealed name of "Father, Son, and

Holy Spirit." In addition to replacing God's word with human words, such changes distort the doctrine of the Trinity. The words of Christ should be used as he spoke them to us, thereby addressing God with the name that he has revealed to human beings. Likewise, we should understand these words in their scriptural sense. Those who use the triune name of God while denying the Trinity only deceive themselves and others. Repeating the name while rejecting the triune God denies baptism.

### Water

The other essential component of baptism is water. The word "baptize" literally means "to wash," or "to apply water." Water is so common and unexciting, that it seems like it cannot accomplish forgiveness. But the Lord has chosen to use this element. It is true, the water is plain water only. There is nothing special or magical about this element. But this ordinary water is included in God's command to baptize and combined with God's word. When the water is applied, God marks the baptized with his own name and he forgives.

### Does Scripture Specify a Mode of Baptism?

While it is obvious that baptism is to use water, how is that water to be applied? The word "baptize" means "to wash or apply water," but is there a specific biblical method of application? Must we immerse someone fully in water? Pour it generously over their head? Sprinkle it on them? Christians have employed a number of different methods in baptism, because the word of God never mandates a certain mode. In fact, "baptize" is an ordinary word used to describe things such as washing hands, dishes, and even furniture (see Mark 7:2-4). Some of these things might be immersed in water, others clearly are washed in other ways. Unless it can be shown that Christ has limited the application of water to a certain method, we dare not restrict his institution. The burden of proof is on those who insist on one method of application. Without clear biblical instruction, Christians are free to use a variety of methods in baptism.

Since Christ did not command a certain mode of application, Christians throughout history have baptized in a variety of ways. Application of large amounts of water may be aesthetically pleasing and evoke the biblical theme that we are "buried with Christ" in baptism (Romans 6:4) but this is not always possible. (For example, imagine trying to baptize someone in a hospital's intensive care unit where immersion would likely be impossible). Aside from logistical issues, Christians should be concerned about giving false impressions about the use of Christian freedom. If some Christians wrongly attempt to force their will on other believers in areas of **adiaphora** (things that Scripture neither commands nor forbids), we should not give in to their demands. Finally, we should be careful that our practices not cause Christians who were legitimately baptized to question the validity of their baptism. Baptism should give confidence and certainly, not doubt and questions. It is sad that while Christ has allowed us great latitude in how the water is applied in baptism, Christians often seem eager to restrict the freedom he has given. Even sadder is the fact that humans are constantly tempted to turn God's gracious act of baptism into a human work by focusing on the mode of baptism rather than the promise of God.

In contrast, God's institution is simple. He gives us the essential components of baptism: water that is applied to a person with the word of God. That word is the name of God himself. Since Christ instituted baptism this way, faithful Christians will strive to keep his institution and not change the element or the word, nor inappropriately narrow his institution. Altering either one can only create doubt where our Lord intended to give confidence.

## The Recipients of Baptism

Baptism is simple: the application of water with the triune name. But who is to be baptized? The Lord commissioned his church to make disciples of "all nations" by baptizing them. There are no limits to this commission. It embraces all people: every nation, ethnicity, culture, sex, and age is included in Christ's institution of baptism. He can adopt any person into God's family

### Is all water equal?

Water is the external element in baptism. God does amazing things in this sacrament, but does them through ordinary water. The baptismal water does not undergo any change. Scripture does not speak of "holy water" nor is the water infused with any special powers. Likewise, the source of the water does not affect the power or validity of the sacrament. Whether the water is drawn from a tap, comes from a river, or even is brought from the Jordan River, the baptism is still the work of God. When the baptism is concluded, the water is still just water, but the person is different. God works through simple water just as he promised.

through this sacrament. As we read the biblical accounts of baptism (such as Matthew 28:18-20), it is clear that baptism and teaching always belong together. Discipleship involves baptism and teaching, but is there an order in which these are to be performed?

When adults are brought to faith and a life of discipleship, they ordinarily hear the word and receive some instruction in the Christian faith before they are baptized since they are able to hear and respond to the word of God. They will not know what baptism is, why it is important, or why they would want to be baptized unless they are first taught about baptism. For this reason, an adult is instructed in Christianity before being baptized. However, the Christian church should not expect that a new convert be fully trained in every aspect of theology before being baptized. If this were the case, no one would ever be baptized! The call to growth and discipleship is a lifelong one. The instruction that precedes baptism is one in the fundamental teachings of the Christian faith.

Adult converts sometimes feel some anxiety at the thought of being baptized publicly. Perhaps this arises from knowledge that others were baptized as infants or children, or out of embarrassment that they have spent much of their lives in isolation from God and his people. They need not feel uncomfortable. As Christ says, there is rejoicing in heaven when one sinner repents (Luke 15:7). In the same way, Christians rejoice when another person is brought to faith and receives the blessings of baptism. This is not a cause for embarrassment but for celebration. In baptism, God enlarges his family.

### Should Infants be Baptized?

While all Christians recognize the importance of baptizing adults, some are confused about the appropriateness of baptism for children and infants. Is it appropriate for children to be baptized or should they wait until they are old enough to decide for themselves? It is noteworthy that such questions are raised in spiritual issues but would never be entertained in other areas of life. A responsible parent would not keep their children out of school until they were old enough to decide whether they wanted to be educated, nor would most allow a minor child to drop out if he did not want to go. They would not withhold medical care from a child until she was old enough to understand the treatment. Parents are responsible for the upbringing and nurture of their children and that includes their spiritual life. Others want to withhold baptism from children because they wrongly insist that baptism must be by immersion. One could not, they argue, immerse an infant completely in water, therefore baptism must wait until they are older. Since biblical baptism is not restricted to immersion, this objection is invalid.

However, we might also note that some churches do baptize infants by immersion. Whatever reasons may be given to avoid infant baptism, there are ample biblical reasons to commend it.

First, children and infants are to be baptized because they are included in Christ's command to make disciples of all nations (Matthew 28:19). Persons of all ages are part of the nations, not simply adults. What's more, we know that Jesus welcomed children. In Luke 18:15-17, he rebuked his disciples for keeping children away from him, saying, "Let the children come to me, and do not hinder them, for to such belongs the kingdom of God." In fact, the word he uses for children (*brephos*) is properly translated, "infants." Jesus welcomes those children and goes on to say, "whoever does not receive the kingdom of God like a child shall not enter it." Notice that Jesus does not say that children should become like adults; adults are to become like children. In Matthew 18:6, Jesus speaks of the little ones who believe in him. Jesus does not limit the kingdom of God to adults. We dare not limit it either.

Another important reason for infant baptism is that infants are sinners in need of forgiveness (Psalm 51:5). While we hate to see the effects of sin in any human life, we may be particularly troubled when we see it in an infant, yet infants do suffer the effects of sin. They are weak, can become ill, and sometimes die. Death is an effect of sin. Sinners need Christ's forgiveness and one of the ways that he promises to forgive sins is through baptism.

To be sure, infants are unable to give a verbal confession of their faith, but this does not mean that they are incapable of believing. Faith is a gift of God and the work of the Holy Spirit. It is by his grace that anyone believes, and not our own works (Ephesians 2:8-10). Infants may not be able to articulate their faith just as they are unable to verbalize their love for their mother, but this does not mean that faith or love are absent from them. With God's power, it will grow in time, but even infants can believe (Matthew 18:6).

Parents are given the wonderful blessing and responsibility of bringing their children to baptism. Just as they make decisions for their children in many other areas and provide what they think is best for them, so they do in baptism. We should remember, however, that baptism is not a "spiritual inoculation" that gives immunity from sin and unbelief. A child who is baptized should be raised in the faith, instructed in God's truth, and nurtured in the Christian faith throughout their lives. Parents promise to raise their children in the faith when they are baptized. When they faithfully fulfill this promise, they again demonstrate the truth that, in Christ's institution, baptism and teaching belong together.

*The Effectiveness of Baptism*

The promises associated with baptism are extraordinary. Forgiveness, life, salvation, and the Holy Spirit are all given through this means of grace. It is able to do these great things because God has instituted it and promised to work through it. The power of God working through his word and the water makes baptism effective. It is his baptism. His word, his name, and his grace make it effective. In light of the simplicity of this gift, it is strange to see that some Christians complicate baptism by ascribing its power or effectiveness to other things. This often happens when humans assign themselves a role that God does not give to us. We should take note of some of these false views and be strengthened in our commitment to the biblical teaching.

### Some False Views of Baptism

Some Christians treat baptism in a mechanical way, maintaining that baptism is made effective simply by going through the right motions and saying the right words. This view is often summarized by the Latin phrase, ***ex opere operato***, or "by the work that is worked." In essence, this views baptism as if it were magic. Said another way, this treats baptism as Law and not Gospel. The focus is on our work and proper performance instead of on God and his work. It also neglects faith. An application of this view might be seen in someone who secretly baptizes another person's child so that they would be saved, regardless of their upbringing. This might also be reflected in a parent who brings their child to be baptized, but refuses to bring him to worship or provide for his Christian instruction. Instead of these mechanistic and faithless views, we receive baptism as a gift from God, used according to his institution.

Another errant view of baptism limits its forgiveness by claiming that baptism only forgives sins committed before baptism. According to this view, when a person commits sins after they are baptized, they need to find another way to secure forgiveness. Often they are directed to **penance** or other human works. While it is true that God provides his grace to us in a variety of means, he does not limit baptism in this way. Certainly, a person who sins after baptism (as everyone does) will seek and receive God's forgiveness. Yet this is not given by means of a human work, but from God's free grace. The absolution we receive is a further application of our baptismal grace.

Yet another faulty view of baptism makes it dependent on the character or the work of human beings instead of on Christ. This may be done by claiming that baptism is based on the moral character or piety of the person who is baptizing. Since we can never be completely certain that another person is pious or sincere, we could never be certain that our baptism is valid. This might also be done by insisting that the person being baptized has to lead a sinless life either before or after they are baptized. Since this is impossible (see Romans 7:14-25), we would never receive God's grace. Still others see the forgiveness and grace as a reward that God gives to the person for their work of being baptized. This makes their work a cause of grace, not a response to it. Either way, we are making baptism and God's grace dependent upon mere humans instead of receiving the promised grace of God.

Another significant error turns baptism into a symbol, thus removing grace from God's gift. In this view, baptism does not grant forgiveness or any gift of God, but is only a symbol that points to Christ's death and resurrection. This error may even sink to the level of making baptism only a symbol of the commitment that the individual has for their God. "I will show how much I love him by going through this ceremony." In such an understanding, God is not working through baptism. It makes baptism a work in which we remember what he has done, and denies the promises of God and the very gifts that he gives.

A related error reduces or denies the power of baptism by insisting on its repetition. If a person drifts from faith and then returns, they may want to be rebaptized. If they join a new church, they may seek to be rebaptized. If they have a significant religious experience, they may ask to be rebaptized. While such desires may arise from important events in their lives, this view again transforms baptism into a human work. It is sadly true that Christians sometimes fall from faith and then happily return later. But in such a case, God did not falter in his promises. The baptism he gave and the grace he gives are certain and continual. If baptism is his work, and if it is performed according to his institution, it does not need to be repeated in an individual life.

A final error may be a semantic issue for many people, but it is important to understand correctly. Many Christians, in speaking of their baptism, will say that they were baptized into a denomination or congregation. "I was baptized as a Lutheran" or "I was baptized as a Presbyterian." While their baptism may have taken place in a Lutheran, Presbyterian, or other Christian church, there is no "Lutheran baptism" or "Presbyterian baptism." There is only Christian baptism. All who are baptized into the triune name according to Christ's institution have received Christian baptism. Consequently, most Christian denominations recognize the validity of each other's baptism.

*Living in Baptism*

Too often, little thought is given to baptism. For many people it is something that happened when they were a baby. Pictures bring back warm memories, but other than that it is treated as something in the past. Baptism is not just a gift of the past but a gift of daily life. It is a gift that was given and in which we live every day.

How do we live in our baptism? This begins, as our baptism did, with confession of sin. As Luther explained in the Small Catechism, "the old creature in us with all sins and evil desires is to be drowned and die through daily contrition and repentance." The Holy Spirit works repentance in us as he uses the Law to convict us of our sin. Our sinful nature is no longer our master. We were buried into death with Christ and are now dead to sin. Yet that sinful nature keeps trying to gain mastery over us. This is why our contrition and repentance is a daily matter. The practice of confession and absolution *is* living in baptism.

But we don't stop there. Luther continued that "a new man should daily emerge and arise to live before God in righteousness and purity forever." God's grace and forgiveness abound in our lives. Baptismal grace constantly flows over us as the Holy Spirit works new life through the Gospel, strengthens our faith, and blesses us with forgiveness. We live in our baptism when we live in Christ's forgiveness.

## 4. Absolution

After his resurrection, Jesus appeared to his disciples, gave them the gift of the Holy Spirit and said, "if you forgive the sins of anyone, they are forgiven; if you withhold forgiveness from anyone, it is withheld" (John 20: 23). James exhorts Christians to "confess your sins to one another" (James 5:16). This forgiveness is not limited in scope or duration. In fact, Jesus tells his disciples that whatever they bind on earth will be bound in heaven and whatever they loose on earth will be loosed in heaven (Matthew 16: 19; 18:18). Based on these and other scriptural passages, Christians have followed Christ's commission and boldly proclaim forgiveness of sins in God's name.

Some Christians associate the practice of **confession** and **absolution** with Roman Catholicism. While Roman Catholics do practice confession and absolution in their sacrament of **penance**, all Christians should confess their sins and hear God's forgiveness in absolution. This may be done corporately in worship, and individually in other contexts. What's important is that we hear God's promised words of full and free forgiveness of sins in Jesus' name.

*To Whom Should We Confess?*

The topic of confession and absolution can evoke some interesting reactions among Christians. Some uncomfortableness may result from false assumptions about this gift of God. One false assumption is that we should only confess our sins to the person that we have sinned against. We cannot speak for another person and offer forgiveness on their behalf, and we certainly cannot speak for God. Or can we? We certainly should confess to those we have sinned against, and seek to forgive those who have sinned against us. The reconciliation that comes from honest confession and gracious absolution is important to our relationships (see Matthew 18:12-19). Yet we should also recognize that every sin is committed against God and also needs his forgiveness. So, for example, when David had committed adultery with Bathsheba and caused Uriah's murder, he confessed that he sinned against God (Psalm 51:4). Furthermore, God has commissioned his church to forgive sins and has committed the "ministry of reconciliation" to us (2 Corinthians 5:18).

We do confess our sins directly to God. Yet God has also commissioned us to confess to other Christians and to pronounce his forgiveness to them. We may confess and receive absolution from any Christian (James 5:16) or from a pastor (2 Corinthians 5:18, John 20:23), and they should respond by declaring God's forgiveness to us. Either way, the forgiveness comes from God through his servant. The absolution is valid whether it is spoken by a pastor or by a layperson, but many Christians find it particularly helpful to confess to their pastor. A pastor has pledged to keep any sins confessed to him in confidence. Additionally, while we should have the confidence to confess our sins to any brother or sister in the faith, we may feel more comfortable confessing to someone who has a deeper theological training and is equipped to offer spiritual counsel. Most pastors hear people confess sins on a regular basis, and are helpful spiritual guides to their members. Additionally, we know that pastors have been called to carry out this ministry. We confess to them in their office as pastor.

While private confession and absolution are "unnecessary," they are a helpful gift that God has given to us. We know that God has forgiven us all our sins, but Christians frequently are troubled by specific sins. They need reassurance and confidence that they are really forgiven. Satan constantly tempts us to doubt our forgiveness and salvation. Private absolution gives us a powerful weapon and reassurance as we hear a fellow Christian embody

Christ's commission to forgive. They forgive us for specific sins in a concrete way. Christians receiving the gift of absolution often describe it as a liberating and uplifting experience. Certainly it is, because it is centered in the liberating and uplifting Gospel.

## 5. The Lord's Supper

When one examines the Scriptures, it is clear that food is an important part of the story of God's people. In the beginning, Adam and Eve lived in paradise where God gave them all the plants in the garden for food except one. They lived with only one command: do not eat of that one tree or you will die. That rebellious eating brought death to them and their descendants. In response, the Lord expelled them from the garden so that they would not eat from the Tree of Life and live in the horrible state of their sin forever (Genesis 3:22-24). On the night that God delivered Israel from slavery in Egypt, they ate a special meal of unleavened bread, roast lamb, and bitter herbs. This Passover meal was to be repeated every year as a lasting remembrance of God's deliverance (Exodus 12:17-20) and is still celebrated to this day. When Israel became hungry in their forty years in the wilderness, God provided them the daily gift of manna from heaven and with a steady supply of quail for meat (Exodus 16:13-15).

When Elijah fled from the evil king Ahab, he took refuge with a poor widow and her son. The small amount of flour and oil that she possessed were sufficient to provide bread for many days (1 Kings 17:9-16). Isaiah looked forward to the reign of the Messiah, describing it in terms of a rich banquet that would be shared by all God's people (Isaiah 25:6).

When the Messiah came, he continued to bless God's people by means of food. In his first miracle, he turned water into wine for a wedding banquet (John 2:1-11). He fed more than five thousand people in the wilderness by miraculously increasing five loaves of bread and two fish, providing enough food for everyone (Luke 9:12-17). He ate in the homes of the "respectable" members of society (Luke 7:36) and with tax collectors and sinners (Mark 2:15). He blessed them with his presence and with food.

These are just a few of the examples of God's blessing of food in Scripture. Yet of all these meals, one stands out as the most significant. On the night he was betrayed, Jesus shared a meal with his disciples. He washed their feet as a servant would. He spent time with them. He blessed the food that they ate together. Then, unexpectedly, he did something else. Giving them bread to eat he said, "this is my body." Taking a cup of wine, he declared, "this is my blood." He told them that this meal would bring forgiveness and that they should repeat it in the future. He blessed them, and us, with an amazing meal.

*The Institution of the Lord's Supper*

The importance of this meal is shown by the detailed attention that the Bible gives to it. Three Gospels (Matthew 26:26-29; Mark 14:22-24; Luke 22:19-20) and one Epistle (1 Corinthians 11:23-25) all describe what happened on that night.

> . . .the Lord Jesus on the night when he was betrayed took bread, [24] and when he had given thanks, he broke it, and said, "This is my body which is for you. Do this in remembrance of me." [25] In the same way also he took the cup, after supper, saying, "This cup is the new covenant in my blood. Do this, as often as you drink it, in remembrance of me." (1 Corinthians 11:23-25)

These words are known as the **words of institution**. All of these accounts present the same essential truths about this meal and what it means. It happened on the night Jesus was betrayed. After this meal, they would go to the garden of Gethsemane where, after praying, Jesus would be arrested. Along with other things, bread and "the cup" were on the table. The context of these verses reveals more information about these elements. Jesus "gave thanks" or blessed the food, and he gave it to his disciples. He said that the bread was his body and the wine in the cup was his blood. He said that this meal was to be done "in remembrance" of him, and that it gave forgiveness (Matthew 26:28).

The context of these passages, along with other sections of Scripture, provides further information about the meaning and use of this meal, but the main points are all here. Our Savior established this meal. He chose the elements that are used. We know what he did with these elements and what he said they were. He promises to give certain blessings. Most of all, he secures those

**Many Names; One Sacrament**

Based on the diversity of descriptions in scripture, Christians use a variety of names to for this sacrament including:

The Breaking of the Bread
Holy Communion
The Eucharist
The Lord's Supper
The Lord's Table
The New Covenant or Testament
The Sacrament of the Altar

blessings for us by leaving that meal and giving his life as a sacrifice on the cross.

Tragically, these simple words of Jesus have become a point of disagreement in his church. What do they mean? Can we take them at face value or must we understand them in a different manner? How should this meal be used today? Many of these questions arise from the different sources of theological information used by various Christians. They are significant questions; questions that call for biblical answers.

## The Elements of the Lord's Supper

One of the first challenges raised by some Christians involves the physical elements that are used in the Lord's Supper. Jesus took bread and took a cup. What are Christians today to use for this meal?

### Bread

The first element in the Lord's Supper is bread. Jesus gave bread to his disciples, but what was this bread? When he instituted the Eucharist, he was celebrating the Passover meal with his disciples in the upper room. Luke tells us that it was "the day of Unleavened Bread" (Luke 22:7). Certainly the bread that they used for this meal was made without yeast, for unleavened bread is an important part of the Passover (Exodus 12:7). However, the words of institution themselves do not specify unleavened bread (in Greek, *azumos*). They simply say "bread" (Greek: *artos*). Because of this, Christians are free to use a variety of types of bread in this meal. Many churches use wafers for several reasons. They are convenient to use, requiring no special storage. They have a long shelf life, so a congregation can have a significant supply of bread on hand for the sacrament. They do not readily crumble and so do not trouble people about how the body of Christ is being handled. The tradeoff for these virtues is that wafers may not seem much like bread at all. Furthermore, the use of many wafers diminishes the biblical imagery of the people of God being one just as there is one bread (1 Corinthians 10: 17). Some churches use other bread, leavened or unleavened. As long as it is bread, it is legitimate for use in the Lord's Supper. Still, we should be concerned that the elements are used respectfully and in a way that enhances worship, not in a manner that might confuse people or detract from worship. It is also important to note that Scripture nowhere specifies the grain used to make the bread. Most congregations today use wheat bread, but this is not mandated in the institution of the sacrament. So, or example, a Christian who had an allergy to wheat might be legitimately given a different type of bread in the sacrament.

## Wine

The other element used is "the cup" (Matthew 26:27). The verses sur-rounding the words of institution make the contents of this cup clear. Jesus refers to it as  the "fruit of the vine" (Matthew 26:29) while Paul notes a horrible abuse of the meal in that some were getting drunk (1 Corinthians 11:20-21). Wine was an ordinary beverage in the biblical world and it was an expected part of the Passover meal.  Moreover, since the grape harvest occurs in late summer or early fall of the year, there was no way for the dis-ciples to have the fruit of the vine unless it had fermented into wine.

Some Christians object to the use of wine in Holy Communion because they mistakenly believe that any consumption of alcohol is sinful. Clearly the Bible condemns the abuse of alcohol (Ephesians 5:18), but it does not bar Christians from a proper, responsible use of wine.  Jesus' first miracle changed water into wine (John 2:1-11), and he was even falsely accused of being a drunkard (Matthew 11:19). The Bible does not reject a responsible use of wine but rather sees it as a gift of God.  In light of the biblical evi-dence, it is clear that Jesus used wine in this meal. As we follow his institu-tion, we will do the same thing.

A special concern may be raised by ministry to those who are addicted to alcohol. Recovering alcoholics are often worried, with good cause, that consuming any alcohol might tempt them to return to drinking. Christians and congregations have responded to this specific concern in a variety of ways.  Some counsel an alcoholic to abstain from the Lord's Supper or to take only the host. Some offer a drop of wine that has been highly diluted with water. Others provide nonalcoholic wine (wine that has had the alcohol removed) for such cases. A communicant who is concerned about the use of wine in the sacrament should, above all, be in contact with his or her pastor. As the pastor ministers to his members, he can not only offer solutions to this immediate concern but, more importantly, provide additional support and vital spiritual care.

## The Body and Blood of Christ

While there are some differences among Christians regarding the bread and wine, the majority of challenges come when discussing the central is-sue of this sacrament. Jesus says, "This is my body" and "This is my blood." Lutherans, along with some other Christians, truly believe that the words of the Son of God are determinative for the meaning of this meal. Jesus says "is" so this is true. Faith trusts the words of our Savior and takes him at his word.

The challenge of this teaching arises not so much when we ask "what did Jesus say?" but when we instead ask, "how can this be true?" When human senses examine the elements of the Eucharist, they see bread and wine, taste bread and wine, and touch bread and wine. How can these elements possibly be the body and blood of Christ? Human reason cannot comprehend how Christ's body can be in the bread of this meal or his blood in the wine. Ordinary human experience may cause us to doubt the biblical teaching that Christ is present in this meal, and also simultaneously present in another congregation's celebration of the sacrament. How can this possibly be the right understanding?

If reason or experience are our main theological influence, we may easily give in to these concerns. On the other hand, if theology is founded in Scripture, we will hear the words of Jesus, listen to his offer to receive him in his body and blood, and trust his words. This is the body and blood of Christ because Jesus says this. At the same time, we believe that it is also bread and wine. St. Paul speaks of body-bread and wine-blood being given and received at the Lord's Table. "The *cup* of blessing that we bless, is it not a participation [or communion, *koinonia*] in the *blood* of Christ? The *bread* that we break, is it not a participation in the *body* of Christ?" (1 Corinthians 10:16). Because of this, we believe that the communicant receives both bread and body. We drink wine and the blood of Christ. Both are present because Scripture says that they are.

How are Christ's body and blood present? The precise mechanism is a mystery to us: a mystery that cannot be explained in terms of human physics, chemistry, metaphysics, or philosophy. We believe the Lord's words even though we cannot explain the presence of the body and blood. Lutherans have frequently used the phrase, "in, with, and under" to describe the body and blood and bread and wine. Each preposition defends against the Lord's Supper being drawn into error. Saying all three of these is, in effect, to say, "don't pin me down. I believe that his body and blood are there. That is enough!" Just as Christ is one person with two natures, so the one food is both bread and the body of Christ.

The bread and wine in the Lord's Supper are the body and blood of Christ. This is not a cannibalistic eating and drinking (John 6:52), but a sacramental eating and drinking. He is truly present. The Lord is at work in his Supper forgiving sins. He has located himself there, as nowhere else, in his body and blood. As we eat this meal we actually receive Christ's body and blood. He does not give us an image or a picture or a symbol. He gives us his body and blood.

This position is generally called **real presence**. Christ is really present, in his body and blood, in this sacrament. However, we should be careful to use this phrase precisely and to define our terms accurately. Other Christians might also say that Christ is really present, but not believe that he is present as he says: in his body and blood. We believe that his body and blood are really present because that is what he has told us.

### Christ is Present to Bless His People

Jesus Christ is distributed and received in the sacrament. Through bread and wine, he literally enters the bodies and lives of those who commune. This is wonderful news for those who believe in him. Almighty God dwells with us. He comes in a tangible, concrete form. We know that he has come to us when we commune because he promises to do this. The bodily presence of Christ is a powerful comfort and assurance in times of trial. It is a source of strength in adversity. Whatever our situation, we know that Christ comes to us. What's more, he comes to us with his promised forgiveness. The same body, once crucified for us and now risen and glorified, is our food. In his institution of the Lord's Supper, Jesus said that the blood that we drink was poured out for the forgiveness of sins (Matthew 26:28). Our Savior promises his grace whenever we receive this sacrament in faith.

In addition to this vertical relationship with God, the Lord's Supper also has a horizontal aspect. While Jesus Christ personally comes to each person who communes, this is not a private dinner for two; it is a banquet shared with others. A communicant is united with all others who share in the sacrament. Paul writes, "Because there is one bread, we who are many are one body, for we all partake of the one bread" (1 Corinthians 10:17). This unity is not limited to those who commune with us at one service. We are united with all Christ's people in the one church. All Christians of all times and places are united in the Eucharistic presence of Christ. The historic liturgy of the church has recognized this, saying, "therefore with angels and archangels and with all the company of heaven we laud and magnify your glorious name, evermore praising you. . ." Christ Jesus graciously unites us in his body as we commune.

### Christ is Received by All Who Commune

The Lord's Supper is pure Gospel to the child of God. The Savior comes to his people, who have faith in him, and blesses them with his grace. Anyone who trusts him receives this blessing. A person with a weak faith is strengthened and blessed; those with a stronger faith are also blessed. This is what he wants to do in the sacrament. He acts according to his proper work: the Gospel.

However, Scripture is careful to note that Christ's body and blood are present in this meal regardless of the faith of the communicant. Faith does not cause him to be present; it recognizes and receives him. His body and blood are given to all who commune, whether they believe him or not. But when Christ is received by someone who does not have faith, Christ is still present. Now the Sacrament is not an application of the Gospel but of the Law. This is due to the recipient. If they take the Supper while rejecting the Gospel, they have rejected his fulfillment of the Law and so stand in their own merit. So immediately after giving the words of institution, St. Paul cautions,

> Whoever eats the bread or drinks the cup of the Lord in an unworthy manner will be guilty of sinning against the body and blood of the Lord. [28] A man ought to examine himself before he eats of the bread and drinks of the cup. [29] For anyone who eats and drinks without recognizing the body of the Lord eats and drinks judgment on himself. [30] That is why many among you are weak and sick, and a number of you have fallen asleep. [31] But if we judged ourselves, we would not come under judgment. (1 Corinthians 11:27-31)

Christ is present, distributed, and received by all who commune. Consequently, it is vital that those who commune have faith and are properly prepared to receive him.

## Other Interpretations of the Lord's Supper

Real presence is not a scientific or philosophical explanation; it is a deliberate position of faith. Jesus says the bread is his body, so we believe it is. It is a challenge, though, to live with what appears to be an unanswered question. How can this be true? Human reason is uneasy with this uncertainty. Because of this, other Christians may offer different explanations of how Christ is (or is not) present in this meal.

### Transubstantiation

During the Middle Ages, the church tried to explain how the body and blood are present using the physics of Aristotle. Aristotle taught that all material things have an inner **substance** which is its basic nature. These things also have **accidents** which give them their own characteristics. Ordinarily, the substance is reflected in its accidents. For example, the substance of bread is its "breadness." That bread has accidents or attributes such as taste, texture, smell and shape. We have an idea what bread will taste like because it is bread. We do not expect that it will taste like an apple. That "accident" would not be consistent with its "substance." Applying this to the Lord's Supper, the church taught that in the Lord's Supper the inner substances of the bread and wine were replaced by, or changed into, the substances of Christ's body and blood even though the accidents (outward characteristics) of bread and wine remain. This explanation is known as **transubstantiation**, and it remains the official position of Roman Catholicism. The question of how Christ is present has been answered with philosophical tools. This change occurs when a rightly ordained priest conducts the service and says the words of Christ properly.

This explanation is not based solely on Scripture, but involves the use of reason (applied in philosophy) to supplement and explain Scripture. We should note that, even though this method is deficient, the end result is that they do believe that the body and blood of Christ are really there and that they are distributed and received by the communicant. However, though the elements still appear to be bread and wine, this is only in appearance. There is no more bread or wine present; it is entirely and fully the body and blood of Jesus.

The teaching of transubstantiation is generally accompanied by the view of the sacraments known as *ex opere operato.* That is, the sacraments are effective "because of the work that is performed." In this view, the Lord's Supper becomes effective based on the actions of the person consecrating it (or sometimes the person receiving it). This error overlooks the importance of faith which receives the grace that God gives in the Supper.

While transubstantiation is an error, it is a minor error compared to its application in the Roman Catholic Mass. Traditional Roman Catholicism (which was in practice at the time of the Reformation) maintained that after the bread and wine were transubstantiated into the body and blood of Jesus, the priest would then take that body and blood and offer it to God as a sacrifice for sin. He did not "kill Jesus" on the altar, but he offered the body of Christ to God to atone for our sins. Participation in this "sacrifice" was a good work that earned merit before God. This notion reversed the Lord's gift. Where Jesus gave us his body and said "take this, eat it," the sacrifice of the mass hands the body back to God and says, "you take this." This clearly is not the Lord's institution. Christ's death on the cross was the sacrifice for the sins of the whole world. He finished the work there (John 19:30). There is no more need to sacrifice for sins.

Modern Roman Catholic theologians no longer teach that the Mass is a repetition of Christ's sacrifice, but instead teach that the Mass "re-presents" his sacrifice to God and to us. This shift in teaching still suggests that the sacrament is a human work instead of divine grace.

### The Spiritual Presence of Christ

A second view of the Lord's Supper was advocated by John Calvin and is still held by some who follow his theology. Calvin rightly thought that the presence of Christ was a direct application of the doctrine of Christology. Unfortunately, his Christology was strongly influenced by reason, and so reason affected his doctrine of the Eucharist as well as his Christology.

Calvin believed that Christ was fully divine and fully human, but he maintained that a finite human nature was incapable of possessing the fullness of the divine nature. "The finite is incapable of the infinite," he claimed. Even though Jesus Christ is the Son of God, his human body limits what he can do. God is omnipresent, but human beings must be locally present. We must be in only one place at one time. Calvin reasoned that because Jesus was human, his human nature needed to be locally present somewhere. Where is Jesus? Scripture teaches that he ascended into heaven and sits at the right hand of the Father (Acts 2:33). If Jesus is locally present there, he cannot be simultaneously present in the sacrament in another place. Consequently, it is impossible for Jesus to be bodily present in the sacrament. This position may seem logical, but it hardly does justice to Christ's words and promise.

If this is true, what is happening in the Lord's Supper? Calvin wanted to believe the words of Christ, so he came up with a new description. In Communion, a Christian receives only bread and wine with his mouth. At the same time, however, the Spirit enables his soul to reach up to heaven by faith where it spiritually partakes of Christ. This idea is based, in part, on a Platonic philosophy that the soul can receive heavenly things but the body can only receive earthly elements. Calvin certainly believed that something happens in the Lord's Supper. He believed that the communicant receives Christ. Christ is, in a way, really present, but he is not present or received in his body and blood. The words of Jesus are thus reinterpreted to fit the limits of logic.

### A Symbolic Meal or Memorial Meal

A final view is more prevalent among Protestants than the view just discussed. Accepting the same limitations that troubled Calvin, some Christians respond by teaching that the body and blood of Christ are not in the bread and wine at all. Instead, they think that the earthly elements only point to or symbolize a heavenly reality. They are only a symbol of something spiritual or a reminder of the work that Christ has done. They do not deliver any gifts such as forgiveness, life, or salvation, because food cannot do such things. The celebration of Communion does not deliver any benefits; it merely helps one remember what Christ has already done. It is, in effect, an object lesson, or a memento to help us recall something very important. But it is not what Jesus said it was: his body and blood given for our forgiveness.

This teaching, along with spiritual presence, robs the Lord's Supper of Christ's body and blood for forgiveness and turns it into a mere symbolic or memorial meal which we do to remember what Christ has done. The focus is upon our work of doing and remembering and not upon the Lord giving his gifts.

## The Use of the Lord's Supper

The belief of what is received in the Lord's Supper affects the use of this sacrament by Christians. One who believes that Christ is truly present will administer and use this gift in a very different manner than someone who believes that it is only a symbol. Christians are often aware of varying Eucharistic practices, but they may not see that these directly result from belief about its meaning and significance. Issues such as who will commune in a Christian congregation, how communion is distributed and in what contexts, and how excess elements are dealt with often reflect the theology of the person doing these things.

## Admission to the Lord's Supper

The Lord's Supper brings Christ to us, but it also unites us with our fellow communicants. Since we are united with him in this meal, we are also united with all who are in Christ (1 Corinthians 10:17) Those who commune together are confessing a common faith and entering into an intimate relationship. For this reason, Christians have always been concerned with a unity of faith, particularly as we commune together. Additionally, while recognizing that the Lord's Supper is a great blessing that can be taken for our good, we also realize that it is possible to take it in a harmful manner (1 Corinthians 11). For these reasons, the Christian church throughout the centuries has been concerned with who communes at her altar.

Historically, the church has never admitted anyone to the Lord's Supper who has not been baptized. Jesus celebrated the first Eucharist with his disciples (Mark 14:17). In the Great Commission, he told his church to make disciples by baptizing and teaching them to observe everything he commanded (Matthew 28:18-20). The Lord's Supper does not bring someone into the kingdom of God as Baptism does, but strengthens and confirms the faith of those already in his kingdom. Similarly in the Old Testament, an uncircumcised male did not partake of the Passover (Exodus 12:48). One who wishes to commune should first be baptized.

Secondly, St. Paul writes that a person should examine himself before he takes the Sacrament. This examination involves faith (what do I believe?) and an examination of sin (which will inevitably lead to confession). The church has always offered confession (self-examination) and absolution in order to prepare those who intend to go the Lord's Supper. For the church does not admit to the Lord's Supper those who do not know why they come or what they seek. It has refused to let those who deceive themselves about God's word or the Christian life believe that there is unity of faith or life where that unity is broken. Thus the church "excommunicates" in order to save the person who confesses contrary to God's word or lives contrary to his word. A person who is unwilling or unable to examine himself should not be communed. For this reason, most Christian churches do not commune young children or others who are incapable of self examination. Likewise, they generally have some period of instruction given to children or adolescents before they are communed. This instruction often ends in the human rite of **confirmation**.

Since one may partake of the Lord's Supper to their harm (1 Corinthians 11:28-31), the church practices **closed communion**. Closed communion is the sharing of the Lord's Supper by those of the same confession of the Lord. Those who confess Christ crucified in every article of the faith are invited to partake of the Lord's Supper. Those who have a different confession should not partake of the Lord's Supper. One cannot confess Christ in one article of the faith and deny him in another article of the faith. That is a contradiction.

Lest anyone take it to their harm, they are asked not to commune. Closed communion is often called **close communion**. These two terms mean the same thing. It is "close" not in the sense of "we believe close to the same thing" but that those who commune are "close together" or "intimate." In other words, they share a common confession and faith. The practice of **open communion**, where all are freely admitted to the Lord's Supper, is a recent practice in the Christian church in which the confession of Christ crucified in every article of the faith is not recognized nor highly treasured.

The practice of admission to the Lord's Supper calls for thoughtful, biblical reflection both on the part of the communicant and on the part of the congregation. It is wrong to commune one who is unprepared for the Lord's Supper and so might take it to their harm. It is likewise wrong to refuse communion to one who is prepared and worthy to receive it and thus keep them from its benefits. For this reason, communicants and pastors alike are to be reminded of the importance of a strong and open pastoral relationship.

We should also note that, while the practice of closed communion is the practice of the ancient church and is practiced by many Christians today, it often is directly related to the view of the presence of Christ confessed. A church (or a Christian) who does not believe that Christ is present would have reason to exclude anyone from the sacrament. If nothing is happening, no harm can result. A church that believes that Christ is bodily present (including Roman Catholics, Lutherans and others) will be much more likely to take the warnings of 1 Corinthians 11 seriously and, out of concern for the communicant's well being, take steps to ensure that those who take the Lord's Supper are properly prepared.

### Preparing to Commune

Self-examination is not only for visitors and guests who might join a congregation for the Eucharist, it is part of the preparation of every communicant. Christians preparing for the sacrament need to be aware of their spiritual condition. Worthiness for partaking of the Lord's Supper does not have to do with how holy we are or ridding ourselves of sin before we go to the Lord's Supper. If we could get rid of our sin before going to the Lord's Supper, we would not need the Lord's Supper because it is for the forgiveness of sin. Worthiness has to do with our confession that we are unworthy and that we are sinful and in need of forgiveness. Thoughtful preparation should focus on the words of Scripture. Contemplation of the Ten Commandments, or example, will reveal the need for grace. That awareness is accompanied by faith in Christ. He is the sacrifice for our sins; he has secured our forgiveness. He feeds us with himself and grants us his forgiveness. Reflection on these truths is part of the preparation for the Supper.

Additionally, there are other disciplines that a Christian may follow in preparation for the Lord's Supper. Many Christians find it meaningful to fast before they commune, so that the first food they receive that day is the body and blood of Christ. Some find it helpful to read specific portions of Scripture and to pray. Some find that the texts of the liturgy (which come from Scripture) are beneficial for reflection. Christians should be encouraged to find practices that are consistent with God's word and that are helpful to them in taking the Supper. We should always be aware, however, that while such preparations may be useful, they are not required. A discipline that is meaningful to one Christian might be an obstacle to another. Christians may legitimately use a diversity of practices. But, as Luther reminds us, one is

truly worthy and prepared when we have faith in the words of Christ. Believing his words, and believing in him, we are ready.

### *The Lord's Supper as a Congregation's Meal*

When Christ instituted the Lord's Supper, it was in the presence of his
disciples; they all communed. As St. Paul teaches the Corinthians about the
Sacrament, he speaks of their use of this gift together. There is no biblical
evidence of the Lord's Supper being administered in any private way. This
meal is always celebrated corporately. The Lord's Supper is a gift to all the
Lord's people in the congregation. It was not instituted for private use or
for use by certain groups within the congregation. When groups within the
congregation take the Eucharist unto themselves and celebrate it apart from
the whole congregation, division or schism may result. This action may
display a partisan spirit which abuses the Lord's gift. Thus a pastor should
never celebrate communion for himself alone. This is not the right use of the
Eucharist. Similarly, it is inappropriate to have a service at which only part
of the congregation (just the bride or groom at a wedding, for example) is
invited to commune. The congregation celebrates this meal together. The
pastor, whom they have called to this public ministry, consecrates the elements and admits to the Lord's Table. Anyone who is eligible and prepared
to commune is then given the opportunity to receive Christ's body and
blood. This is the normative practice of the Lord's Supper.

There is, however, an important concession that needs to be made in
special circumstances. The church has always taken the Lord's Supper to
those who are ill or infirm and unable to join the congregation at the celebration of his meal. This is not a case of divisiveness, but of inability to come
to the main service. In such a situation, a member should confidently ask for
communion and the pastor should gladly serve it. In fact, when this is done,
other eligible communicants may also participate, thus reminding the ill or
homebound person that they are part of the larger church, even while they
also receive the benefits of the Sacrament.

### The Blessings of the Means of Grace

The means of grace demonstrate the lavish love of God. He has freely
saved us through the work of Christ alone. He makes the benefits of that
saving work freely and commonly available through human language, water,
bread, and wine. He does not hide his grace or put difficult conditions on it.
He does not ask for mystical quests, impossible tasks, or obscure things. He
comes to us simply, gently, lovingly. Indeed, He gives us his grace over and
over again in so many ways that we do not lack opportunity to receive it.

All of the means of grace convey the full forgiveness of all sins. You don't get part of your sins forgiven through each gift or each means of grace. Either you have forgiveness or you have rejected it. It is not helpful to play one gift off against another and act as if, when forgiveness is received through one gift, the other gifts are not needed. This might easily lead to a despising of the gifts and rejection of the forgiveness the Lord gives. Rather than receive forgiveness through one gift and then see no need of the other gifts, each means is received uniquely. Each gift is treasured for all that the Lord gives in the way he has promised. The Christian does well to ponder the unique ways in which God gives his grace in each of the means and the unique way in which we receive and experience it. How does the Lord give forgiveness in baptism differently than anywhere else and how do we experience it? How does he uniquely forgive in the Lord's Supper? In what way is his grace given uniquely in the preaching of the Gospel? Seen in such a way, each gift is treasured, sought after, and received with joy.

He gives us the perfect gift: Christ and his righteousness. He gives this gift in many ways. And his gift is always available, just where he promised it would be.

---

### Key Terms

| | |
|---|---|
| Absolution | Gospel |
| Accidents | Means of Grace |
| Adiaphora | Open communion |
| Baptism | Penance |
| Close/closed | Real presence |
| communion | Sacrament |
| Confession | Substance |
| Confirmation | Transubstantiation |
| Eucharist | Words of institution |
| *Ex opere operato* | |

## For Review and Discussion

1.  God is free to act apart from the means of grace, but we should always "test the spirits" to see if something really is from God. How should Christians evaluate whether something really comes from God? How might it endanger faith to assume that any miraculous, supernatural, or revelatory event comes from God?

2.  Why do you think people are so willing to make baptism into a mere symbol or a human work? What might you do or say to help them view baptism in a more biblical way?

3.  A friend delays baptism for their newborn baby, saying that they want to wait until their child is old enough to choose for himself and to understand baptism. What might you say to help these parents see the legitimacy and importance of infant baptism? How could you keep the Gospel dominant in this conversation?

4.  Absolution is sometimes referred to as "the forgotten sacrament." How can a recovery of a biblical understanding of this gift strengthen our faith? How might it strengthen our churches, families, and other relationships?

5.  When presented with the Lord's Supper, some Christians ask, "how often do we have to commune?" How does this question demonstrate a confusion of Law and Gospel? How would you respond to their question?

## For Further Reading

*Admission to the Lord's Supper: Basics of Biblical and Confessional Teaching* A report of the Commission on Theology and Church Relations of the Lutheran Church – Missouri Synod. St. Louis, Missouri: The Lutheran Church – Missouri Synod, 1999.

Bartels, Ernest. *Take Eat, Take Drink: The Lord's Supper through the Centuries.* St. Louis: Concordia Publishing House, 2004.

Chemnitz, Martin. *Ministry, Word, and Sacraments: An Enchiridion.* Translated by Luther Poellot. St. Louis: Concordia Publishing House, 1981.

Das, Andrew. *Baptized into God's Family.* Milwaukee: Northwestern Publishing House, 1992.

Jeremias, Joachim. *Infant Baptism in the First Four Centuries.* Philadelphia: Westminster Press, 1962.

_____. *The Origin of Infant Baptism.* Naperville, Illinois: A. R. Allenson, 1963.

Saarnivaara, Uuras. *Scriptural Baptism: a Dialog Between John Baptstead and Martin Childfont.* New York: Vantage Press, 1953.

*Theology and Practice of the Lord's Supper.* A report of the Commission on Theology and Church Relations of the Lutheran Church—Missouri Synod. St. Louis, Missouri: The Lutheran Church—Missouri Synod, 1983.

# 13

# The Church

I can be a Christian all by myself. I have faith, God hears my prayers, forgives my sins, and I read my Bible. If I want to hear what someone else has to say, I can read a book, listen to the radio, watch TV, or search the internet. Why do I need the church or any organized religion?

Our society prizes individualism and personal responsibility. We are taught not to depend on other people and to take care of ourselves. Individualistic attitudes affect our understanding of the church and other areas of life. The arguments raised in the previous paragraph are common, and they have a point: a person can be a Christian without associating with other Christians. However, this attitude overlooks a wonderful gift of God. From the beginning of creation, God has shown us that we are meant to live in relationship with him and with other people. Knowing our need for other people, and wanting to unite us as his body, he calls us to be the church. This chapter will explore the nature of the church and the blessings that God gives his people as we examine:

1. The Nature of the Church—*Created by God for the good of his people*
2. Attributes of the Church—*Biblical and credal descriptions*
3. Marks of the Church—*God's people gather around word and sacraments*
4. Is the Church Visible?—*Two important realities concerning the church*

## 1. The Nature of the Church

   "Church" is a rather imprecise word. In common speech, it can mean a worship service, a building, a local congregation, or a denomination. Properly speaking, the **church** is the body of Christ, consisting of all true believers from all times. Any of these definitions might be intended by the word "church." Part of the reason that "church" has so many meanings is that the New Testament uses a fairly generic word to describe this gift of God: *ecclesia*. This Greek word originally denoted a meeting or assembly of people—those who have been "called out" from one place to another. It is interesting that Scripture chooses such a neutral, secular word to describe God's people. It could have relied on Hebrew concepts like synagogue or temple, but these words tended to be viewed in a Jewish context. It could likewise have used a number of different Greek words that were common in other religions, but these would also carry baggage. Instead, the New Testament calls the church a gathering. It is the assembly of God's people, called out of the world to be his own. Having chosen this word, it then describes this gathering.

### *Established by God*

   Though human beings are an integral part of the church, it is not a human idea. God establishes the church. He has redeemed us in Jesus Christ, called us to faith, and placed us into relationship with each other. He equips the members of the church with spiritual gifts and calls ministers to serve in his church (1 Corinthians 12:28). The true church belongs to God (Acts 20:28, 1 Corinthians 1:2). She includes human beings, but humans do not establish the church, bring her into being, or cause her success. God does all this.
   Christ Jesus is the Savior and head of the church (Ephesians 5:23). He "loved the church and gave himself up for her that he might sanctify her, having cleansed her by the washing of water with the word. . . that she might be holy and without blemish" (Ephesians 5:25-27). While the Savior graciously allows his people to serve in his church, he says "I will build my church" (Matthew 16:18). Descriptions of the earliest days of the Christian church show that as they worshipped together, God was daily adding people to this body (Acts 2:42-47). Together they shared in God's blessings, proclaimed his word, were fed with the body and blood of Jesus and baptized in the triune name of God. God established his church, and through her, he blesses his people.

*Describing the Church*

To help us understand the church and the blessings that God provides in and through it, the Bible describes the church with a number of images. All of these pictures demonstrate two aspects to the church: "vertical" and "horizontal" dimensions. The "vertical" is our relationship with God. Unless we belong to him and believe in him, we are not part of the church. The "horizontal" consists of the relationships that we have with other Christians in the church. Without the "vertical," the church would be just another human organization—a social club or association. Without the "horizontal", we might be Christians, but we would not be the church; we would be unable to carry out the tasks that our Lord has placed before us. While our relationship with our Savior is primary, both of these dimensions are important to our understanding of the church, and both are part of God's plan for us.

One biblical image for the church is a flock of sheep being led by a shepherd. Jesus himself used this description. "My sheep hear my voice and I know them, and they follow me. I give them eternal life and they will never perish" (John 10:27-28). Jesus is the Good Shepherd (John 10:11, 14) who seeks the lost sheep to give them life and safety (Luke 15:4-7). This image is also reflected when Christians refer to their clergy as pastors, since "pastor" is derived from the Latin word for "shepherd." Pastors care for God's flock under the guidance of Christ the Good Shepherd.

Another biblical image for the church is a bride. Ephesians 5 compares the relationship of Christ to the church with the relationship of a husband to his bride. He loves the church, gives everything for her, even his own life, so that she will live in beauty and holiness with him forever (Ephesians 5:23-32).[1] Revelation likewise describes the church as a beautiful bride (Revelation 21:2,9,10). This metaphor richly portrays the vertical relationship of love that we receive from God himself. A similar familial relationship is that of the family. Ephesians 2:19 calls Christians members of God's household and fellow citizens. God's people live together as one family. He is our Father, Jesus is our brother (Hebrews 2:11). Christians are part of one family together.

Many biblical passages compare the church to a building. Jesus is described as the foundation (1 Corinthians 3:11), or as the cornerstone that holds the rest of the building together (Ephesians 2:20). The apostles and prophets, grounded in Christ, are next in the building (Ephesians 2:20).

---

[1] The fact that Ephesians 5 is often seen as a controversial passage about the relationships of husbands and wives shows that we have not read this in light of Christ. Our human relationships always fall short of the perfection of the Savior.

> The Church has tra-
> ditionally been described
> with feminine pronouns.
> The Church is not an "it"
> but a "she." This reflects
> the biblical image of the
> church as the bride of
> Christ. Retaining this
> biblical vocabulary helps
> us understand that the
> Church is in a loving rela-
> tionship with her God and
> Savior.

Other Christians are the "living stones" from which the rest of the building is built (1 Peter 2:5). The building would not exist at all without Christ, nor would it be complete if he did not build it. We might be stones, but we would not be the intended building. This image is intensified when Scripture describes us as not simply any building but as a Temple (2 Corinthians 6:16). The Temple is the dwelling place of God—he lives in his church.

Yet another familiar image of the church is the body of Christ. Individual members are like the parts of a body. Each is connected to the others and is needed by the rest of body (1 Corinthians 12:12-27, Romans 12:4-5). This image is often used as a way to discuss the uniqueness of gifts of individual members of the body. This is a legitimate application but it should never be forgotten that this passage teaches that we are not many separate individuals but one body. Our calling is to be part of the whole church. Above all, we should recognize that these passages teach that while there are many individual parts of the body, there is only one head: Jesus Christ (Colossians 1: 18, Ephesians 1:22-23). It is his body, and he is in control.

## 2. Attributes of the Church

These metaphors of the church all reveal important things, showing us the horizontal and vertical relationships that are found in the church. Scripture also offers direct descriptions that aid understanding. These have often been summarized in the language of the Nicene Creed: "I believe in. . . one, holy, catholic and apostolic church." These attributes are taught by Scripture, but they may be hard for us to recognize in this world. It may appear that these are only an ideal or a goal which has not yet been attained. Yet in the Creed, the church confesses what we believe to be true according to God's word. These are valid descriptions of the church when she is viewed with his standards.

### One

The first attribute of the church may seem like an unusual claim. How can Christians say they believe in one church when there are so many denominations and divisions in the church? The answer is that there are two perspectives from which we view the church. When we look from a merely human point of view, we see many congregations, denominations and other groups. But when we examine the church from God's perspective, something else is seen.

> There is one body and one Spirit—just as you were called to the one hope that belongs to your call —⁵one Lord, one faith, one baptism, ⁶one God and Father of all, who is over all and through all and in all. (Ephesians 4:4-6)

Since the true church consists of all believers in Christ, from God's perspective (and properly speaking) there is only one church. This will be discussed in more detail below under the heading, "Is the church visible?"

### Holy

If the belief in one church is surprising, the credal confession of a holy church may seem utterly absurd. Scandals, betrayals of trust, and repeated acts of sin make many skeptical of any claims that the church is holy. Those who avoid churches often note the presence of hypocrites and sinners inside the church. Is the church holy? Once again, it is necessary to consider things from God's perspective. The church consists of forgiven sinners. We may recognize sin in their lives, but if they are in Christ Jesus, they are holy and forgiven. So it is with the church. Jesus does not find the church holy and love her because of this. He finds her sinful and makes her holy (Ephesians 5:25-27). The church is holy because her members have been clothed with the holiness of Jesus.

### Catholic

A third credal affirmation of the church is that it is **catholic**. This description may make some Christians uncomfortable because they consider it to be the name of one particular denomination. Properly speaking, catholic is not the name of a denomination (that is more accurately called the Roman Catholic church), but is a statement of the universality and unity of the one church that transcends denominational lines. Catholic refers to the completeness of the church. Her members come from all nations and languages (Revelation 5:9,10) throughout the world. When we confess that we believe in the catholic church, we proclaim that Christianity does not belong to one nation, ethnicity, language group or even denomination. All who belong to Jesus are part of the catholic church.

## Apostolic

The fourth creedal characteristic of the church is that she is **apostolic**. This simply means that the things that were taught by the first Christians are still being taught today. The apostolic and prophetic Scriptures are still the only infallible source of doctrine. The church is built on the foundation of the apostles and prophets (Ephesians 2:20). The true Christian church is not to invent new teachings, but to remain faithful to the inspired Scriptures, the teaching of the apostles (Acts 2:42).

## Enduring

One further attribute of the church, though not explicitly mentioned in the Creed, is nonetheless worthy of consideration at this point. Christ establishes his church. He builds her, blesses her, and causes her to prosper. He also promises that his church will endure. Though she may face persecution and trials, the true church will endure until Jesus returns. There will always be Christians on earth. Jesus promises that even the gates of hell will not overcome his church (Matthew 16:18). This does not mean that every congregation will exist forever, but that there will always be Christians on earth, and they will always be joined together in Christ's church.

## 3. Marks of the Church

The church exists, by Christ's commission, to minister to his people, but what is this ministry? Congregations today are often involved in a wide range of activities including worship, education, social ministry, fellowship activities, counseling, family programs, entertainment and any number of additional functions. Some of these things may be distinctly Christian, others less so. While Christians and congregations can legitimately join in many activities together, these may not all be the specific tasks prescribed by Scripture.

## Word and Sacrament

The means of grace are consistently at the heart of biblical descriptions of the church. The reason for this is simple: without God's grace, the church would simply be another human organization. The church exists to gather God's people around his grace, and to ensure that his grace is continually applied to individuals who need it. For this reason, the means of grace are often called the **marks of the church**. Christians, and the church, may be found where the means of grace are found.

Christians gather around the word of God. The Bible, and particularly the proclamation of the Gospel, is one of the marks of the church. Without God's word, we would hear only the words of humans. God's word, rightly preached, is an essential treasure of the church. Acts 2:42 says that the early Christians devoted themselves to the apostles' teaching—in other words, to the Scriptures. Jesus tells us that his disciples will abide in his word (John 8:31). While we can, and should, read the Scriptures individually, we are also called to read and hear them together.

As we hear and apply the word of God, we also learn of other marks of the church. The Christian church is marked by baptism, since Christ commissioned us to baptize (Matthew 28:18-20), and baptism incorporates us into the church. The church will proclaim the forgiveness of sins since this is part of his will for us (John 20:23). Christians will share in the Lord's Supper as they gather together as the church, since this, too, is part of Christ's gracious will for us (1 Corinthians 11:23-26). When we see the marks of the church—the means of grace—being used according to Christ's institution, we are seeing the church.

*Other Activities of the Church*

The means of grace, and therefore Christ, are always at the center of the church. They are publicly administered in worship. They are present in the biblical teaching of the church, and in many other activities. Scripture describes many other things that Christians do either individually or together. They serve God by helping each other and the world around us (Ephesians 4:12). They work together to spread the Gospel throughout the world (Acts 1:8). They serve in various vocations in society. Many of the activities of the church are things done in addition to the ministry of word and sacrament. These can be helpful and wholesome activities, and may serve many good purposes. Christians should be careful, however, that other activities do not replace or eclipse the divinely given means of grace. Without the true marks of the church, we are only a human organization. When we use the gifts that he gives us, and apply them according to his word, he promises his blessings.

## 4. Is the Church Visible?

The marks of the church are visible things. One can see that the sacraments are being administered and hear the word proclaimed. Does this mean that we can identify the church in its entirety? The marks of the church present the same challenge already seen in the attributes of the church. Both reveal that the church presents us with two realities: human and divine. Because the church is made up of sinful human beings, the effects of that sin are seen in the church. Likewise, the church is the creation of God, made and redeemed by him. His word describes it in terms that reflect this reality. An individual Christian can be described as both justified and sinful at the same time. Similarly, the church is holy and sinful, united and divided, faithful and straying. The tension between these two realities can be difficult. Much of this difficulty stems from the fact that we simply cannot see the things that God sees. He alone knows the hearts of all humans. When we speak of the church, it is important to distinguish the full reality that God sees from the things that we are able to see. Two different aspects of the church reveal themselves. These are often described as the "invisible" church and the "visible" church.

### The "Visible" and "Invisible" Church

A distinction such as this must be made when we account for the differing types of knowledge that we have. Properly speaking, the church consists of all true believers in Christ from all times. There is only one church, and it includes every single Christian—even those not yet born. Since membership in this church is determined by faith, only one who can truly see the heart of each person can truly know who belongs to it. A person might give false witness about their belief, claiming to belong to God, but in reality be a hypocrite or an unbeliever. Sadly, people sometimes join churches for wrong reasons. They may want to impress another person, increase their business contacts, or want to find a spouse. They may become members of that congregation, but if they do not truly have faith, they are not truly members of the one, holy, catholic, and apostolic church. God alone sees the heart, and he knows if a person is a hypocrite. He knows who really belongs to him (2 Timothy 2:19). For this reason, the one, catholic, true church is often called the **invisible church**—only God can truly see it.

This one true church transcends all human boundaries. It includes people who are members of different denominations, and people who have not joined any congregation. By God's grace, it can even include people who are part of heretical churches and cults. If they have true faith in Christ and trust in him, they are Christians and part of this church. (Of course, it is difficult to be in this position. Heretical churches and cults lead people away from the Gospel. A person would need to be ignorant of what their church believes, or reject it to be in this position. Discovering the truth, they should seek an orthodox church.)

We cannot see the heart or judge the sincerity of faith of another person, and we cannot see the completeness of the "invisible church." Yet this does not mean that we have no knowledge about the identity of other Christians or the presence of the church. Through the marks of the church and the confession of Christians, we can identify the presence of the church on earth. This is frequently called the **visible church**, because it is manifest before our eyes. The visible church is identified by the marks of the church. Where the means of grace are present and people confess their faith, we see a manifestation of the visible church. Because we cannot see the heart, the visible church will include hypocrites and unbelievers (Matthew 13:24-29). It will include people who do not always present the Scriptures accurately or administer the sacraments faithfully. We evaluate visible churches on the basis of their confession and teaching. If they are presenting the Gospel of Jesus Christ rightly, they are part of the visible church. We will also assume that all who share in this confession are part of the invisible church, while remembering that only God has the ability to know this completely.

*One Church, Many Churches*

These two realities give rise to a challenging problem for Christians. If there really is only one church (the invisible church) how do we account for the many divisions in that one church. If the truth is found in Scripture, why are there so many different descriptions of it? Where do all these visible churches come from?

*Geographical and Functional Divisions*

One reason for the many churches is natural and even positive. There are many churches and congregations because there are many Christians. If there were no denominational differences, there would still be many different congregations in different places. Cities would likewise have multiple congregations to effectively minister to the many people who live there. This simple truth is often overlooked by those who use the number of congregations as an argument against Christianity. Even in the New Testament era there were many congregations—some in the same city (see 1 Corinthians 16:19).

## Doctrinal Divisions

There are, however, serious and sinful reasons for divisions between churches as well. One of the most significant reasons is that Christians do not always agree on the content of Christianity. Doctrinal disagreements cause division in the church. Often such disagreements have their root in disagreements about the inspiration or authority of Scripture. They may likewise involve reliance on non-biblical sources of information. One need only consider some of the topics in the previous chapters to see that different denominations and churches have radically different theological positions. These differences of doctrine can easily divide the church.

Other divisions occur when some Christians insist that everyone reach identical conclusions on issues of adiaphora. Demanding uniformity on matters that the Scriptures leave open can be a sign of weakness or immaturity of faith. In other cases, it might indicate a desire to restrict the legitimate Christian freedom of other people. When human opinions are elevated to the level of God's word, divisions often follow.

When a doctrinal disagreement continues without resolution, a more permanent schism may be introduced into the church. This may result in a **denomination**, or organized religious group. While there are independent Christian congregations, most choose to affiliate with other like-minded congregations in a denomination. Congregations join in such groupings to enable them to do work together that they would not be able to do alone. Ordinarily, denominations share a common confession of faith (though in some denominations, it may be very loosely defined) and a common vision for ministry. Recent years have seen more "non-denominational" churches. While these appear to be independent congregations, many non-denominational churches affiliate with other congregations in cooperative agreements, networks, or other organizational structures. While such arrangements are often more flexible than the traditional denominations, they are, for all practical purposes, denominations.

All Christians should be disturbed by doctrinal divisions and should pray and work for unity of faith (see John 17:21). Christians should continually study the Scriptures to ensure that they are teaching according to God's word and not merely presenting our own ideas. We should listen carefully to other Christians to ensure that we understand them correctly. But we should not simply agree to disagree or pretend that doctrinal differences do not matter. If theology was a human system of thought, the differences might not matter, but we should be careful to hold to the true word of God. We are not free to remove biblical teachings just so that we can get along better with those who deny them.

## Sin Causes Divisions

Yet we would do well to admit that not all divisions are entirely doctrinal. Many divisions and tensions in the church are caused, or increased in severity, by the sinful actions of those involved in them. Certainly it is sinful to teach false doctrine, but sin goes beyond this. Congregations and larger church bodies can be torn apart by the sinful acts of their members, and by the equally sinful refusal to forgive those who are penitent. At times human pride and arrogance can hide behind a doctrinal argument. As we strive for the true unity of the church in word and sacrament, we should be willing to examine our own sinful contributions to divisions.

## Two Opposite Errors

The many divisions in Christianity should disturb us. Jesus prayed that his disciples would be one. We also should pray and work for the true unity of the church. As we strive for unity, two opposite errors may emerge. The first is to forge an external unity without resolving doctrinal disagreements. This places a higher value on external unity than on a unity of faith. This may take the form of **unionism**, which seeks to hide doctrinal division in an external gathering. Those involved in unionism may "agree to disagree" or may say that an issue cannot be settled, even when Scripture addresses it. Certainly there are issues where Christians may legitimately disagree, but unionism ignores the need to share a common faith in areas where the Scriptures are clear. Unionism looks good externally, but it denies the truth of Scripture. A related error, known as syncretism, takes this even further. Instead of simply allowing people to hold different teachings, as unionism does, **syncretism** mixes features of different religions together, in effect creating a new religion. Unionism and syncretism are appealing to our culture, but they compromise the truth of God's word.

An opposite error may be made by those who are rightly wary of unionism or syncretism. A desire to share a common faith that is grounded in the Scriptures may be distorted to include things that Scripture does not demand, or to insist on interpretations that may not be justified by a biblical text. While divisions may be a sad necessity in the case of some disagreements, it is perilously easy to make the standard of faith higher than the Scriptures. This may lead to **sectarianism**, an unnecessary and sinful divisiveness. It is wrong to pretend we have doctrinal agreement with those who believe differently than we do. It is equally wrong to create division without biblical reason. Both of these extremes are inconsistent with Holy Scripture.

## *Church Fellowship*

When congregations and denominations have doctrinal agreement, they should acknowledge this, rejoice in it, and gladly work together in Christ's kingdom. Churches that are in doctrinal agreement may formalize this agreement by joining in church fellowship. "**Fellowship**" may mean many different things, but in this context, it refers to churches that share a common confession of faith and a willingness to work together. Churches that are in fellowship together may cooperate in a variety of different areas, they may share pastors and resources, and their members may be encouraged to worship and commune in the other churches. Fellowship is a formal recognition of biblical agreement. By definition, congregations that are part of a denomination are in fellowship with the other congregations in their denomination. (Though this may be doubted and even shattered in time of controversy.) Fellowship agreements may also include other denominations, or churches in other countries.

Because fellowship is a function of the "visible" church, it is based on the faith that is confessed and taught by each church. It is not a judgment of the sincerity of the church. It is not to be based on simple emotion or will, but on the faith that is publicly proclaimed. When an individual Christian joins a congregation, he confesses the faith of that congregation and joins in their fellowship. As part of the "body," each member should be aware that their actions affect the other members of their church. Because of this, individual members should ordinarily follow the fellowship practices of their congregation.

## *Choosing a Congregation*

**Congregations** are groups of Christians who share a common faith. As they gather around the means of grace, they proclaim that faith and seek to bring other people to be disciples of Jesus and to confess that faith with them. Because of the eternal significance of these things, church membership is a serious matter. No congregation is perfect, but a Christian should seek a congregation that faithfully proclaims God's word and administers the sacraments according to Christ's institution. If errors arise, they should be corrected on the basis of God's word. While God's word is present in many places, the faithful Christian should seek a congregation where it is proclaimed in its truth.

## The Beauty of the Church

A close examination of the church can be frustrating. When we look at the past and present of the church, we often see things that we wish we could ignore. We see the effects of sin, and we see weaknesses. Yet if we look with a divine perspective, we see something different. St. Paul wrote:

> . . .Christ loved the church and gave himself up for her, [26]that he might sanctify her, having cleansed her by the washing of water with the word, [27]so that he might present the church to himself in splendor, without spot or wrinkle or any such thing, that she might be holy and without blemish. (Ephesians 5:25-27)

This is what God sees when he looks at the church. He sees his bride. He does not find the church as a holy and beautiful thing. He finds sinners who are lost without him, and in his grace, he loves them. So Christ comes, gives himself for the church, cleanses her with baptism, teaches her in the word, and feeds her with his body and blood. He makes the church something new: a beautiful, holy bride. Just as he makes each one of us his people, so he sanctifies his church.

| Key Terms | |
|---|---|
| Apostolic | Invisible church |
| Catholic | Marks of the church |
| Church | Sectarianism |
| Congregation | Syncretism |
| Denomination | Unionism |
| Fellowship | Visible Church |

## For Review and Discussion

1. This chapter noted a certain vagueness to the word "church." Sometimes Christians will insist that we not say "I went to church on Sunday." Why do you think they object to this phrase? Do you think it is a legitimate concern?

2. The book of Ephesians devotes considerable attention to the church. Read through this Epistle, paying particular attention

to what St. Paul teaches about the church. What insights do you gain as you do this?

3.  The church has both horizontal and vertical dimensions and relationships. How does this distinction help explain some of the complexities and benefits of the church?

4.  There are many biblical metaphors for the church (such as a flock, bride, family, building or body). Choose one of these metaphors and search the Scripture for examples of how it describes and illustrates the church.

5.  Sadly, some people have been hurt by their experience of the visible church. What counsel would you give to someone who was avoiding fellowship with other Christians because of past negative experiences?

# 14

# The Christian in Society

One of the most basic human longings is the desire to know our place in the world. How do we fit in? What is expected of us, and what can we expect from others? How do we relate to other people? As the people of God, Christians know that we find our identity and meaning in him, but we may be more confused when we seek to know our place in this world.

Some people speak as if the holiest activities of Christians take place in isolation from the world. A "good" or "serious" Christian is in church all the time or spends a lifetime in silent contemplation and prayer. If this is true, then lesser (or even "bad") Christians are those involved with "worldly" pursuits such as careers, jobs, or families. Perhaps we soften this but still think that those who pursue vocations in the church are serving God while those who have secular vocations are doing something less significant.

These might be common ideas, but they are not biblical. When God calls us to himself, he does not remove us from the world, nor does he call us to abandon all human contact. In fact, this is exactly the opposite of the truth. Instead of isolating us from other people, he places us in significant relationships of love and service in families, friendships, communities, societies and churches. Consequently, the Christian life is not just a matter of how an individual relates to God; it includes involvement with other people. We will consider the role and place of the Christian in society as we examine:

1. One King, Two Kingdoms—*God rules the world in different ways*
2. Vocation—*God provides for our needs through human beings*
3. Government—*God establishes worldly order for our benefit*

## 1. One King, Two Kingdoms

It can be a challenge to deal with the complex issues of life in this world. Christians frequently feel tensions between paradoxical truths. The world was created by the triune God and belongs to him, but it does not recognize or acknowledge him. Christ died to redeem all people, but many reject him and his ways. As the children of God, we know that this fallen world is not really our home, yet God has placed us here. How can we live with these paradoxes?

Some people try to sort out these issues by compartmentalizing their lives. God is for spiritual things. He is proclaimed in worship and Bible studies. He is available to listen to prayers, to forgive, and bless people, but he has no real interest or involvement in the rest of life. Those things are left up to human beings and our efforts. While this may be a popular understanding, it is not how God deals with humanity. God is not interested only in "spiritual" matters. He created the material world. He loves and provides for both Christians and non-Christians (even while desiring that non-Christians come to faith in him). He provides for all creatures. God is not limited by our categories or our understanding. All aspects of our existence are dependent upon him. Yet there is some truth in the idea that we can distinguish between different areas of life. Even though God is interested in both "sacred" and "secular" realms, he works in them in different ways.

### God Rules His Church

God is indeed Lord of the church. All of his people, whom he has called to faith, acknowledge him as savior and king. Though we daily fall into sin and fail our king, he freely forgives us for Christ's sake and blesses us as we live and serve in his kingdom. In this kingdom, he rules by his Gospel. By his grace, he continues to bless and equip us for service. While God can act directly and miraculously to do this, he promises that he will act in his church through the means of grace. Moreover, his word tells us that he wants to give these fatherly blessings to all people. Christ has died for all, and offers all people a place in this kingdom, though only those who receive him in faith will know the blessings of life in this kingdom. Many of the blessings that Christians receive and experience in this life are given to them in this kingdom, and we rejoice that God gives them so freely to us. Because God's greatest desire for human beings is that we hear the Gospel and come to faith, this aspect of his work is sometimes called his "right hand" reign, or "the **kingdom of the right**."

*God Rules Over All Creation*

Of course, we know about the blessings that God gives us in his church. We have already examined these things in more detail in a number of chapters. As wonderful as these gifts are, the Scriptures do not confine God and his work to the church. Indeed, the Lord rules over all creation. As he cares for believers in the church, so he cares for all creatures in this wider kingdom. God gives the gift of life to all creatures. Whether they acknowledge him or not, all creatures owe their existence to the creative work of God. In the same way, he provides for all creatures. All people receive his care and blessings in this life, not just Christians. Jesus reminds us of this, saying,

> Or which one of you, if his son asks him for bread, will give him a stone? [10]Or if he asks for a fish, will give him a serpent? [11]If you then, who are evil, know how to give good gifts to your children, how much more will your Father who is in heaven give good things to those who ask him! (Matthew 7:9-11)

Despite their sinfulness, human parents take care of their children. God, who is holy, provides greater care for all people. Moreover, his gifts are not conditional. They are not a reward for good behavior. Instead, ". . .your Father who is in heaven. . . makes his sun rise on the evil and on the good, and sends rain on the just and on the unjust" (Matthew 5:45). God cares for all people even though none of us deserves his blessings.

God provides for us through these blessings of nature, but these are only the beginning of his providential care. He protects and cares for people through families. He rules and cares for us by providing protection, order and safety through the work of governments. He provides for our daily needs through the work and service of people who strive to perform their jobs well. We tend to consider these things as the work of human beings, but Scripture shows us that God provides for us in these and many other ways.

In our "secular" lives, just as in the church, God can work directly (immediately) or through means (mediately). For example, he may provide us with food by performing a miracle. The Israelites were given the gift of manna by God's direct, immediate action. God can also provide us with food through the labors of farmers, shippers, grocers, and cooks. Either way, our hunger is satisfied. When a person is sick, they rightly pray to God for his healing. God may cure them miraculously, but is the outcome any different if he heals them through the service of doctors, nurses, and pharmacists? Either way, God has cared for them.

God is truly working in his world, but we should recognize that he works in different ways. Here in the world, God works not through the

Gospel but through Law. Governments care for people not by administering the sacraments or forgiving sins but by administering justice. Here God
works mediately by restraining sin and providing order. To distinguish this
work of God from his work in the church, this is sometimes called his "left
hand" rule, or "the **kingdom of the left**." These distinctions are remind-
ers that God works in different ways and with different goals in these two
kingdoms.

*Christians Live in Both Kingdoms*

While God works with different means and objectives in both of these
kingdoms, he works for our good in both. He is the one king who reigns
over both of these kingdoms. Christians are more accustomed to speaking
of God's work in the church than in the world, but we should recognize his
action in both kingdoms. By doing this, we will see more of our Lord's loving care. In addition, we should recognize that he works in both kingdoms
because we live in both kingdoms. We receive his blessings in the church,
but we also are under his care and his rule in the world.

But this is where we often experience tension and challenges. The two
kingdoms operate with different purposes and objectives. The workings
of a government have different aims than the ministry of the church, yet
Christians are called to obey the government (Romans 13:1). In addition, all
institutions that have human involvement are prone to experience the effects
of sin. Governments, families, marriages, and jobs are all prone to failure,
and disappointment. People who serve in the kingdom of the left, and those
who serve in the kingdom of the right are apt to confuse their authority and
their role. So we see Christians trying to advance the mission of the church
through political power, or politicians exploiting religion to gain control or
influence. We may be confused as we live simultaneously in these two kingdoms. These are common problems in this fallen world.

While human sinfulness can frustrate and confuse us, God still reigns
in both kingdoms, and his will is done in spite of human foolishness. We
know great blessings through both his left hand and right hand rule. We have
already examined the rule of God in his church in detail. In this chapter we
consider the workings of God in our lives as we live together in society. We
see God's providential care in our vocations, marriages, families, and in
government. In all of these institutions, God works for our good.

## 2. Vocation

One of the most enduring questions asked by human beings concerns the purpose of our existence. Why are we here? What are we supposed to do in life? As Christians we know that we are here because God loves us and wants us to be his own. Our chief purpose is to be loved by God and, in response, to believe in him and love him. Yet this is not the complete purpose of human existence. We are also here to love and serve other people. The Scriptures continually remind us that we are to serve other people in love. This service includes sharing the Gospel with them, but it also includes caring for physical needs. One of the most significant ways that we serve other people is through vocation.

Many people think of "vocation" only as a synonym for a job, but it is a much broader concept. **Vocation** means a calling. We do not simply function in various jobs; we are called to do certain things. God calls us to service in this world; he has a purpose in mind for us. Our vocations can give us pleasure as we carry out meaningful tasks in the world, they can help provide for our own physical needs, and they can help and serve other people. A person's vocation may include a career, but it is not limited to one job. In fact, all people have multiple vocations. God calls us to various tasks, relationships and responsibilities. Some vocations come at different times of life. For a time, a person may have the vocation of a student. Later (often simultaneously) they may be an employee, and perhaps even later, an employer of other people. All of these are vocations. We may also hold some vocations simultaneously. We may be called to be a member of a family, an employee, and a friend of numerous people. All of these are vocations. Seemingly ordinary tasks, jobs, or relationships can be great blessings from God to us and to others when we see them as he does: as vocations or callings. They are opportunities to serve him by serving other people (see Matthew 25:37-40).

### The Vocation of Work

The work that a person does can be a significant part of their identity. When we meet someone new, we often ask, "what do you do?" Our jobs and careers take up a significant portion of our lives, and are part of the contribution that we make to this world. While our careers can be an important part of our identity, we should be careful to recognize that they are only part. Many people have made their entire identity synonymous with their occupation, but this frequently leads to shallow and unfulfilling lives. Equally shallow, however, is the attitude that sees one's occupation as essentially

*Luther on Vocation*

Martin Luther often spoke of the vocations of lay people and noted that their "ordinary" tasks were often more pleasing to God than the works of monks, nuns, and priests, because they carry out these humble tasks in faith.

"The household tasks of a single faithful servant are more pleasing to God than the contemptible worship and fasts of monks, since the servant's tasks are performed in the Spirit and in faith. And the significance and value of works is in faith and in the Spirit, not in how great or many they are. So a serving girl, who sweeps the floor and milks the cows, worships God in a beautiful way. . . . A student who listens to his teacher in faith should know that he is doing a precious thing." (Lectures on Genesis, chapter 45:24)

meaningless or just a means to make money. Such a narrow view fails to see that our careers and our daily activities can be blessings from God.

As you read this, your thoughts may wander to those whose careers involve professional service in the church. Those called to serve as pastors, teachers, or other positions of ministry and service are rightly said to have a divine calling and vocation. God does raise up these servants for ministry in his church. As important and beneficial as their calling is, these are not the only careers that are vocations. God works through the ministry of pastors and teachers, but he likewise works through the vocations of bankers, cooks, janitors, sales clerks, and countless others. God calls people to service in many careers.  Consider how many vocations are mentioned in Scripture. The Bible is filled with depictions of farmers, shepherds, merchants, musicians, fishermen, judges, kings, tax collectors, soldiers, scribes, tent makers, artists, and many other vocations. In fact, Jesus himself was a carpenter. All of these "jobs" were really vocations: opportunities to serve.

*Christians are Called to Productive Work*

Christians have always been tempted to consider "church work" or "spiritual tasks" to be more important or more holy than "secular" things. Naturally, we want our priorities to be in order. It doesn't matter how good a job we do in our careers or relationships if we lack faith. Yet Christians are often tempted to ignore or neglect their vocations. From the beginning, some Christians have struggled with the idea that the urgency of Christ's return means that we do not have the time to engage in non-spiritual vocations. Some Christians in the early church stopped working in order to wait for Christ's return. Others, even today, think that secular work should be avoided so that we have more time for spiritual tasks. But the Bible warns that we not flee from our vocations under the guise of spirituality. St. Paul taught the Thessalonians,

> Now we command you, brothers, in the name of our Lord Jesus Christ, that you keep away from any brother who is walking in idleness and not in accord with the tradition that you received from us. [7]For you yourselves know how you ought to imitate us, because we were not idle when we were with you, [8]nor did we eat anyone's bread without paying for it, but with toil and labor we worked night and day, that we might not be a burden to any of you. [9]It was not because we do not have that right, but to give you in ourselves an example to imitate. [10]For even when we were with you, we would give you this command: If anyone is not willing to work, let him not eat. [11]For we hear that some among you walk in idleness, not busy at work, but busybodies. [12]Now such persons we command and encourage in the Lord Jesus Christ to do their work quietly and to earn their own living. [13]As for you, brothers, do not grow weary in doing good. (2 Thessalonians 3:6-13)

Earlier, Paul had told the same Christians to work with their own hands so that they would be respected by outsiders and not be dependent on others (1 Thessalonians 4:11-12). While Christians should gladly and willingly help those in need, Paul is concerned that some may exploit their Christian faith, using it as a pretense for laziness. So even though Paul was an apostle, he also made tents to support himself. This does not mean, however, that we should not pay those working in full-time church vocations. In these and other passages, Paul notes that it is appropriate to compensate those who labor in the church (2 Thessalonians 3:9, 1 Corinthians 9:11). He does warn, however, that we do not hide laziness behind a show of piety.

Our vocations allow us to serve the world in very tangible ways. We should also note that Christian involvement in "secular" vocations is often used by God for very sacred purposes. In addition to the productivity of their vocation, these tasks and careers are often a very effective point of contact between believers and unbelievers. Many people in our world will not visit a church. They may resist a visit from a pastor or church worker. They likely will not read materials sent out by a Christian congregation. Yet they may meet and get to know individual Christians as these Christians carry out

their vocations. They may see the lives and hear the witness of these believers who serve in vocation. Countless people have heard the Gospel and
come to faith because of the involvement of Christians in various secular
callings.

## The Vocation of Relationships

As important as the vocation of work is, however, it would be a grave
mistake to limit the concept of vocation to this one aspect of life. Our vocations put us in contact with many people. We now focus on vocations that
place us in deeper relationships with other people, beginning with the very
first human relationship: marriage.

From the beginning of human history, God established marriage as the
cornerstone of society and as a blessing to us. Genesis says that when God
created Adam, he first placed him in Eden and called him to care for the
earth. Yet God also decreed, "It is not good that the man should be alone; I
will make a helper fit for him" (Genesis 2:18. Note that the word "helper"
does not indicate an inferior status but a complementary one. In fact, God
describes himself as our helper). Through marriage, God blesses his children with love, support, companionship, sexual intimacy, and often the gift
of children. God's institution of marriage was meant to bring joy and happiness to his people. Husbands and wives are called to love each other and
be a blessing to each other for the rest of their lives. It is not meant to be a
temporary relationship, but a union of one flesh that endures as long as both
spouses live. To be sure, there are times when they will be unhappy with
their spouse. Husbands and wives will not always have warm feelings for
each other, but they are called to love and forgive each other. With God's
grace, marriages can and do last as relationships of joy and gladness.

Like all of our experiences in this life, however, marriage is also affected by sinfulness. Even the marriage of Adam and Eve, who were joined
directly by God, was affected by the fall into sin. All relationships since then
have been tainted by sin. Some break their marriage vows in unfaithfulness
or divorce. Some remain married but fail to love and care for their spouse
as they promised to do. Even couples with "happy" marriages have conflict
and difficulty, but by grace, they have learned how to deal with these effects
of sin. Those who are called to the vocation of marriage are called by God to
be his agent in caring for their spouse. This is one of the ways God blesses
his people.

Similarly, those called to the vocation of parents are called by God to
care for their children with his love. Parents are to protect, nurture, and teach
their children. They are called to bring them up in a relationship with God.

They model forgiveness and faith to their children. As their children mature, Christian parents can know the joy of knowing their children as fellow-believers and children of God.

Children also are called in a vocation to their parents and their siblings. They are to honor, love, and forgive their parents. They are called to serve them in Christian love and to be a blessing to their parents (even as their parents are to them). These vocational relationships in the family are never to be an excuse for sinful or wicked behavior. The authority of parents and the obedience of children is not absolute. For example, God's word gives no room for abuse in the family. But it does lift up our families and invites all to see these relationships as opportunities to serve him.

Of course, not everyone is called to the same vocations. Some are not called to be married, but are called by God to a single life. Some married couples are not called to be parents. Some children are raised in families that fall short of God's standards and calling. But all people live in relationships that are gifts of God and can be opportunities for service and love. When friendships are seen as vocations from God, we view them in a new light and are given additional opportunities to serve God and others. God can use all of our relationships to his glory and our good.

## Sin Affects Our Vocations

Vocations are a blessing from God, but sinful people can twist God's good gifts into something he never intended them to be. God gives us the vocation of work for our benefit and enjoyment, but many find no joy or satisfaction in their occupation. When they see no meaning or significance in the work that they do, vocation becomes only a way of making money, a means to an end, or just a job. Yet even if we find our vocations meaningful and fulfilling, there remain aspects in every vocation that are unpleasant or a burden. This is not God's design, but the result of sinfulness.

Before the fall into sin had taken place, God called Adam and Eve to vocation: "Be fruitful and multiply and fill the earth and subdue it and have dominion over the fish of the sea and over the birds of the heavens and over every living thing that moves on the earth" (Genesis 1:28). Their creator gave them important and meaningful work to do. They were to fill and subdue the earth, taking care of it and of the other creatures. This responsibility was a gift of God and would bring them great happiness and fulfillment. But their fall into sin affected everything, even their vocation of work. Confronting them with their sin, God says,

> . . .cursed is the ground because of you; in pain you shall eat of it all the days of your life; [18]thorns and thistles it shall bring forth for you; and you shall eat the plants of the field. [19]By the sweat of your face you shall eat bread, till you return to the ground, for out of it you were taken; for you are dust, and to dust you shall return. (Genesis 3:17b-19)

Their sin had transformed the joy of vocation into painful toil and labor. Sin cursed mankind with the burden of frustrating work. In this life, the child of God knows both of these aspects of work. We can experience the delight of a satisfying and productive vocation, but also will know the difficulty and frustration that comes with work in a fallen world.

There is another way in which sin affects vocation. There are some activities and jobs that cannot be seen as a vocation at all, yet are chosen by sinful people for their own purposes. Jobs that are inherently sinful are not vocations. God does not call people into activities that violate his will. One cannot sin to the glory of God! So criminal occupations or jobs that entail a breaking of God's commands are illicit and are not part of God's calling.

## The Freedom of Vocation

Through legitimate vocations, God blesses humanity and provides for our many needs. As we have a responsibility to faithfully engage in the vocations to which we are called, so we also have the joy of allowing others to serve in their vocations. Our society prizes self-reliance. We want to be able to provide for ourselves so that we are not dependent on other people. Yet we are never really self-sufficient. We all depend on other people. Certainly, we should be ready and eager to use our talents and abilities to support ourselves, but we also need to recognize our need for other people. One person simply cannot do everything. God provides us with people in many vocations so that we can serve each other. Christians can legitimately rely on the vocations of other people in this life. We can allow those who have greater ability or expertise in certain areas to be a service to us. (We should also remember to compensate them appropriately). A healthy attitude regarding vocation means that we do not have to do everything ourselves. Allowing others to fulfill their vocations in our lives frees us to carry out our own vocations.

We should allow others to fulfill their vocations. In fact, there are times when we must recognize that we cannot carry out the work of another person's vocation for ourselves. Vocations sometimes include the authority to do certain things. A physician has the authority to administer medications to her patients. While that is a vital part of her vocation, it would be wrong for a teacher to prescribe medication to his students. The teacher lacks the expertise and the authority to usurp the physician's vocation. A police officer has the authority to stop or redirect traffic. A pedestrian who tries to do the same thing might well be arrested, since he does not have the authority to do this. While we serve in our God-given vocations to the best of our ability, we also will let others carry out their vocations in the same way.

## 3. Government

Families provide and care for their members. They bring order and protection to the lives of the family members. That same care, order, and protection is needed when individuals and families live together in larger societies. Such cultures might thrive for a time without a government, but eventually situations will emerge that involve the whole society or that bring two or more individuals or families into conflict. The more people that live in a society, the greater the need for a system of government that will protect and serve all the citizens of that society. The powerful and the strong may be able to protect their own needs, but the measure of a society is how it cares for the needs and preserves the rights of the weak and underprivileged. Additionally, opportunities to be affected by lawless or criminal behavior increase in larger societies. Governments help provide structure to care for and protect citizens.

### God Establishes Government for the Good of All People

Scripture teaches that God has established governments for the benefit of all people. At times this is obvious in the narrative of Scripture. Exodus shows how God established a government for Israel through Moses. When they entered the promised land they were governed by judges and eventually kings. These rulers governed in a **theocracy**. God was the ultimate king, and his Law was the standard of the land. When Israel frequently drifted from the ways of the Lord, he recalled them to the truth of his word. It is relatively easy to see that God established government in Israel. But this theocracy is not the only government established by God. In a critical passage, Romans shows us the extent of God's establishment of governments.

> Let every person be subject to the governing authorities. For there is no authority except from God, and those that exist have been instituted by God. [2]Therefore whoever resists the authorities resists what God has appointed, and those who resist will incur judgment. [3]For rulers are not a terror to good conduct, but to bad. Would you have no fear of the one who is in authority? Then do what is good, and you will receive his approval,

⁴for he is God's servant for your good. But if you do wrong, be afraid, for he does not bear the sword in vain. For he is the servant of God, an avenger who carries out God's wrath on the wrongdoer. ⁵Therefore one must be in subjection, not only to avoid God's wrath but also for the sake of conscience. ⁶For the same reason you also pay taxes, for the authorities are ministers of God, attending to this very thing. ⁷Pay to all what is owed to them: taxes to whom taxes are owed, revenue to whom revenue is owed, respect to whom respect is owed, honor to whom honor is owed. (Romans 13:1-7. See also 1 Peter 2:13-14)

Israel's theocracy was established by God, but so are all other governments. They rule by and with his authority and Christians are commanded to be obedient to them. Those in authority over us are God's servants. These words really are startling when their full meaning is considered. They do not claim merely that good governments are God's servants, or that Christian leaders are his servants. Paul teaches that *all* governments are established by God and serve him. When we remember that the Roman government that Paul knew was persecuting and murdering Christians, these words become even more remarkable. All governments are established by God for the good of human society.

## The Responsibilities of Government

God establishes these governments for a reason. Those placed in positions of authority by God have specific duties and responsibilities. Governments have the responsibility to protect and care for their citizens. In 1 Timothy, Paul writes that we should pray for all people including prayers "for kings and all who are in high positions, that we may lead a peaceful and quiet life, godly and dignified in every way" (1 Timothy 2:1-2). Governments provide for their people by allowing nations and citizens to live in times of peace. They do this by protecting their land from hostile forces outside of it, and from criminal or dangerous activity inside. In order to do this, the government has considerable authority over the life of its citizens and those who would harm them. Romans teaches that the government has the power of the sword, and that it is "an avenger who carries out God's wrath on the wrongdoer" (Romans 13:4). Governments have the power to impose capital punishment (Genesis 9:6) and to wage war against other nations that threaten its citizens. This does not mean that governments *must* impose the death penalty or engage in a particular war, but these powers are legitimately granted to governments by God. He will also hold them accountable for the way in which they use these responsibilities. Additionally, because the government needs resources to carry out its duties, it is empowered to gather taxes from its citizens. Jesus teaches that we are to "render to Caesar the things that are Caesar's" (Matthew 22:21) and Paul tells us, "pay to all what is owed to them: taxes to whom taxes are owed, revenue to whom revenue is owed, respect to whom respect is owed, honor to whom honor is owed" (Romans 13:7).

## Obeying the Government

God calls Christians to be obedient to the government, and gives a great deal of authority to our leaders. He tells us to honor, respect, and pray for our leaders, and reminds us that they have the power to punish evil doers. Yet reflection on the actions of human governments may lead us to question just how these principles apply in our modern world. We all know of governments that have acted unjustly or immorally. Can these passages really mean that Christians must obey governments at all times? What about governments that persecute Christianity? What about governments, such as the Nazis, who carried out acts of great evil? Do these verses apply to them also?

Many Christians are familiar with the response of St. Peter to an illegitimate government order. When the Jewish Sanhedrin ordered the apostles not to preach about Jesus, they did not obey. Instead, they responded "we must obey God rather than men" (Acts 5:29). When the commands of a government and the commands of God are in conflict, the Christian must follow the same principle: God's word is supreme. However, many Christians have used this as an excuse to disobey laws that do not contradict the Scriptures. If we invoke this defense, we should be sure that God really does teach that we do so. Additionally, we should note that this does not free us from the penalty of the government. There are times when Christians must disobey the commands of unjust governments, but that disobedience may require that the sentence be paid. Many Christians forget that in Acts 5, the disciples were flogged before being set free (Acts 5:40). They left rejoicing, and continued to preach about Jesus, but they had faced the unjust punishment for disobeying the government. In the same way, we should remember that the disciples who wrote that we should obey the government and that God had established the government lived in societies that persecuted Christians. Peter and Paul wrote these things about the government that would eventually martyr them both.

These examples have all focused on the reaction of Christians to governments that forbade the practice of Christianity. What of governments that are involved in other immoral activities? Certainly Christians do not want to condone or support the evil activities of a corrupt government. To the extent that is allowed, Christians can seek to change and influence their governments. In a democracy, Christians can work to change the government or influence its laws. In more controlling governments, response may be more difficult, but a Christian should always strive to stand on the side of God's word. Whenever a government asks a Christian to violate God's commands, the Christian must refuse.

## The Christian in Society

Our Lord, who has redeemed us and who equips us with his gifts, calls Christians to serve others as we are a part of society. As we do this, it is obvious that we are in the world, but not really a part of it. We always walk out of step with those who do not know our Savior, but we can still be a blessing to them. As we serve this world, we are part of God's providential plan for the world. He blesses all people through marriages, families, and governments. The vocations of individual Christians can likewise be a blessing to many people and bring glory to God. Most of the vocations examined in this chapter may be engaged in by Christians and non-Christians alike. Yet the Christian is able to recognize something that the non-Christian will easily overlook: in all these vocations, God is providing for his creation. Seeing that, the Christian can joyfully go about his daily life, confident that as we do these things, we work not merely for human beings, but for the Lord himself (Colossians 3:23).

### Key Terms

| | |
|---|---|
| Kingdom of the left | Theocracy |
| Kingdom of the right | Vocation |

## For Review and Discussion

1.  What is meant by the "right hand" and "left hand" rule of God? How do we relate to these two kingdoms? In what way does this teaching inform our understanding of the relationship between church and state? How does it help us understand our place in the world?

2.  Most Christians have multiple vocations. What vocations do you currently have? How are these vocations avenues for serv-

ing God and others? What aspects of your vocations need to be evaluated in light of God's word?

3. The Biblical teaching on marriage and on sexual behavior is often at odds with the beliefs and examples of our society. How can Christians winsomely and faithfully demonstrate and proclaim their faith in such a context?

4. Christians are called to be obedient to the government as long as it does not require them to violate God's word. How does this relate to situations of civil disobedience? When should a Christian refuse to obey a law? What are the limits of this disobedience? Should Christians work to change laws that they believe are unjust?

## For Further Reading

Billing, Einar. *Our Calling*. Minneapolis: Fortress Press, 1964.

Huegli, Albert G., ed. *Church and State Under God.* St. Louis: Concordia Publishing House, 1974.

Menuge, Angus, ed. *Christ and Culture in Dialog: Constructive Themes and Practical Applications.* St. Louis: Concordia Academic Press, 1999.

Niebuhr, H. Richard. *Christ and Culture*. San Francisco: HarperSan-Francisco, 1956.

*Render Unto Caesar. . . and Unto God: A Lutheran View of Church and State*. A report of the Commission on Theology and Church Relations of the Lutheran Church—Missouri Synod. St. Louis, Missouri: The Lutheran Church—Missouri Synod, 1995.

Veith, Gene Edward. *God at Work*. Wheaton: Crossway, 2002.

Wingren, Gustaf. *Luther on Vocation*. Philadelphia: Muhlenberg Press, 1957.

# 15

# The Last Things

The end is near. This world, and the people who live in it, will not continue in its present form forever. The time is coming when God will bring an end to this existence, and will judge all humanity. People often react to this biblical truth in two different ways. One is denial: acting as if this life and world will exist, just as they are, forever. They live as if Christ will never return and do not watch for or expect his coming. Lives grow complacent, focused on today, not listening to God's word for the future. The opposite reaction is obsession with ideas about the end of the world. Hollywood has long known that movies about the apocalypse, Armageddon, and the end of the world can make a lot of money. Many Christians seem fixated on the end times, working hard to find connections between biblical prophesies and newspaper headlines. Some seem to imply that teachings about the end times are the most important thing in Scripture.

There are many conflicting views about the end times. These debates can be complicated and confusing—but the message of God's word is far simpler. He does not want us to deny reality or to obsess on our own ideas and systems. Instead, he reveals his gracious truth to us. This life is not all that there is. Our Savior will return for us, and we eagerly wait for that day of great joy! He prepares us to meet him by teaching us about:

1. Death—*The last enemy to be defeated*
2. Signs of the End—*How will we know when the end is near?*
3. The Return of Christ—*Our Savior returns in glory*
4. The Resurrection of the Dead—*All humanity will rise again*
5. The Final Judgment—*The Savior is king of all*
6. Hell—*An eternity apart from God*
7. Heaven—*God's children live with him forever*

These topics summarize the biblical teaching on the last things (or **eschatology**). According to Scripture, the last days began with Jesus' first coming and continue today. 1 Peter 1:20 says that Christ "was made manifest in the last times for your sake" (see also Hebrews 1:2, and Acts 2:16-21). For generations, Christians have lived in the last days while watching for the return of their Lord on *the* last day, but they died before his return. Their own last day, the end of their lives, came before the end of the world.

Christ has promised that he will return, and prepares us to meet him. We do not know if his return will occur today, or later in our lifetime, or after we have died. Yet no matter when he returns, we will see our Lord and receive the salvation he has won for us. Regardless of when he comes, the child of God is eager and ready to meet him in faith.

## 1. Death

You are mortal. At some point, you are going to die. Many people spend a lot of time and money in foolish attempts to hide this basic truth. Unless Jesus returns first, every one of us is going to die. Our first parents brought death to all of their descendants by their sin, and we have lived in the shadow of death ever since. Romans teaches that ". . .sin came into the world through one man, and death through sin, and so death spread to all men because all sinned. . ." (Romans 5:12). We may die of illness, accident, violence, or old age, but the root cause behind them all is sin. Advances in medicine may devise therapies and treatments for some of these secondary causes, but medicine cannot cure death itself. Human efforts treat the symptoms but not the real problem: sin.

Human understanding does not fully comprehend the seriousness of death. Sin brings three types of death to humanity: physical, spiritual, and eternal death. Physical death, the death of the body, is obvious. Human reason has more trouble discerning that sin has also brought spiritual death. The life humans once had with God was lost when we fell. "You were dead in the trespasses and sins in which you once walked" (Ephesians 2:1,2). Because we are spiritually dead, we are unable to save ourselves or deal with our spiritual needs. Our situation does not improve in the life to come. When life on earth is over, we still deserve nothing but death. Our sins have earned an eternal sentence of death. God's word calls hell "the second death" (Revelation 20:14). These three deaths are all part of the just sentence for our sin.

Of course, this is not the whole story. Death is a consequence of sin, but Christ Jesus has redeemed us. God's grace has been "manifested through the appearing of our Savior Christ Jesus, who abolished death and brought life and immortality to light through the gospel" (2 Timothy 1:10). Because of

## Good Grief

Since death is a consequence of sin, experiencing the death of someone we love is a painful experience. We know that all who are in Christ Jesus will be in heaven, but we still may miss them here on earth. Some well meaning Christians, hoping to comfort those who mourn, will say something like, "don't be sad. They are with Jesus." Certainly they are, but that does not eliminate our feeling of loss.

St. Paul instructs us not to grieve like those who have no hope (1 Thessalonians 4:13). Notice that he does not tell Christians not to grieve, but he does tell us that our mourning will be different because we have the assurance of salvation.

It is normal for a Christian to grieve. Even Jesus cried at the grave of Lazarus (John 11:35). As we mourn, a Christian will remember Christ's promises of the resurrection. We might also remember the promise of Jesus that mourners are blessed because they will be comforted (Matthew 5:4). He is our comfort.

Jesus, the sting of death is removed (1 Corinthians 15:55-57) and those who die in faith are truly called blessed (Revelation 14:13). Since Jesus has paid the penalty for sin, the Christian has died to sin and been raised with Christ. He has given us new life. Because of him, we will not face the eternal death of hell, and because he has died and risen for us, physical death is now the door to everlasting life.

The Christian lives in the tension of these two facts. We know that we have life in Christ but we still face the death of our bodies. Physical death is not the end, and it will not hold us. Still, death is "the last enemy to be destroyed" (1 Corinthians 15:26). Death should make us uncomfortable. God did not create us for death, but for life. Death is a consequence of sin, but our Savior has taken its power and given us his life.

### Death Defined

What is death? We recognize it when we see it, but what is it? To understand the nature of death we need to understand the nature of humanity. In our discussion of humanity, we examined the biblical descriptions of human nature. A human being has a body and a soul (or spirit). The soul is the life and consciousness of the body. Without a soul, the body is simply a corpse. Death is the separation of the body and the soul. That which gives a person life, uniqueness, personality, and identity, is removed from the flesh. The body that remains looks similar to the person (though a lifeless body never really looks like the living person), but it does not live, relate to others, or reveal its full identity.

Scripture describes death as the separation of body and soul. James remarks that "the body apart from the spirit is dead" (James 2:26). Ecclesiastes teaches "the dust returns to the earth as it was, and the spirit returns to God who gave it" (Ecclesiastes 12:7). Jesus teaches us not to fear those who can kill the body but not the soul (Matthew 10:28). At his death, Scripture says that Jesus "gave up his spirit" (John 19:30) while his lifeless corpse remained on the cross.

Once separated, the body decays into its natural elements. Genesis 3:19 shows that because of sin, humans will ". . .return to the ground, for out of it you were taken; for you are dust, and to dust you shall return." This reality will not change until Christ returns and raises the dead. The soul has a different experience. It does not decay like the body, but continues to live. God has created us to live eternally. The nature of this eternal existence varies, depending on whether the individual has received or rejected God's gift of salvation. At death, believers are with the Lord (Luke 23:43, Philippians 1: 23; Revelation 6:9) while those who rejected Christ's salvation are in hell (Luke 16:19-31).

It may seem that death is out of place in this chapter. Is this really one of the last things? While the death of an individual is not the last event to take place on earth, it is the last thing that person will experience on earth. There is little difference for the individual if they personally experience the return of Jesus or if they die. That moment marks the end of their earthly life, and the end of their opportunity to receive salvation in Christ (Hebrews 9:27). Whether our lives end with the return of Christ or by our own death, we need to be prepared to meet our Savior. No matter how we leave this life, we need his grace.

## 2. Signs of the End

An individual may experience death at any moment. We may not live in expectation of death, but our earthly life is fragile and passing. We are prepared to die, or to live, when we are in Christ Jesus. Of course, there will be a generation that is alive when Christ returns. These people will not experience death but will go directly from life to the afterlife. For believers, this will be a day of joy and gladness. Sin, death, and Satan will be removed from us forever, and we will know the presence of God himself. Knowing this, believers of all times have wondered, "when will Christ return?" Wanting us to be prepared at all times, God has not told us the precise timing of Christ's return, but he has told us that there will be a number of signs that will warn us of the approaching last day. These signs are found in many sections of Scripture including Matthew 24:4-35 (with parallels in Mark 13: 6-31, and Luke 21:8-28), 2 Timothy 3:1-4, 2 Thessalonians 2, and the book of Revelation. Because there are many signs, it may help us to organize them into several categories: signs in nature, signs in society, signs against the church, and signs in the church. All of these signs demonstrate that we live in the last days.

*Signs in Nature*

The fall into sin did not just affect human beings; all creation was altered by human disobedience (Romans 8:19-21). Consequently we should not be surprised to see changes and signs in nature. In the last days there will be famine (Matthew 24:7), pestilence (Luke 21:11), earthquakes (Matthew 24:7), and a roaring and tossing of the sea (Luke 21:25). We are so used to the effects of sin in our lives that these things may seem natural, but they are not. They are signs that the earth is not functioning as God intended. Moreover, there will be signs in the heavens. The sun and moon will be darkened, stars will fall from the sky, and the heavenly bodies will be shaken (Matthew 24:29). These events, described from our earthly perspective, also announce that the end is near. It may be that this prophecy is fulfilled when the sun grows dim. It would also be fulfilled if the sun and moon were obscured from our view in some way. Likewise, Jesus is not necessarily saying that every star in the universe will fall onto the surface of the earth. Rather, it will appear to humans as if the stars are falling. Some of these signs in nature are simple, others are more remarkable, but all are heralds that the end is near.

*Signs in Society*

Other signs show the effects of sin in human society and relationships. In the last days there will be an increase in wickedness and a decrease in love (Matthew 24:12). St. Paul particularly notes the sinfulness of humanity:

> In the last days there will come times of difficulty. [2]For people will be lovers of self, lovers of money, proud, arrogant, abusive, disobedient to their parents, ungrateful, unholy, [3]heartless, unappeasable, slanderous, without

self-control, brutal, not loving good, ⁴treacherous, reckless, swollen with conceit, lovers of pleasure rather than lovers of God. (2 Timothy 3:1-4)

This sinful behavior on the individual level also affects societies and nations. There will be wars and rumors of wars (Matthew 24:6), rebellions, and revolutions (Luke 21:9). Societies and governments fail and fall in the last days.

## Signs Against the Church

Already we have seen some fearsome signs. Some Christians have tried to exempt the Christian church from these experiences, but Jesus does not teach this. While all of the signs already listed will be experienced by believers and unbelievers alike, some of the signs will be directed against Christians themselves. As a sinful and unbelieving world hates our Lord, so they will mistreat his people. Jesus warns of coming persecution. Believers will be mistreated, tortured, arrested and killed (Matthew 24:10). They will be betrayed by their family, parents, children, and friends (Mark 13:12). The world will irrationally hate Christians because of Jesus (Mark 13:13), and there will be efforts to exterminate Christianity. Nobody longs for persecution, but through this persecution, Christians will be given the opportunity to testify of Jesus before religious leaders, kings, and many people (Luke 21: 12). This witness is another sign of the end.

## Signs in the Church

Christians will feel the wrath of a sinful world in the last days. But we must also remember that Christians are sinners. While some things are done against the church, there are also signs of things done *in* the church. In the face of persecution, some Christians will forsake their faith and deny their Lord (Matthew 24:10). False prophets will distort the teachings of Christianity (Matthew 24:11). False teachers will arise, claiming to be Christ (Matthew 24:5). They will perform counterfeit miracles (Matthew 24:24) and will lead others into unbelief and false teachings.

These things happen inside the church, and are done by people claiming to be Christians. Yet in these last days the church will not abandon her commission. Sent to make disciples of all nations, Christians will continue this work, even in the face of persecution, for before our Lord returns, the Gospel will be preached in the whole world (Matthew 24:14).

### The Antichrist

Another sign within the church is the appearance of the Antichrist. This frightening figure is described in several places of Scripture as the **Antichrist** (John's Epistles), the **man of lawlessness** (2 Thessalonians), the beast (Revelation) and the abomination that brings desolation (Daniel). All describe someone who is opposed to Christ and his people. There are, in fact, several meanings to the title antichrist. In the broad sense of the term, anyone opposed to Christ is an antichrist. St. John warns,

> Children, it is the last hour, and as you have heard that antichrist is coming, so now many antichrists have come. Therefore we know that it is the last hour. [19]They went out from us, but they were not of us; for if they had been of us, they would have continued with us. But they went out, that it might become plain that they all are not of us. (1 John 2:18-19)

Note that John uses "antichrist" in two senses. *The* Antichrist is coming, and *many* antichrists have come. Christians have sometimes been so focused on the coming of the Antichrist that they forget about the dangers of the many antichrists, but John reminds us that anyone who opposes Christ is dangerous. This is not an external threat; they were once part of the church. They know Christianity from the inside, but these false teachers do not confess the faith of the true church. John describes their teachings: "Who is the liar but he who denies that Jesus is the Christ? This is the antichrist, he who denies the Father and the Son" (1 John 2:22). The antichrist rejects Jesus as the Messiah. He is literally anti-Christ. According to 1 John 4:3, the antichrist does not acknowledge that Jesus is from God. In other words, his deity is denied. Second John 7 adds, "Many deceivers have gone out into the world, those who do not confess the coming of Jesus Christ in the flesh. Such a one is the deceiver and the antichrist." John is using the term antichrist in a broad sense. Anyone who is opposed to Christ and who teaches falsely about him is antichrist. Whether they deny his deity, the incarnation, or his office as the Messiah, they are false teachers who try to deceive the people of God. John warns that such teachers will be well known in these last days, and their blasphemy must be rejected.

While anyone opposed to Christ is antichrist, Scripture also warns us of one great Antichrist. Paul describes this figure in 2 Thessalonians 2. It seems that some false teachers had tried to convince the Thessalonian church that the last day had already come. Paul shows them that this is false. The day of the Lord will not come until

> . . .the man of lawlessness is revealed, the son of destruction, [4]who opposes and exalts himself against every so-called god or object of worship, so that he takes his seat in the temple of God, proclaiming himself to be God. . . [9]The coming of the lawless one is by the activity of Satan with all power and false signs and wonders, [10]and with all wicked deception for those who are perishing, because they refused to love the truth and so be saved (2 Thessalonians 2:3-4, 9-10).

When Paul wrote these words, the man of lawlessness, or Antichrist, had not come. He was being held back by God's power (2 Thessalonians 2: 7), but the time would come when this person would appear. Scripture tells us the signs by which this person will be recognized. First, the Antichrist will act in opposition to Christ. But this opposition alone does not make a person the Antichrist. This one "takes his seat in the temple of God (2 Thessalonians 2:4). In the New Testament era, the Temple is not a building in Jerusalem, but the place where God dwells—his church (1 Corinthians 3: 16-17). The Antichrist is not a danger from outside—he comes as part of the church. Third, the Antichrist exalts himself over God and everything else, and even proclaims himself to be God (2 Thessalonians 2:4). These claims will be backed up by counterfeit miracles, signs and wonders (2 Thessalonians 2:9) which deceive some people.

The Antichrist, as a leader in the church, will try to blend in. He will act and speak like he belongs, but he will really be teaching doctrines that are opposed to the Gospel. He will exalt his own authority and teachings over the word of God. He will gradually lead people away from God's truth in such a way that it seems right and pious. People will believe this false teacher and be led astray, but his teachings will not endure. Christ will preserve his church and ultimately will destroy this great false teacher.

Any candid look at church history will show that Christ's church has seen teachers that have opposed God and have devised doctrines in conflict with the Gospel. Scripture teaches that Christ will not return until this man is revealed, but we have seen people meet these criteria. Others may fulfill them again, but the sign has been met.

*Have the Signs been Fulfilled?*

Signs in nature, society, against the church, and signs in the church have all been foretold as things that will precede the coming of our Lord. Jesus tells us that such signs are like "birth pains" (Matthew 24:8). They precede the big event: his return. At the time the signs were revealed there was little doubt that the signs were future events. Is that still true today, or have the signs been fulfilled? The question is vital because it will shape our understanding of Jesus and his return. For two thousand years, Christians have looked at the signs and believed that they lived in the end times. Modern Christians should share this conclusion. The signs of his coming have been fulfilled. We have seen signs in nature: earthquakes, famines, and disease. The signs in the heavens (the darkening of the sun and moon and the falling of the stars) might be seen as fulfilled signs, but even those who think they have not yet been fulfilled may realize that these signs could be fulfilled in a few minutes. We have also seen the chaos of signs in society. The loveless and selfish lives that 2 Timothy describes are commonplace. Wars, rebellions, and discord are everyday occurrences. Christianity has repeatedly seen the world's opposition. Believers have been persecuted, betrayed, and martyred. Indeed, in many parts of the world, Christians today face persecution and martyrdom. While we should be more zealous in spreading the Gospel, it has been taken all over the world. There are individuals who have not yet heard, but the Gospel is being taken to all nations. (Colossians 1:23 says that the Gospel "has been proclaimed in all creation under heaven.") The signs within the church are also being fulfilled. We have seen apostasy, false teaching, and even seen the marks of the Antichrist fulfilled.

The signs have been met. Christ could return at any moment or his return may not come for some time. If he delays, the signs will continue to be fulfilled again and again as he warns the world that time is running out. We may even see a greater fulfillment of some signs than has been seen in the past. Yet it is important for us to realize that there is no sign that restrains our Savior. He could return at any moment.

So why hasn't he come yet? What is taking him so long? Peter answers, "The Lord is not slow to fulfill his promise as some count slowness, but is patient toward you, not wishing that anyone should perish, but that all should reach repentance" (2 Peter 3:9). He waits to give ample opportunity for people to believe. He waits because he is patient with humanity, but his patience is not eternal. He will return when he chooses. It may be today, it may be in the future, but our Savior will return.

### 3. The Return of Christ

Jesus reveals one final sign in Matthew 24:30: "They will see the Son of Man coming on the clouds of heaven with power and great glory." This is the final sign, but it is not a sign of warning; it is the end of the warnings. Christ has promised that he will return visibly to the earth. As Hebrews summarizes it, he "will appear a second time, not to deal with sin but to save those who are eagerly waiting for him" (Hebrews 9:28). The return of Christ (or **parousia**) is a simple teaching, but it is sadly complicated by those who go beyond Scripture. Our Savior wants us to know that he is coming for us, and he wants us to be ready.

While all of the other signs can be ignored and rejected in unbelief, there will be no mistaking the return of our Savior. Matthew 24:30 says that the nations will see him. No one will overlook his coming, for ". . .every eye will see him, even those who pierced him. . ." (Revelation 1:7). He warns us not to believe people who tell us that he has already come. If we have not seen him, he has not come. His return will be visible to all (Matthew 24:26-27).

It will be a great and glorious day. Our Lord tells us to be ready and watchful for his return. He tells us the signs so that we will be prepared. Yet he does not give us a schedule. Christians are not given the exact time and date of Christ's return (Acts 1:6-7). The timing is unknown by the angels, and even Jesus in his state of humiliation did not know the timing of the parousia (Mark 13:32). No, the moment of his return will be a surprise.

> Now concerning the times and the seasons, brothers, you have no need to have anything written to you. ²For you yourselves are fully aware that the day of the Lord will come like a thief in the night. ³While people are saying, "There is peace and security," then sudden destruction will come upon them as labor pains come upon a pregnant woman, and they will not escape (1 Thessalonians 5:1-3).

Paul's image is a particularly fitting one. The time of Christ's return is like the onset of labor pains. A woman does not know exactly when her labor will begin, but she has ample sign that her delivery is close! The child growing within her needs to be born. Likewise, Christians will not know the precise timing of Christ's return. We will all be surprised by the timing, but we will not be surprised that he does return.

Since he has already justified us in his first coming, he does not come to suffer for sins again (Hebrews 9:24). No, the purpose of his coming is to bring salvation to his people. He comes to judge the nations and to bring us to live with him eternally.

### 4. The Resurrection of the Dead

Scripture teaches that when Jesus returns he will raise the dead to life again. God who created us body and soul, will restore our bodies on the last day. All people will rise again. As Jesus said, ". . .an hour is coming when all who are in the tombs will hear his voice and come out, those who have done good to the resurrection of life, and those who have done evil to the resurrection of judgment" (John 5:28-29 see also Daniel 12:2 and Acts 24:

15). While the eternal fate of those raised will vary (based on their faith), all people will be raised from the dead.

Human logic may stumble over the idea of the resurrection. How will God raise up bodies that have decomposed, been scattered, or been destroyed? The simple answer is that God has the power to do what he chooses. Job prophesied, "I know that my Redeemer lives, and at the last he will stand upon the earth. And after my skin has been thus destroyed, yet in my flesh shall I see God, whom I shall see for myself, and my eyes shall behold and not another" (Job 19:25-27). Job knew that God is able to do this miracle— a miracle that is possible because his Redeemer lives. We will live because our Redeemer lives (see also 1 Corinthians 15:12).

Christ will raise all the dead. We will have bodies for all eternity. Yet we must remember that these bodies will be different than the ones we have now. Our current bodies have been affected by sinfulness. We are mortal, we age, get ill and become injured. These are effects of sin. But the children of God are promised glorified, immortal bodies (1 Corinthians 15:35-37).

### 5. The Final Judgment

All humanity, body and soul, will stand before their Lord on that day. Christ comes to judge all humanity: those who are alive when he returns and those whom he has raised to life (Acts 10:42). All humanity will be judged by Christ (Romans 14:10), but the judgment will be a vastly different experience for different people.

For those who trust in Christ their Savior, judgment day is simply one more affirmation of the Gospel. They enter a joyous eternity in heaven because their sins have been forgiven. John's Gospel describes it well.

> God did not send his Son into the world to condemn the world, but in order that the world might be saved through him. [18]Whoever believes in him is not condemned, but whoever does not believe is condemned already, because he has not believed in the name of the only Son of God. . . . [36]Whoever believes in the Son has eternal life; whoever does not obey the Son shall not see life, but the wrath of God remains on him. (John 3: 17-18, 36)

Salvation was freely available to all people through Christ. Those who received his grace are clothed in his righteousness. They have already been forgiven and are given the gift of eternal life for Christ's sake. Because of Jesus, there is no question what will become of Christians. We will be granted eternal life. There is no doubt about this verdict. God has already accepted us for his Son's sake. Those who choose to stand apart from Christ on that day will lack the righteousness and holiness that God demands. They will be condemned because they have rejected their only hope. Both believers and unbelievers were sinners in need of redemption. Christ died for all. But those who reject his grace will not receive salvation on that great day.

We are saved by the grace of God and not by our works. Scripture does say, however, that works will be mentioned on that day. In Matthew 25: 31-46, Jesus says that he will separate the nations as a shepherd separates the sheep from the goats. He then tells the sheep that they will enter heaven and that in this life they had fed, clothed, visited and cared for him. Since the bewildered sheep cannot remember doing these things, Jesus explains that things done for the least of his brothers were done for him. In contrast, the goats are told that they did not do any of these things and are accordingly banished to hell. Many read this passage and draw the false conclusion that salvation is based on works such as feeding the hungry. Yet this is not what is portrayed in Matthew 25. Before Jesus discusses the works done by people, he has already separated the sheep from the goats. He knows who belongs to him because the sheep have believed in him and he has forgiven them. When he examines the lives of forgiven sinners, nothing remains but the good things they have done. These works only exist because they are forgiven. The sheep know that they cannot be saved by their works. This is why they protest that they do not remember doing the things Jesus describes. The goats rejected Christ's grace, and so they stand on that day in all of their human sinfulness. Because they have not been forgiven, nothing they could have done would be sufficient to earn their salvation. In fact, their actions in this life deserve only damnation. The same thing is true of the sheep, but the sheep are saved by Christ's works and not their own.

*The End of the World*

When the judgment is complete, this life as we know it now will end. All human beings will be welcomed into heaven or will be banished to hell. But what is to become of the rest of God's creation? Since all creation has been subject to the effects of sin (Romans 8:19-22), it too needs to change. Scripture speaks of the destruction of the universe, and of the future existence of a new heaven and new earth. In the days of Noah God destroyed and remade the earth through the great flood. At the last day God will destroy the universe with fire.

> But the day of the Lord will come like a thief, and then the heavens will pass away with a roar, and the heavenly bodies will be burned up and dissolved, and the earth and the works that are done on it will be exposed. .

. . the heavens will be set on fire and dissolved, and the heavenly bodies will melt as they burn! [13]But according to his promise we are waiting for new heavens and a new earth in which righteousness dwells (2 Peter 3: 10, 12-13).

Jesus taught us that "Heaven and earth will pass away, but my words will not pass away" (Luke 21:33). Paul likewise teaches that "the present form of this world is passing away" (1 Corinthians 7:31). While Scripture gives us few details about the new universe, it tells us all that we need to know. As God will transform our sin-affected bodies into glorified bodies, so he will transform the rest of creation. The effects of sin on all creation will be undone by the power of God.

## 6. Hell

Scripture naturally provides us with more information about the experience of human beings. Following the judgment of Christ, there are only two possibilities: a human being may spend eternity with or without God. Those who have rejected God's gifts of grace and salvation will ultimately come to the tragic realization of what they have really done. God will not force them to receive his blessings. He will allow them to spend eternity apart from him if that is their choice. Eternity without the presence of God is hell.

Many people are troubled by the existence of hell. They ask, "how can a loving God condemn people to hell?" This question overlooks important information. God provided for the salvation of all people. It is only the rejection of his presence that has caused damnation. By rejecting Christ, they have rejected heaven (John 3:36). Still, we should note that God did not create hell in order to punish human beings. Some humans will be condemned to hell, but God did not create us for damnation. In fact, Jesus tells us the reason for hell's existence. It is "eternal fire prepared for the devil and his angels" (Matthew 25:41). Because of Christ's victory, no human needs to go to hell. Yet those who choose it will finally receive damnation.

### Descriptions of Hell

While there have been many descriptions of hell in human history, imagination, and literature, the Bible doesn't give us many details. If we believe the message of the Scriptures, we will never see hell! It simply tells us enough to know that we never want to be there. As Martin Luther once remarked, no description of hell could ever be as bad as its reality.

The reason that hell is such an awful place is that it is an existence apart from the presence of God. Second Thessalonians says that those who do not know God "will suffer the punishment of eternal destruction away from the presence of the Lord and from the glory of his might" (2 Thessalonians 1: 9). In Matthew 25 the goats are told "depart from me, you cursed, into the eternal fire. . ." (Matthew 25:41). While this detail is often overlooked in descriptions of hell, it is actually the worst part of damnation. All good things that we receive in this life (whether we are believers or unbelievers) are gifts of God. Humanity has nothing without the blessing of God. Even in our worst moments on this earth, we still receive God's fatherly care. But hell is banishment from God's presence. All of his gifts are gone. He is absent.

All other descriptions in Scripture reveal the despair and hopelessness of a godless existence. Hell is described as a place of unquenchable fire (Mark 9:43, Matthew 25:41), agony (Luke 16:24), and darkness (Matthew 8:12). Without hope, humans will be filled with despair. They will weep and gnash their teeth (Matthew 8:12). They will cry out for relief, but no relief is available to them (Luke 16:24-26). This horrible existence will continue for all eternity (Matthew 25:41; 2 Thessalonians 1:9).

## *False Views of Hell*

These are disturbing images, but they are biblical descriptions of eternity without God. Many Christians are disturbed by the reality and idea of hell. We should be disturbed by the idea of hell. God does not want humans to go there, and he has commissioned his church to bring the Gospel to the nations. But we go too far if we alter God's word in order to make it more palatable to our reason or emotions. We do not advance the Gospel by removing the threat of hell that is clearly taught in Scripture.

Some people have tried to avoid the biblical teaching about hell by removing it from their theology. This may be done through **universalism**, teaching that every single human will be in heaven, no matter what they believe. Another way is **annihilationism**, teaching that God will simply destroy those who are not in heaven. Others try to work around hell by teaching a "**conditional immortality**" which claims that God will only raise believers to life again. While all of these options would result in an empty hell, none of them are biblical.

Another way people have tried to avoid the biblical teaching of hell is by removing the eternity of hell. This false teaching would claim that God will sentence people to hell for their sin and unbelief, but that their sentence has a time limit. He will eventually parole them and allow them to leave hell. Such a view of hell is really one of purgatory, though in this case, the individual need never have known Christ at all. This description may sound more compassionate, but it is not in agreement with God's word.

Still others would accommodate their reason or feelings by making hell a metaphor for pain and suffering on earth. But this waters down the reality of hell that is discussed in Scripture. None of these human explanations does justice to the biblical doctrine of hell. In fact, a denial of hell also impacts our understanding of salvation. Damnation is a real possibility, but Christ came to suffer and die so that we don't have to face it. If we reject the Scriptures and deny hell, we ultimately take away from the work of Christ. The proper response to the horrors of hell is not to ignore or reject this biblical teaching, but to rely on the grace of Christ.

## 7. Heaven

Holy Scripture is far more concerned with the wonders of heaven than the horrors of hell. God desires the salvation of human beings, and he has done all that is necessary for our salvation in Jesus Christ. All who receive his grace will be given his reward on the last day: heaven. But what is heaven? Scripture is filled with many descriptions and images of the joys that lie before us, but words cannot fully embrace the joys of heaven. "No eye has seen, nor ear heard, nor the heart of man imagined, what God has prepared for those who love him—these things God has revealed to us through the Spirit" (1 Corinthians 2:9, 10).

God reveals many things about heaven. It is easy to get so caught up in the details that we miss the greatest feature of all. In heaven, we will be in the presence of God our creator and redeemer. He will bring us into his kingdom where we will see his face (Revelation 22:4) and his glory (John 17:4). In this life, sinful humans cannot bear the holy presence of God, but in his kingdom we will see him and live with him forever. There in his presence we will gladly worship and glorify him eternally (Revelation 7:15).

In heaven we will be completely free of sin and its effects. In this life we know God's continual forgiveness, but we still live with the consequences of sin. As God's new creation, we will live without those effects. In this life we know hardship and difficulties. There we will be free of hunger, thirst, pain and sorrow (Revelation 7:16-17). Here we continue to face the last enemy— death. But in heaven, "He will wipe away every tear from their eyes, and death will be no more, neither shall there be mourning nor crying nor pain anymore, for the former things have passed away" (Revelation 21:4). We will be immortal, free from temptation, sin, disease, death, and all the other effects of sin. Our current lives are so affected by sinfulness that we may find it hard to comprehend the difference with our eternal life, but it will affect every aspect of our existence.

Scripture often describes heaven as our eternal home. It is the home of our Father, and we belong there with him. Peter calls it the place in which "righteousness dwells" (2 Peter 3:13). Jesus tells us that there are many rooms in his Father's house, and he goes to prepare a place there for us (John 14:2). While hell is a place of darkness and isolation, heaven is filled with the light of God and the fellowship of his people (Revelation 21:23-25). Jesus described heaven in many parables. Often these descriptions are images of a great communal or family celebration. Heaven is a banquet or feast (Isaiah 25:6, Matthew 8:11). This is often described as a wedding feast—the celebration of the marriage of Christ and his church (Revelation 19:7-9). Christ, our beloved, makes us his own. All of these images show us an important fact about heaven. Not only will we be with God, we will be with all the people of God.

By the grace of God he will bring us into his eternal kingdom. Free from sin and all its effects, joined together with all of God's people, we will live with God forever. It will be a beautiful place because it is his place. These images only begin to describe the wonders of heaven. The Psalmist summarized these things, saying, "You make known to me the path of life; in your presence there is fullness of joy; at your right hand are pleasures forevermore" (Psalm 16:11). These are God's promises to us. Here on earth, the church waits in eager expectation, knowing that our God is faithful to his promises. He is preparing all of these things for us, and he will bring them to pass. In faith, his church cries out, "Amen. Come, Lord Jesus!" (Revelation 22:20).

---

### Key Terms

| | |
|---|---|
| Annihilationism | Eschatology |
| Antichrist | Man of lawlessness |
| Conditional | Parousia |
|    immortality | Universalism |

---

### For Review and Discussion

1.  Why do you think there are so many misconceptions and false teachings about the end times? How can Christians appropriately counter these ideas?

2. Scripture discusses many signs of the end times. Review the signs presented in this chapter and the biblical texts from which they come. What specific things that have occurred or are occurring presently suggest that these are indeed the end times?

3. Many false teachings suggest that people may have second chances to do what God desires. This is seen in teachings of purgatory, in millennialism, in schemes that limit the duration of hell, and in other issues as well. What do these attempts show about our human condition? Do these theories imply a deficiency in the work of Christ and justification?

4. Some Christians seem obsessed with the end times; others seem to avoid the topic. Why do you think this subject generates such opposite reactions?

5. Read the description of heaven found in Revelation 21 and 22. How do these chapters fill Christians with hope and joy?

**For Further Reading**

Brighton, Louis. *Revelation*. St. Louis: Concordia Publishing House, 1999.

*The End Times: A Study on Eschatology and the Millennium.* A report of the Commission on Theology and Church Relations of the Lutheran Church—Missouri Synod. St. Louis, Missouri: The Lutheran Church—Missouri Synod, 1989.

# Appendix

# The Ecumenical Creeds

From the very beginning, Christians have formulated Scriptural summaries as statements of their beliefs. These statements are known as **creeds** or **confessions**. They proclaim the core beliefs and values of those who hold them, and they present the fundamental teachings of a person's faith in an orderly form.

The New Testament word for "confess" (*homologein*) literally means "the same words." A person who makes a confession says the same words as another, agreeing that these words are correct. We use this word to describe our admission of sinfulness before God. We agree with his verdict and confess that we are sinners (1 John 1:9). The same word is used for agreement with other biblical truths. Christians confess that "Jesus is Lord" (Romans 10:9). Paul speaks about Timothy making his "good confession in the presence of many witnesses" and also notes that Jesus made "the good confession" before Pontius Pilate (1 Timothy 6:12-13). A person may say many things, but when they confess something, they are proclaiming belief in its truth.

All Christians are called to confess the faith. Sometimes this is done individually as we declare our faith to other people. Groups of Christians also confess the faith corporately as together they affirm the content and meaning of the faith they share. A proper Christian confession is based on Scripture, summarizes Scripture, and is always in a lesser position than Scripture. This is what we believe the Scriptures teach. Good confessions will clearly proclaim biblical truth, and will direct those who hear them back to the Bible.

While different groups of Christians may have their own creeds and confessions, the three **ecumenical creeds** are confessions of all Christianity. ("**Ecumenical**" means worldwide or universal. It refers to all Christian groups, not just one denomination). Many Christians confess these creeds in their worship services. Others groups do not use them so regularly, but the content of these Creeds is nothing less than basic Christian teaching. The doctrine presented in the creeds separates Christians from non-Christians. These confessions are called creeds, which comes from the Latin word *credo,* meaning, "I believe." They are not merely descriptions of a doctrinal system, but rather personal and corporate confessions of faith.

## The Apostles' Creed

The shortest and most ancient of the Creeds is known as the Apostles' Creed. While there is no direct historical link of this document to the apostles themselves, it summarizes the apostolic teaching found in Scripture. It was first called the Apostles' Creed in A.D. 390, but this Creed is far older than that. In the latter half of the second century, an early version now known as the "Old Roman Symbol" was used in Christian congregations. This early form of the Creed was associated with baptism. As people were baptized, they were asked to confess their faith in the triune God. The questions and their answer demonstrated that they knew and believed the Christian faith. The words that they confessed focused on the doctrine of the Trinity and on the person and work of Jesus Christ. After their baptism, they would continue to confess their faith using the same summary of faith.

This ancient baptismal formula remains a confession of faith today. We still ask adults who are baptized to confess their faith (or sponsors to speak on behalf of young children who are baptized). They still summarize basic Christian teaching in the words of the Apostles' Creed. Whenever the baptized children of God confess this Creed, they remember their baptism and the God who has made them his own. In his Small Catechism, Martin Luther offered an explanation of this Creed, and urged that Christians say it as part of their prayers when they rise in the morning and when they lie down at night. We also confess this Creed together. By custom, this Creed is ordinarily used in services that do not celebrate the Lord's Supper. Together we remember our baptism, our Christian faith, and our part in his church.

> I believe in God, the Father Almighty
>     maker of heaven and earth.
>
> And in Jesus Christ, His only Son, our Lord
>     who was conceived by the Holy Spirit,
>     born of the virgin Mary,
>     suffered under Pontius Pilate,
>     was crucified, died and was buried.
>     He descended into hell.
>     The third day He rose again from the dead.
>     He ascended into heaven
>     and sits at the right hand of God the Father Almighty.

From thence He will come to judge the living and the dead.

I believe in the Holy Spirit,
    the holy Christian[1] Church
        the communion of saints,
    the forgiveness of sins,
    the resurrection of the body,
    and the life everlasting. Amen.

## The Nicene Creed

While the Apostles' Creed arose liturgically, the Nicene Creed was written in response to a specific theological controversy. In AD 313, the Edict of Milan declared that Christianity would be tolerated as a religion within the Roman Empire. The Emperor Constantine soon realized that this religion could be a strong unifying force in his empire, but theological divisions could bring chaos. During these early years of Christianity, a presbyter in Alexandria named Arius (256-336) became quite influential. Wanting to uphold the unique deity of God the Father, Arius taught that the Son was subordinate to the Father. He began to teach that the Son was not fully God, but a creature. The first thing that God did was create the Son. All other creatures were created by the Son. Thus the Son is greater than everything else, but less than God the Father. Put another way, the Son was *a god* but not God. Other Christians quickly recognized that **Arianism** reduced Christ's deity while also suggesting a kind of polytheism. Such a position denied Scripture and threatened salvation since the deity of Christ is an essential component of mankind's redemption. But the Arians were strong, and a great division was growing in Christianity.

In response, in AD 325, Constantine called the bishops of the church to a theological council in Nicea. This council discussed the claims of Arianism in the light of Scripture. Concluding that Arianism did not teach the biblical truth of Christ's deity, they drafted a creed that described the person of Christ in biblical terms. Christ is "…God of God, Light of Light, true God of true God, begotten not made, being of one substance with the Father…" Each of these statements confronts the Arian heresy with the biblical truth. Christ is not a creature; he is fully divine.

---

[1] the ancient text reads "catholic," meaning the whole Church as it confesses the wholeness of Christian doctrine.

The document that emerged from this council was signed by almost everyone in attendance. The first and second articles are the same as we confess today. However, in this early version of the creed, the third article is largely missing. It confesses faith in the Holy Spirit but lacks the detail that we confess today. The creed concluded with specific condemnations (known as **anathemas**) of Arian teachings.

Nicea is known as the first **ecumenical council**, since representatives of the entire Christian church were present. At the second ecumenical council, held in Constantinople in 381, the Nicene Creed was reiterated and expanded. The third article was lengthened to the form that we know today, directly confessing the deity and work of the Holy Spirit.

In later years, a further addition was made to the Nicene Creed in the Western church. At Constantinople, the creed said that the Holy Spirit "proceeds from the Father." Arian teachers soon tried to exploit this wording to teach that the Son was not fully God. In response, many congregations inserted the Latin word *filioque*, which means "and the Son." The Western church continues to confess that the Holy Spirit "...proceeds from the Father *and the Son....*" Unfortunately, this addition was not made at an ecumenical council or with the consent of churches in eastern Christianity. Consequently, these churches have never agreed with the insertion of these words. This division, known as the *filioque* controversy, remains a point of contention between eastern and western Christianity. While the change should have been made in consultation with other Christian leaders, we should note that the idea it expresses is biblical (John 15:26; 1 Corinthians 2:12; Romans 8: 9; Galatians 4:6).

Since the Nicene Creed developed as a response to the Arian heresy, it is more polemical than the Apostles' Creed. It makes its theological points with care, precisely noting the differences between orthodoxy and heresy. This confession of faith is commonly used today at celebrations of the Lord's Supper and at festival services of the church. We confess the faith in the triune God, and in our Redeemer who is truly God.

> I believe in one God,
>     the Father Almighty,
>     maker of heaven and earth
>         and of all things visible and invisible.

> And in one Lord Jesus Christ,
>         the only-begotten Son of God,
>         begotten of His Father before all worlds,
>         God of God, Light of Light,

very God of very God,
begotten, not made,
being of one substance with the Father,
by whom all things were made;
who for us men[2] and for our salvation came down from heaven
and was incarnate by the Holy Spirit of the virgin Mary
and was made man;
and was crucified also for us under Pontius Pilate.
He suffered and was buried.
And the third day He rose again according to the Scriptures
and ascended into heaven
and sits at the right hand of the Father.
And He will come again with glory to judge both
the living and the dead,
whose kingdom will have no end.

And I believe in the Holy Spirit,
the Lord and giver of life,
who proceeds from the Father and the Son,
who with the Father and the Son together is worshiped and glorified,
who spoke by the prophets.
And I believe in one holy Christian[3] and apostolic Church,
I acknowledge one Baptism for the remission of sins,
and I look for the resurrection of the dead
and the life of the world to come. Amen.

## The Athanasian Creed

The third ecumenical creed may not be as well known as the other two. It is considerably longer and is not used in worship with the frequency of the previous two Creeds. Like the Apostles' Creed, its name is perhaps misleading. It is called the Athanasian Creed. Athanasius (ca 293-373) was an assistant to the bishop of Alexandria at the council of Nicea and later became the bishop of Alexandria. He was a strong opponent of Arianism and helped guide the Council of Nicea to an orthodox confession of the Trinity. Thus

---

[2] us men does not mean "males" but "all people"
[3] the ancient text reads "catholic" meaning the whole Church as it confesses the wholeness of Christian doctrine.

when Christians later saw this Creed that so strongly presents the doctrine of the Trinity, many assumed that it must have come from Athanasius.

The evidence, however, suggests that someone else wrote this Creed. The earliest known copies of the Creed (from the early sixth century) were found in southern France, not in Northern Africa where Athanasius ministered. While the rest of Athanasius' writings are in Greek, the earliest copies of this creed are in Latin. It seems to address heresies that were not known in his time. Furthermore, Athanasius' followers never mention this creed. All of this suggests that this creed, while expressing theology in agreement with Athanasius' teaching, was written by someone else.

Regardless of who wrote the creed, the content is that of Christian orthodoxy. Its forty propositions strongly present the doctrine of the Trinity and the deity of Christ. The Creed is precise, carefully closing loopholes that heretics used to distort the Christian truth. It also includes anathemas of heretical views in the body of the Creed (lines 1, 2, 26, 40). The Athanasian Creed is traditionally confessed in public worship on the festival of the Holy Trinity, but its theology should be reflected in all trinitarian teaching.

[1] Whoever desires to be saved must, above all, hold the catholic faith.

[2] Whoever does not keep it whole and undefiled will without doubt perish eternally.

[3] And the catholic faith is this,

[4] that we worship one God in Trinity and Trinity in Unity, neither confusing the persons nor dividing the substance.

[5] For the Father is one person, the Son is another, and the Holy Spirit is another.

[6] But the Godhead of the Father and of the Son and of the Holy Spirit is one: the glory equal, the majesty coeternal.

[7] Such as the Father is, such is the Son, and such is the Holy Spirit:

[8] the Father uncreated, the Son uncreated, the Holy Spirit uncreated;

[9] the Father infinite, the Son infinite, the Holy Spirit infinite;

[10] the Father eternal, the Son eternal, the Holy Spirit eternal.

[11] And yet there are not three Eternals, but one Eternal.

[12] just as there are not three Uncreated or three Infinites, but one Uncreated and one Infinite.

[13] In the same way, the Father is almighty, the Son almighty, the Holy Spirit almighty;

[14] and yet there are not three Almighties, but one Almighty.

[15] So the Father is God, the Son is God, the Holy Spirit is God;

[16] and yet there are not three Gods, but one God.

[17] So the Father is Lord, the Son is Lord, the Holy Spirit is Lord;

[18] and yet there are not three Lords, but one Lord.

[19] Just as we are compelled by the Christian truth to acknowledge each distinct person as God and Lord, so also are we prohibited by the catholic religion to say that there are three Gods or Lords.

[20] The Father is not made nor created nor begotten by anyone.

[21] The Son is neither made nor created, but begotten of the Father alone.

[22] The Holy Spirit is of the Father and of the Son, neither made nor created nor begotten, but proceeding.

[23] Thus, there is one Father, not three Fathers; one Son, not three Sons; one Holy Spirit, not three Holy Spirits.

[24] And in this Trinity none is before or after another; none is greater or less than another;

[25] but the whole three persons are coeternal with each other and coequal, so that in all things, as has been stated above, the Trinity in Unity and Unity in Trinity is to be worshiped.

[26] Therefore, whoever desires to be saved must think thus about the Trinity.

[27] But it is also necessary for everlasting salvation that one faithfully believe the incarnation of our Lord Jesus Christ.

[28] Therefore, it is the right faith that we believe and confess that our Lord Jesus Christ, the Son of God, is at the same time both God and man.

[29] He is God, begotten from the substance of the Father before all ages; and He is man, born of the substance of His mother in this age:

[30] perfect God and perfect man, composed of a rational soul and human flesh;

[31] equal to the Father in respect to His divinity, less than the Father with respect to His humanity.

[32] Although He is God and man, He is not two, but one Christ:

[33] one, however, not by the conversion of the divinity into flesh, but by the assumption of the humanity into God;

[34] one altogether, not by confusion of substance, but by unity of person.

[35] For as the rational soul and flesh is one man, so God and man is one Christ,

[36] who suffered for our salvation, descended into hell, rose again the third day from the dead,

[37] ascended into heaven, and is seated at the right hand of the Father, God Almighty, from whence He will come to judge the living and the dead.

<sup>38</sup> At His coming all people will rise again with their bodies and give an account concerning their own deeds.

<sup>39</sup> And those who have done good will enter into eternal life, and those who have done evil into eternal fire.

<sup>40</sup> This is the catholic faith; whoever does not believe it faithfully and firmly cannot be saved.

### Key Terms

| | |
|---|---|
| Anathemas | Ecumenical Council |
| Arianism | Ecumenical Creeds |
| Ecumenical | *Filioque* |

# Glossary

**Absolution** — The proclamation of the full forgiveness of sins on account of Christ's saving work.

**Accidents** — Aristotelian term for an attribute or characteristic of something; the effect it has on human senses. This is distinct from its **substance**.

**Active obedience** — Christ's complete fulfilling of the entire Law of God for the rest of humanity (see also **passive obedience**).

**Actual sin** — any sinful deed, word, thought or intention, as distinguished from **original sin**.

**Adiaphora** — "indifferent things." Things that God has neither commanded nor forbidden.

**Adoptionism** — the false teaching that the man Jesus was not always the incarnate God. Instead, he was "adopted" as the Son of God at some time during his earthly life. This results in denying his complete deity.

**Agnostic** — someone who believes that it is impossible to know whether or not God or gods exist.

**Alien righteousness** — the righteousness of Christ that is imputed to sinful humans from outside of themselves. They are declared righteous, but the righteousness belongs to Christ alone.

**Alien work** — a description of the Law of God. It is his word and work, but it crushes the sinner. Since God desires to be gracious to all, this work of the Law is described as "alien."

**Amillennialism** — literally "no millennium." Refers to the belief that the thousand year reign of Christ depicted in Revelation 20 is not a literal thousand years on earth, but depicts the ongoing and lasting rule of Christ.

**Anathemas** — condemnations. Most early creeds and confessions not only confessed their belief but also condemned false teachings through anathemas.

**Annihilationism** — the non-biblical teaching that individuals who are not saved will eventually cease to exist and not be damned to eternal hell.

**Anthropology** — the study of humanity.

**Anthropomorphism** — describing God in human terms. This may be done in ways that are consistent with biblical imagery or in ways that distort the biblical data.

**Antichrist** — one who is against Christ. Scripture speaks of many antichrists, but also of one great Antichrist who opposes Christ and his people.

**Antilegomena** — biblical books whose canonical status has been disputed over the course of Christian history. Examples include Hebrews (whose author is uncertain) and Jude (which quotes from non-canonical books) (see also **ho-mologoumena**).

**Antinomianism** — "against Law." Refers to a variety of beliefs that reject any place for God's Law in the life of a Christian.

**Apocrypha** — books from the intertestamental period that are generally not regarded as canonical by Protestants. While they purport to be part of the Old Testament, they seem to have been written much later. Luther commended the apocryphal books for reading, but not for use as a source of doctrine.

**Apostasy** — falling away from faith

**Apostolic** — coming from the apostles of Jesus or from the time period in which these apostles were alive.

**Arianism** — the heretical teaching that the Son of God was not fully God in the same sense that the Father is God, but was instead the first thing that God created. This heretical teaching is condemned in the Nicene Creed. Groups such as the Jehovah's Witnesses continue in the Arian heresy today.

**Arminianism** — A theological system named for Jacob Arminius (1560-1609) who developed his theology to oppose the views of both Lutheranism and Calvinism. It teaches that human beings freely choose or reject salvation and that **election** is based on God's **foreknowledge** of these human choices. Arminianism thus places human freedom at the center of theology. Its opponents sometimes call it "decision theology."

**Atheist** — one who is convinced that there is no God or gods. Since this conclusion cannot be verified empirically, atheism is an inherently religious belief.

**Atonement** — the work of Christ in dealing with the problem of human sinfulness and reconciling humanity to God. Various biblical (and sometimes non-biblical) descriptions of this work are known as "atonement theories."

**Autographs** — the technical name for the first copy of a biblical work — the document personally written by the human author.

**Baptism** — a means of grace, instituted by Christ, in which water is applied with the word of God, in which God promises forgiveness of sins.

**Begotten** — a term of procreation or origin. A person begets something that has the same nature as him or herself but makes or creates something of a different nature. Christ is the only begotten Son of God; this means that he himself is also God.

**Bondage of the will** — Martin Luther's description of the human will. Fallen humans never truly have free will; we are always affected by our fallen nature, the world and the devil.

**Born again** — or born from above. Refers to the new life that the Holy Spirit gives to the Christian.

**Canon** — literally a "rule" or "standard." Refers to the biblical books that are received as the inspired word of God. Most Protestants accept 39 Old Testament and 27 New Testament books as canonical.

**Catholic** — properly speaking, refers to the entire Christian **church** on earth (the universal or world-wide church).

**Ceremonial Law** — portions of Old Testament Law that pertained to worship in the tabernacle or Temple or to other religious practices of Jews before the coming of the Messiah. The ceremonial law has been fulfilled by Christ and is no longer binding.

**Christ** — Greek word meaning "anointed one;" equivalent to the Hebrew word "Messiah."

**Christology** — the study of the person and work of Jesus Christ.

**Christocentric** — Christ-centered. True Christian doctrine is always christocentric.

**Church** — in its proper sense, refers to the total of all believers in Christ in all times and places. More broadly, it can mean a **congregation**, a group of congregations that share a common **confession**, or a worship service held in a congregation.

**Civil-political law** — Laws in the Scriptures that apply to a specific temporal society. Generally, these laws were addressed to the nation of Israel. These laws no longer apply to Christians today, but they demonstrate the importance and authorities of civil governments today. If one's own government adopts these or similar laws, they are then binding on their citizens.

**Civil righteousness** — acts that are beneficial to society or recognized as good works by the world (but not necessarily by God). Any human being, Christian or non-Christian, can practice civil righteousness.

**Clarity of Scripture** — an attribute of Scripture also known as **"perspicuity."** The Bible is written in such a way that its message is clear to a person of average intelligence who makes a reasonable effort to read and understand it.

**Close/Closed Communion** — the practice, employed by a number of Christian groups, of restricting admission to the Lord's Supper to those who mutually confess a common faith, and are able to examine themselves according to Scriptural standards.

**Concupiscence** — the desire to sin or inclination to sin. Concupiscence is part of **original sin**.

**Conditional immortality** — the non-biblical teaching that God will grant immortality only to those who believe in Christ. Consequently, unbelievers cease to exist when they die (similar to **annihilationism**).

**Confession** — "to say the same." When confessing sin, we agree with Scripture that we are sinners. When confessing our faith, we state that we believe certain things to be true, along with other believers.

**Confirmation** — a rite in which a Christian gives a public affirmation of faith after a period of catechetical instruction. Confirmation is a helpful rite of human origin, but is not classified as a sacrament in Lutheranism.

**Congregation** — a local "church" made up of Christians gathered together around word and sacrament.

**Consubstantiation** — mischaracterization of the Lutheran doctrine of the Lord's Supper. Consubstantiation uses Aristotelian philosophy to identify the exact way in which the body and blood of Christ are present with the bread and wine.

**Contrition** — true sorrow and repentance over sin.

**Conversion** — the Holy Spirit's gracious work of changing an unbeliever into a believing child of God, apart from the cooperation or works of the individual.

**Cosmological argument** — this argument for the existence of God uses the existence of the universe as evidence of a divine creator.

**Cosmology** — the study of the origins of the universe.

**Creed** — from the Latin word *credo*, "I believe." Creeds are summary confessions of faith.

**Cross, bearing the** — suffering, affliction or persecution experienced by Christians for the sake of Christ and the Gospel.

**Curb** — the first use or function of the law. In this use, the law restrains some but not all sin by threatening punishment on those who violate its commands.

**Day-age theory** — belief that equates the days of Genesis one with longer periods of time.

**Deism** — religious position that believes in a God who is responsible for the creation of the universe but who is not involved with creation on an ongoing basis. Instead, the universe largely runs according to a set of natural laws without the providential involvement of God.

**Denomination** — A group of Christian congregations that have joined together in a common **confession**. They typically identify themselves with a common name such as Lutheran, Presbyterian, or Baptist.

**Depravity** — the corrupted, sinful state of human nature that has existed since the **Fall**.

**Docetism** — heretical teaching that claimed that Christ did not truly become human but only appeared to have a human body.

**Dominion** — the position of headship and stewardship that human beings have over creation.

**Ecumenical** — world wide, universal, **catholic** Christianity. Not restricted to any denomination.

**Ecumenical Council** — gatherings of theologians from the entire Christian **church** to discuss theological issues. Protestants generally recognize four councils as ecumenical: Nicea (AD 325), **Constantinople** (381), Ephesus (431), and **Chalcedon** (451).

**Ecumenical Creeds** — the three creeds commonly accepted by most Christians, namely the Apostles, Nicene, and Athanasian Creeds.

**Effective** — actually producing an effect, accomplishing a result. For example, Scripture is effective when someone hears its message and believes (see also efficacious).

**Efficacious** — having the power to produce and effect. Something can be efficacious without necessarily being effective (producing that effect). For example, Scripture always has the power to call someone to faith, even though an individual may reject its message (see also effective).

**Epistemology** — the study of the sources and means of gaining knowledge about a subject.

**Epistle** — a New Testament book that was written as a letter to a person or church.

**Eschatology** — the study of the "last things." On an individual level, this includes the study of death, the intermediate state, judgment, and heaven or hell. On the broader level, it refers to all creation and includes the teachings of the last days of the earth, the second coming of Christ, judgment, heaven, and hell.

**Essence** — from the Latin word *esse* which literally means, "to be." Essence refers to the basic nature of something – that which makes something what it is. Theologically, this word is most often used in the doctrine of the **Trinity**. All three persons share the divine essence.

**Eternal** — properly speaking, free from the constraints of linear time; without beginning or end.

**Eucharist** — the Greek word for "thanksgiving," Eucharist is a synonym for the **Lord's Supper**.

**Eutychianism** — a christological heresy that confuses the divine and human natures of Christ. Eutyches taught that the divine nature of Christ absorbed the humanity into itself. Eutychianism essentially denies both the perfect deity and the full humanity of Christ.

**Evolution** — in its most fundamental definition, simply refers to biological change.

**Evolution, atheistic** — the belief that the universe originated and developed through random change and natural selection without the involvement of a god or any other directing power or purpose.

**Evolution, theistic** — the belief that the universe has developed through evolutionary change and natural selection, but that this was begun or has been directed by God.

*Ex nihilo* — Latin for "from nothing." Describes the biblical account of creation that states that God created all things, out of nothing, by his powerful word.

*Ex opere operato* — Latin for "by the work that is worked." This is an improper way of describing the effectiveness of the sacraments. It maintains that sacraments are effective when the right words are said and the right ritual performed, regardless of the faith or intent of those saying or hearing the words. It essentially treats the sacraments as a magical incantation.

**Exaltation** — the teaching that, after the saving work of Christ was complete, he resumed the full and constant use of the divine powers and prerogatives that he had voluntarily limited in his state of humiliation.

**Exegetical theology/exegesis** — the branch of theological studies devoted to the direct study of the biblical text. Exegesis, which literally means, "to lead out," seeks to understand the text on its own terms and not to insert meaning from outside of the text (see also eisegesis).

**Experiential argument** — the notion that human experiences of emotion, beauty, or inner peace give evidence to support the existence of God.

**Faith** — reception of and relational trust in the grace of God. Faith is a gift of the Holy Spirit.

**Fall, the** — Adam and Eve's willful disobedience of God's command in the garden of Eden. This act brought sin, guilt, and depravity to all of humanity.

**Fellowship** — at its most basic level, fellowship means participation in common things and activities. At its most profound level, fellowship among Christians refers to joint participation in the word and sacraments. The type of fellowship requires a common **confession** of the Christian faith.

**Fideism** — faith that does not have Christ as its object but rather trusts in itself. "Faith in faith."

**Filioque** — literally "and the Son." This word was added to the Nicene Creed in the West to teach that the Holy Spirit proceeds not only from the Father but also from the Son. The Eastern churches have never accepted this statement.

**Forensic justification** — the description of Christ's work as a legal or forensic act. For Christ's sake, God declares human beings righteous in his sight, apart from any merit of our own.

**Formal freedom** — the ability of human beings to freely make choices regarding their life and experiences. Freedom from coercion. Due to the **Fall**, formal freedom does not apply to spiritual issues (see **material freedom**).

**Formal principle** — the ultimate source of information in a belief system or philosophy. In Lutheran theology, Scripture alone is the formal principle.

**Fruit of the Spirit** — gifts given by the Holy Spirit that are available to all Christians. Galatians 5:22-23 states these are love, joy, peace, patience, kindness, goodness, faith, gentleness, and self-control.

**Functions of the Law** — also known as "uses of the law." Refers to ways that the law functions in restraining sin in society (curb), revealing our need for a Savior (mirror), and instructing Christians (rule). All three uses are still applications of God's Law, not the Gospel.

**Gap theory** — belief of some dispensationalists that a considerable amount of time passed between the events of Genesis 1:1 and 1:2. Among other things, proponents of this view maintain that the demons fell during this time.

**Gnosticism** — Greek religious movement that emphasized secret knowledge for its initiates. Gnosticism had and has many variants. Gnostics commonly emphasized a radical distinction between the material world (which was evil) and the spiritual dimensions (which were good).

**Good work** — a work done by a Christian that proceeds from faith, is in conformity with God's will, and is motivated by love of or gratitude to God

**Gospel** — in the wide sense, refers to the first four books of the New Testament. In its proper sense, Gospel refers to the doctrine that humanity has been saved from sin and death by the work of Christ alone and that this benefit is given solely by his grace, apart from human works.

**Grace** — God's undeserved favor, love, and mercy towards humanity because of the work of Christ.

**Great Commission** — Christ's words in Matthew 28:18-20 in which he commissions his church to make disciples of all nations by baptizing them in the name of the Father, Son, and Holy Spirit and teaching them to observe everything he has commanded.

**Guilt** — an objective status belonging to one who has violated a law, regardless of their subjective feelings of **shame**.

**Hereditary sin** — the guilt and **depravity** that all human beings possess as part of the fallen nature which was passed on to all people after the **Fall** of Adam and Eve. Synonym for **original sin**.

**Heresy** — a teaching that is contrary to the teachings of the Bible and has, therefore, been rejected by orthodox Christianity. Heresy is not simply an error; it is persistent error that refuses to be normed by the biblical text.

**Hermeneutics** — principles of textual interpretation.

*Hexameron* — Greek word for "six days," referring to the days of creation.

**Historical argument** — a rational argument that suggests that the existence of God is demonstrated (or even proven) by historical events. It may claim that there is an overall triumph of good over evil.

**Historical-grammatical method** — proper method of biblical interpretation that seeks to understand the meaning of a text and its vocabulary within its specific historical context. This is to be distinguished from the historical-critical method which places human reason in judgment over the content of Scripture and treats the inspired word with skepticism.

**Historical theology** — A branch of theology that focuses on the past events, challenges, and theological understanding of the Christian church.

**Holy** — perfect according to God's standards.

**Host** — the bread used in the **Lord's Supper**.

**Humiliation** — the doctrine that, during his earthly life and ministry (from conception to burial), Jesus Christ possessed the attributes and abilities that were his as true God, but for the sake of human redemption, he did not always or fully use these attributes.

**Hypostatic union** — the doctrine of the union of a human nature and a divine nature in the one person of Christ. This is also known as the personal union.

**Image of God** — certain attributes of God which he imparted, to a degree, to humanity before the **Fall** and fully possessed by Adam and Eve in their **prelapsarian** state. These attributes included morality, intelligence, relationality and immortality.

**Immaculate Conception** — Roman Catholic doctrine that says that Mary was born without the stain of sin. This doctrine should not to be confused with the **virgin birth**.

**Imputed righteousness** — the doctrine that God imputes or credits us with Christ's righteousness (see also **infused righteousness**).

**Incarnation** — God's assumption of human nature in the person of Jesus Christ.

**Inerrant** — without error. This is an attribute of Scripture.

**Infallible** — incapable of error. Since Scripture is inspired by God, it is infallible.

**Infused righteousness** — the false teaching that God transforms a person and makes them holy so that he can love them and save them. This is not to be confused with the doctrine of sanctification (see also **imputed righteousness**).

**Inspired** — literally "God-breathed." Refers to the Holy Spirit's work of revealing and preserving God's word in the Bible. Because of inspiration, the Bible is the very word of God.

**Invisible church** — term referring to the complete number of believers in Christ throughout the world and of all times. Because membership in this one true **church** is based on faith alone, which cannot be seen by human beings, this church is said to be invisible.

**Just** — right, fair, and perfectly aligned with God's will.

**Justification** — God declares sinners to be just or righteous for Christ's sake. He imputes our sins to Christ and credits Christ's righteousness to us.

**Kingdom of glory** — Christ's current and eternal rule in heaven.

**Kingdom of grace** — Christ's rule in and over his **church** through the means of grace.

**Kingdom of power** — Christ's rule over all creation by his almighty power.

**Kingdom of the left** — another term for the kingdom of power.

**Kingdom of the right** — another term for the kingdom of grace.

**Law** — in its wide sense, is a synonym for the entire word of God. In its proper sense, it refers to God's word of command. While the Law is perfect, fallen humans are unable to fulfill its demands.

**Legalism** — a distortion of biblical teaching that overemphasizes God's Law and eclipses the Gospel.

**Limited atonement** — false view of the **atonement** that maintains that Christ died only for the elect or for those who would eventually believe in him.

*Logos* — Greek word for "word." Logos can refer to spoken or written words. It is also a title for the Son of God who is the "Word made flesh" (see John 1:1-14).

**Macro-evolution** — the belief that the entire universe originated and developed through random change and natural selection. Views all biological life on earth as interconnected, evolving from common sources. This should be distinguished from **micro-evolution**.

**Magisterial use of reason** — an over-reliance on human reason which allows it to be superior to the word of God.

**Man of lawlessness** — alternate title for the **Antichrist** used in 2 Thessalonians.

**Marks of the church** — synonym for the word and sacraments. The **church** is found where the marks are faithfully used according to Christ's institution.

**Materialism** — philosophical explanation of life that views everything as part of the physical, material world. Excludes the existence of spiritual or supernatural things.

**Material freedom** — the complete freedom of human beings to make free, unco-erced decisions in all matters of life including spiritual issues. This view rejects the **bondage of the will** and the fallenness of human nature. See also **formal freedom**.

**Material principle** — the main, essential teaching. Justification by grace through faith is the material principle of Lutheranism.

**Means of Grace** — specific ways in which God has promised to give us the for-giveness, life, and salvation which Christ has won for us. The **Gospel** and the **sacraments** are means of grace.

**Mercy** — the compassionate act of withholding a justly deserved punishment or be-stowing an undeserved blessing. An attribute of God and a virtue commended to humans.

**Messiah** — Hebrew word meaning "anointed one." The Greek equivalent is "Christ."

**Micro-evolution** — evolutionary change within parts of creation such as within spe-cies or within the "kinds" described in Genesis. A scientifically demonstrated fact that is compatible with scriptural accounts of creation.

**Ministerial use of reason** — the use of human reason that submits to the authority of God's word when reason and Scripture are in conflict.

**Ministry** — from a Latin word meaning, "service," ministry is sometimes used as a synonym for any service done by a Christian. More narrowly, ministry refers to the work of specific Christians who are called to specific offices in the church. In its most proper sense, ministry refers to the ministry of word and sacrament, namely the pastoral office.

**Mirror** — the second use or function of the Law. In this use, the Law reveals human sinfulness and need for God's salvation.

**Missiology** — the study of missions and Christian outreach.

**Modalism** — Trinitarian heresy that denies the three persons. It teaches that the one person of God assumes different "modes" or plays different "roles" when dealing with human beings, but that there is no distinction between the three persons.

**Monergism** — description of conversion that maintains that the Holy Spirit works conversion and faith in a person without their cooperation. The opposite of **synergism**.

**Moral argument** — this logical argument suggests that a universal sense of moral-ity or the individual's experience of a conscience means that there must be a universal law-giver (and therefore, a god).

**Moral Law** — divine laws that are binding on all people of all times. Moral Law is distinguished from **civil-political law** and from **ceremonial law**.

**Narrow sense** — when a term has a range of meanings, the narrow sense is the meaning of the word in its most proper, specific, or technical sense.

**Natural knowledge** — information about God from a source other than Holy Scripture or God's direct **revelation**. This includes things such as the evidence of nature or the conscience.

**Nature** — a description of the essential qualities that make something what it is. For example, a human nature is the "humanness" of the person.

**Nestorianism** — christological heresy that completely separates the two natures of Christ and thus effectively denies the personal union.

**Objective justification** — Christ's work of reconciliation in which he justified the entire world by his death and resurrection. See also **subjective justification**.

**Offense** — anything done to cause a Christian to sin, doubt, or stumble in faith.

**Office** — a particular calling in which a person is "officially" authorized and obligated to perform certain tasks (for example, the office of the pastoral ministry).

**Omnipotent** — all powerful or almighty. One of God's attributes.

**Omnipresent** — present everywhere. One of God's attributes. He is fully present in every place.

**Omniscient** — all knowing. The perfect knowledge of God.

**Ontological argument** — argument for the existence of God that emphasizes the logical nature of believing in God or the need for a "first cause" or "unmoved mover" of the universe.

**Open communion** — the practice of communing any individual regardless of their confession of faith or self-examination.

**Original Sin** — the guilt and **depravity** that all human beings possess as part of the fallen nature which was passed on to all people after the **Fall** of Adam and Eve.

**Orthodox** — literally "right worship," orthodox generally has the meaning of "correct belief" that is grounded in God's truth, as opposed to heresy. It can also be used as the name of a denomination such as Greek Orthodox or Russian Orthodox.

**Panentheism** —the belief that everything God is *in* everything but is not limited to the universe.

**Pantheism** — the belief that everything in the universe *is* God or is a manifestation of God.

*Paraclete* — Greek word for "comforter." Paraclete is generally a title for the Holy Spirit.

**Paradox** — Two statements that may appear to be in contradiction, but actually address different questions, and thus are not contradictory. For example, God is three persons but one God. Paradoxes in Scripture should not be removed but both truths are to be believed.

**Parousia** — Greek word meaning "coming." The Parousia is another word for the second coming of Christ.

**Pastor** — from the Latin word for "shepherd," a pastor is a called minister of word and sacrament.

**Pastoral Epistles** — writings of St. Paul that address the pastoral ministry (among other things): 1 & 2 Timothy and Titus.

**Passive obedience** — Christ's redemptive work of suffering and dying for the sins of humanity (see also active obedience).

**Pelagianism** — heresy that denies **original sin** and elevates the role of the human being in **conversion**. A person is, essentially, able to convert himself.

**Penance** — sacrament of the Roman Catholic Church that includes confession, absolution, and works done as a consequence of sin. Lutherans practice confession and **absolution**, but do not impose the works required in penance. Instead, Lutherans see good works as a response of gratitude.

**Perfectionism** — the belief that Christians are able to be perfectly sanctified or completely obedient to God in all aspects of their lives.

**Person** — someone who exists as a unique, distinct individual. A person is not a part of another being and is usually in relationship with other persons.

**Personal Union** - the doctrine of the union of a human nature and a divine nature in the one person of Christ. This is also known as the hypostatic union.

**Plenary inspiration** — the "full" inspiration of the Bible. Indicates that the entire biblical text is inspired.

**Pluralism** — in theology, pluralism describes the view that various or all religious are equally valid means to reach salvation and encounter God or the gods.

**Polytheism** — the worship of multiple gods.

**Postlapsarian** — refers to events or persons after the **Fall**.

**Postmillennialism** — **eschatological** view that teaches that Christ's visible second coming will occur after a thousand years of peace on earth.

**Practical theology** — division of theology that focuses on the application of theological content in means such as preaching, worship, or education. Sometimes known as "pastoral theology."

**Predestination** — the doctrine that, based solely on his grace, God elects or predestines some individuals to salvation before the creation of the world. Those who are elect come to faith and are saved. This biblical teaching should not be confused with double predestination.

**Prelapsarian** — refers to events and persons before the **Fall**.

**Preservation (in creation)** — God's ongoing involvement with and care for his creation.

**Preservation (in faith)** — biblical teaching that the Holy Spirit works through the **means of grace** to keep Christians in the Christian faith.

**Priest** — one who offers sacrifices and makes intercession between God and humans.

**Priestly Office** — that portion of Christ's work in which he offered himself as a sacrifice for humanity's sin and in which he continues to intercede between God and humanity.

**Primeval** — original, unfallen, pristine state.

**Proceed** — word describing the relationship of the Holy Spirit to the other two persons of the **Trinity**. The Spirit proceeds from the Father and the Son, coming from both, while still being fully and equally God.

**Proper sense** — when a term has a range of meanings, the proper sense, or narrow sense is the meaning of the word in its most proper, specific, or technical sense.

**Prophet** — one appointed by God to proclaim his word. Prophetic ministry may foretell future events but also may interpret present events from God's perspective.

**Prophetic Office** — that portion of Christ's work in which he reveals God's truth to humanity.

**Quickening** — making alive or giving life to a lifeless body.

**Real Presence** — the belief that the **Lord's Supper** is the true body and blood of Jesus Christ in, with, and under the bread and wine.

**Reconciliation** — the work of Christ in which he restored the relationship between God and humanity that had been broken by human sinfulness.

**Reductionism** — an overly simple explanation that ignores the complexity of an issue to offer an easy answer.

**Regeneration** — biblical image of salvation that emphasizes the new life that the Holy Spirit gives to the child of God. See also "born again."

**Revealed knowledge** — knowledge that is not gained from observation of nature or any part of creation but is revealed directly by God. Jesus Christ and his word are God's chief means of self-revelation.

**Revelation** — God's disclosure of his will, purpose, and will to human beings.

**Righteous** — perfectly just and holy according to God's standards.

**Royal Office** — that portion of Christ's work in which he reigns (in different ways) over all creation, over believers, and over heaven.

**Rule** — the "third use" of the Law, in which a Christian uses God's Law as a guide for life and practice. The third use of the Law is always a response to the Gospel, but since it continues to function as the Law, it often transforms into the second use (the mirror).

**Sacrament** — variously defined. A common definition calls it a sacred act that was instituted by God, has a physical element combined with the word of God, and conveys the forgiveness of sins. Another definition calls them rites commanded by God with his promise of grace.

**Sanctification** — the work of the Holy Spirit of making people holy. In its wide sense, sanctification included everything God does for our salvation and preservation, including the work of justification and conversion. In its proper sense, sanctification refers to the inward, spiritual transformation of a believer that is accomplished by the work of the Holy Spirit.

**Sect/sectarianism** — a sect is a group that has separated from some other group, and generally refers to a fringe group of Christianity which has split from a denomination. Sectarianism is overzealous commitment to this sect and extreme isolation from the rest of the group, coupled with a refusal to acknowledge true elements of the other group.

**Semipelagianism** — a heretical view of conversion that maintains that a person must start their own conversion by their own power (apart from the Holy Spirit) but needs God's assistance through the sacraments in order to be fully converted.

**Shame** — the subjective feeling that may accompany **guilt**. Shame may be felt properly (when truly guilty) or improperly (in the case of an erring **conscience**).

*Simul iustus et peccator* — "Simultaneously justified and sinful," or "simultaneously saint and sinner."

*Sola Scriptura* — "Scripture Alone;" the formal principle of Lutheranism.

**Soul** — the aspect of humanity that is not material but spiritual; that which is not the body.

**Spirit** — a word with diverse meanings in Scripture. It is a name of the third person of the **Trinity**, or can refer to beings that have no material body (such as angels). It can also refer to the life or soul of a human being.

**Spiritual gifts** — special gifts, abilities, roles, offices, or functions given by God to individual Christians for use in his church.

**Stewardship** — biblical concept of recognizing the world and our possessions as things given by God to be used in his service. Stewardship sees human beings as caretakers of God's good gifts.

**Subjective justification** — the application of Christ's work of justification of the whole world (**objective justification**) to an individual person. A person who is subjectively justified receives the benefits that Christ won in objective justification.

**Subordinationism** — heretical depiction of the **Trinity** that places the three persons in a hierarchy. In such a depiction, the Son and Holy Spirit are generally seen as subordinate or less than the Father.

**Substance** — the essential nature of something. Theologically, this word describes the common deity of all three persons of the **Trinity**. They share one divine substance or essence.

**Syncretism** — mixing of diverse or contradictory elements of different religions into one hybrid religion. Syncretism, in essence, denies the integrity and exclusivity of diverse belief systems.

**Synergism** — false view of **conversion** that depicts God and human beings "working together" to enact conversion. Distinct from the biblical teaching of **monergism**.

**Systematic theology/systematics** — discipline of theology that organizes a belief system by various topics.

**Teleological argument** — argument that sees the order and intricacy of the universe as evidence for the existence of God.

**Textual criticism** — hermeneutical method that attempts to establish the original text of a document. Textual criticism is an important step in **exegesis**.

**Theocracy** — governmental form in which God is seen to be the head of the government and divine law is civilly binding. Ancient Israel was a theocracy.

**Theology** — literally the study of God. Christian theology is the study of God through his self-revelation.

**Third Use of the Law** — function of the Law in which a Christian uses God's Law as a guide for life and practice. The third use of the Law is always a response to the Gospel, but it continues to function as the Law, and so often transforms into the second use (the mirror). This use is also known as the "rule."

**Torah** — Hebrew word for "Law." Torah is often used as a synonym for the first five books of the Old Testament.

**Traditionalism** — a distorted view of tradition that uncritically accepts the traditions of the past as binding on us today.

**Transubstantiation** — view of the Lord's Supper which teaches that the bread and wine are completely transformed into the body and blood of Jesus, yet they continue to retain their former appearances and external properties.

**Trinity** — the doctrine that God is three persons in one God.

**Tritheism** — the false teaching that there are three gods: the Father, Son, and Holy Spirit.

**Unionism** — joint worship and Christian fellowship among churches or individuals who are not in doctrinal agreement.

**Unitarianism** — A non-Christian religion that denies of the personal distinctions in the **Trinity**.

**Unity/*unitas*** — external fellowship without doctrinal agreement.

**Universalism** — non-biblical teaching that asserts that all humans will be saved, regardless of their belief.

***Verba*** — Latin for "word." Generally used as an abbreviation for the **words of institution** in the **Lord's Supper**.

**Verbal inspiration** — indicates that in the doctrine of inspiration, the actual words themselves are inspired and not simply the ideas of the text.

**Virgin conception and birth** — the work of the Holy Spirit whereby Mary miraculously conceived and bore Jesus while she was a virgin.

**Visible church** — the aspect of the **church** that can be seen by humans. It consists of all who profess faith in Jesus Christ.

**Vivification** — making alive or giving life to a lifeless body.

**Vocation** — from the Latin word for "calling." Theologically, it refers to a person's occupation or duties before God. This concept is not limited to called churchworkers; all Christians have a vocation.

**Wide sense** — when a term has a range of meanings, the wide sense is the broadest or more general meaning of the term.

**Words of institution** — the words of Jesus recorded in Matthew 26:26-29, Mark 14:22-24, Luke 22:19-20, and 1 Corinthians 11:23-25 in which he instituted the **Lord's Supper**. The words of institution, or **verba**, are said at every celebration of the Lord's Supper.

29727592R00174

Made in the USA
San Bernardino, CA
26 January 2016